once a·day

at the table

FAMILY DEVOTIONAL

365 daily readings and conversation starters
for your family

ZONDERVAN®

We want to hear from you. Please send your comments about this book to us in care of zreview@zondervan.com. Thank you.

ZONDERVAN

Once-A-Day At the Table Family Devotional
Copyright © 2012 by Zondervan

This title is also available as a Zondervan ebook.
Visit www.zondervan.com/ebooks.

Requests for information should be addressed to:

Zondervan, *Grand Rapids, Michigan 49530*

Library of Congress Cataloging-in-Publication Data

Once-a-day at the table family devotional / written by the Livingstone Corporation.
      p. cm. — (Once-a-day)
   Includes bibliographical references and index.
   ISBN 978-0-310-41917-4 (softcover : alk. paper)
    1. Families—Prayers and devotions. 2. Devotional calendars. I. Title.
  BV255.L58   2012
  249—dc23   2012024204

Cover design: Jamie DeBruyn
Interior design: Sherri Hoffman and Jamie DeBruyn
Content provider: Chris Hudson

Printed in the United States of America

---

15 16 17 /DCI/ 20 19 18 17 16 15 14 13 12 11 10 9 8 7 6 5 4 3

introduction

Families gather around the table to spend time together, reflect on their day, nourish themselves and grow together as a family. This makes meal time a perfect place to dig into God's perfect Word together.

The family devotions in this book are short enough to complete as you sit together around the table but poignant enough to leave a lasting impression on each member of the family.

Because the Bible is a complex book, Bible passages never become old. No matter your age or spiritual maturity, God's Word has something to offer. People of all ages will find these devotions accessible and meaningful—children will learn from parents, siblings will learn from one another, and parents will refresh their faith through the eyes and hearts of their children.

It is my prayer that your family will grow closer together and closer to God through the Scripture excerpts, thought-provoking devotions and questions to ponder included in this book.

May God richly bless you and your family as you journey together.

—Christopher D. Hudson

about the author

Christopher Hudson's mission is to help people read, understand and apply the Bible. Chris leads a team of Christian publishing professionals at Hudson & Associates, which exists to create Bible resources that strengthen the church. Chris served as general editor for the *Voices of Faith Devotional Bible* (Zondervan) and *College Devotional Bible* (Zondervan) and is a regular contributor for the daily inspiration found at Facebook.com/TheBiblePeople. Chris has been an active teacher in his church for nearly 20 years and lives outside Chicago with his wife and three children.

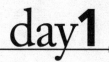

AFTER GOD'S OWN HEART

- What do people mean when they say, "I'm too busy *not* to pray"?
- When is the best time for you to pray? Why?

In the morning, LORD, you hear my voice; in the morning I lay my requests before you and wait expectantly.   PSALM 5:3

In 1 Samuel 13:14, God describes David as "a man after [God's] own heart." One of the ways that King David sought God was through prayer. David's conversations with God were notable.

In Psalm 5, we find three clues to David's prayer success. The first is found in the words, "In the morning." David didn't pray whenever he felt like it; he prayed every day. More specifically, he prayed every morning. He dedicated the first part of his day to God.

The second clue is found in the words, "I lay my requests before you." David wasn't shy about telling God what he needed. He approached God with confidence, the way he would approach a friend. He shared what was going on in his life and what he thought he needed.

The third clue is found in the words, "wait expectantly." David didn't drop his requests at the Lord's door and then go on his way. He waited for God's response. Sometimes God said "yes"; sometimes God said "no." Either way, David listened to God.

If you want to be a person after God's own heart, you need to devote yourself to prayer as David did. ❖

PRAYER

Dear God, thank you for meeting with us any time we approach you. Let us never forget what a privilege it is to talk to you. Amen.

day2

DEVOTED — WHOLEHEARTEDLY

- What are some things that people are devoted to?
- What gets in the way of devotion to God?

"And you, my son Solomon, acknowledge the God of your father, and serve him with wholehearted devotion and with a willing mind, for the LORD searches every heart and understands every desire and every thought. If you seek him, he will be found by you; but if you forsake him, he will reject you forever."   1 CHRONICLES 28:9

Devotion is the word we use to describe participating in a short Bible study and discussion, like the one we're having now. But the word *devotion* also refers to the attitude that drives us to seek God.

To be devoted means to be dedicated. And in this verse, David is telling his son Solomon to wholeheartedly dedicate himself to God. King David knew that people can't halfheartedly serve God.

When we do serve God with wholehearted devotion, God will reward us. When we make him the focus of our lives, he will bless us. That's his promise. The more devoted we become, the more he blesses us.

To devote our life to God means that we live completely for him. It means that we live our life to please and honor him. We seek him, worship him and love him — with our whole heart. ✤

PRAYER

Dear God, you are the only one who deserves our wholehearted devotion. Help us clear the obstacles in our lives that keep us from being wholeheartedly devoted to you. Amen.

TRANSFORMERS

- Share a time when someone knew you were a believer without having been told. What gave you away?
- Share a time when you knew someone was a believer without having been told by that person. How did you know?

Therefore, I urge you, brothers and sisters, in view of God's mercy, to offer your bodies as a living sacrifice, holy and pleasing to God—this is your true and proper worship. Do not conform to the pattern of this world, but be transformed by the renewing of your mind. Then you will be able to test and approve what God's will is—his good, pleasing and perfect will. ROMANS 12:1-2

How much can we learn about people by observing them? If we followed someone around for a day, we would quickly learn what food that person likes to eat, what music they listen to and what makes them laugh. We would be able to see what that person read, who their friends were and how they spent money. Before long, we would be able to give a full report on our subject.

What if someone followed *you* around for a day? What might they learn about you? What would your daily choices say about you? How long would it take your observer to figure out that you're a Christian?

There's an old expression that says, "If you were on trial for being a follower of Christ, would there be enough evidence to convict you?" What would you say to that? Is there evidence in your life that you have been transformed? ❖

PRAYER

Dear God, thank you for changing our lives completely. Let us remember that we are always being watched by people who want to know what it means to be transformed by you. Amen.

day**4**

ONE PURPOSE

- Why does God want your worship?
- How can we become a more worshipful family?

The people rejoiced at the willing response of their leaders, for they had given freely and wholeheartedly to the LORD. David the king also rejoiced greatly. 1 CHRONICLES 29:9

If you ask someone, "What were you put on this earth to do?" chances are you'll find out what that person *likes* to do: "I was put on this earth to play soccer." Or you might find out what that person feels responsible to do: "I was put on this earth to take care of my family." But neither answer is correct. As human beings, we were created for one purpose: to give glory to God.

That means worship—and that's what God wants from us more than anything. The Israelites discovered how important worship is to God. When King David announced that he was building a temple where the people could worship God, the Israelites leapt at the chance to be a part of it. They gave the best of everything they had to use in the construction. They devoted themselves to worship. As a result, God blessed their nation with peace, wealth and respect among the other nations of the world.

God is pleased by our worship and blesses us. Receiving his blessing gives us cause to worship him more, which gives him reason to bless us more. It's a beautiful cycle! ✤

PRAYER

Dear God, we worship you for your love and goodness. Thank you for taking care of your people in the past, for taking care of us today and for taking care of us in the future. Amen.

DECISIONS, DECISIONS

- Who's the first person you turn to when you don't know what to do?
- How do you know when you've made a wrong decision?

If any of you lacks wisdom, you should ask God, who gives generously to all without finding fault, and it will be given to you. JAMES 1:5

We live in a complicated world. We will face complicated decisions. Fortunately for us, we have a resource we can use. God, the source of all wisdom, invites us to share our dilemmas with him. He makes his wisdom available to us.

In order to take full advantage of the opportunity, though, we first need to empty ourselves of our own "wisdom." Sometimes when we ask for advice, we have already made up our minds, and we're just looking for someone to agree with us. That might work with friends, but not with God. If we're going to tap into his wisdom, we need to forget about what we want or what we think should happen. We need to let him guide us.

If you're not sure how to recognize God's voice, try talking to him from different perspectives about the situation you're facing. Talk about the pros, the reasons you should do something. Then talk about the cons, the reasons you shouldn't do it. Let him work in your heart and mind to help you realize which direction is best.

If you really want God's wisdom, just ask him for it. ✤

PRAYER

Dear God, thank you for sharing your wisdom with us. Never let us forget that your help is available whenever we need it. Amen.

day6

KEEPING AN OPEN MIND

- Describe a time when you changed your mind about something. What made you change your mind?
- When something is new to you, how do you decide whether it's right or true?

The heart of the discerning acquires knowledge, for the ears of the wise seek it out.
PROVERBS 18:15

In order to acquire knowledge, we must be open to new ideas. If people weren't open to new ideas, consider the following repercussions:

All movies would still be in black and white.
We would still be writing letters instead of texting.
Computers would still be the size of refrigerators.

Thankfully, many who have gone before us have been open to new ideas. In Proverbs 18, King Solomon tells us that being open to new ideas is also important in our spiritual lives.

This can be a challenge sometimes. It's easier for us to stay in our comfort zones, to hang out with people who act, think and believe like we do. New ideas can be disruptive and uncomfortable. They challenge us to look at the world, other people and ourselves in ways we may not want to.

But new ideas also stretch us and help us grow. That's why wise believers are open to new ideas. If you want to be wise, surround yourself with God-honoring people who challenge you. Push yourself to read different kinds of books than you would normally choose. Ask God to open your eyes to new ways of thinking that give you more insight into his truth. ✤

PRAYER

Dear God, thank you for creating us with the ability to learn new things. Protect us as we explore new ideas and help us recognize your truth when we find it. Amen.

day7

YOUR WILL BE DONE

- What do you think God wants you to do with your life?
- What happens if you ignore God's will?

Trust in the LORD with all your heart and lean not on your own understanding; in all your ways submit to him, and he will make your paths straight. PROVERBS 3:5–6

Have you ever gotten lost? Even though you really thought you knew where you were going? Would you have gotten lost if you had had good directions?

We can get lost in life if we don't use the guidebook God has provided us with—the Bible. We were not designed to be "know-it-alls." None of us were. We were designed to rely on God's instructions and on his will.

This isn't always simple. God's will isn't always obvious, but that doesn't mean that we should put our lives on hold while we wait for him to reveal his plan for our lives. God's Word gives us plenty to go on. The Bible tells us how to behave, how to treat others and how to live wisely. When we follow the instructions God has already given us, he will further reveal his will to us. ✤

PRAYER

Dear God, thank you for caring enough about us as individuals to create a plan for each of our lives. Guide us as we strive to determine your will. Amen.

day8

BETTER THAN A GPS

- Has God ever led you anywhere that surprised you? Explain.
- What's the best thing to do when you don't understand why the Lord is leading you in a certain direction?

I will instruct you and teach you in the way you should go; I will counsel you with my loving eye on you.　　　　　　　　　　　　　　　　PSALM 32:8

While God gives us direction through the Bible, he is not a GPS that we can stick on the windshield. God won't say, "In three and a half years, turn left and attend this college." God leads us in a more subtle way, through our hearts.

God's leading may not always make sense to us. For one thing, his choice of route may not be a straight line. He may lead us off the highway, against traffic or through a random desert. He may take us in a complete circle and bring us right back where we started. He may lead us out into the middle of the ocean and then tell us to make a U-turn.

The GPS only considers where we want to go and the shortest way to get there. God considers an infinite eternity that includes where we begin, where he wants us to go and what we need to learn along the way.

If we trust God to guide us, one day we'll look back on our life and see just what an incredible journey it was. ✤

PRAYER

Dear God, you are amazing because you know the best route for every person's life. Guide our steps so that we go exactly where you want us to go. Amen.

THE CREATOR

- What's your favorite—whether it's an animal, plant, rock formation, beach or something else—of all the works of creation?
- How do you feel when you think about everything God has created?

In the beginning God created the heavens and the earth. Genesis 1:1

Think about what it's like to bring an art project home from school—something you've worked hard to make, all by yourself. You've poured your own unique creativity and skills into designing your masterpiece.

How would you feel if you brought it home, hung it in the middle of the living room, and then watched as everyone completely ignored it? Think about it. Not one gasp of amazement. Not one "Wow, how did you do this?" Not one comment about the colors you used or the skill of your design or the amazing talent behind the work. How would you feel?

Do you suppose God feels the same way when people ignore his creation? After all, he created the world and everything in it. Every day we are surrounded by the beauty of his work and the incredible detail of his design. But how often do we mention it? How often do we even notice it?

Let's start a habit of giving God his due. Let's make a commitment to noticing something new, something beautiful, something incredible in creation every day and thanking him for it. Let's see what that does for our relationship with him. ♣

PRAYER

Dear God, we are in awe of your creation. Every day we see something incredible that you made. Let us never lose our sense of wonder at your creative power. Amen.

THE WARRIOR KING

- If you were in a battle, who would you want by your side? Why?
- How does God want you to respond to the evil and suffering in this world?

Who is this King of glory? The LORD strong and mighty, the LORD mighty in battle.
PSALM 24:8

When we hear the words, "God is love" or "God brings peace to our hearts," we get a sense of God's gentle, healing nature. But if we stop there, we don't get the whole picture of what God is like. In this psalm, David describes God as a King who is "mighty in battle."

That's not just a poetic description, either. The fact that God is a warrior King has very real meaning for us, his followers. If God leads the way into battle, we must be prepared to join him.

Who is the enemy? Satan is God's enemy. So is sin. The Bible says that anything that is not for God is against him (see James 4:4). This means that he has a lot of enemies!

Our battle armor is God's truth, righteousness and faith. We fight for God with the "sword of the Spirit, which is the word of God" (Ephesians 6:17). We join this King of glory by obeying his commandments and by loving others.

The battle will not be easy, but we already know the end of the story. God wins. And so will we. ✤

PRAYER

Dear God, we praise you for your love and your willingness to fight for what is right. With your truth and love, prepare us for battle against the evil and suffering all around us. Amen.

THE ALL-KNOWING ONE

- What do you know now that you didn't know one year ago?
- If you could choose one thing to know a year from now, what would it be? In other words, what would you like to learn more than anything else?

Oh, the depth of the riches of the wisdom and knowledge of God! How unsearchable his judgments, and his paths beyond tracing out! ROMANS 11:33

Has it ever occurred to you that nothing new ever occurs to God? He already knows everything there is to know. This is a difficult concept for us because we learn something new every day. And we could learn a million new things each day and still not know what God knows.

God knows everything from the past, everything that's happening in the present and everything that will happen in the future. He can read every thought we have. He knows more about how we feel than we do. We may be able to fool ourselves, but we can never fool God.

The fact that God, and God alone, is all-knowing makes him the only one we should entrust with our future. He knows the destination of every possible path we could take in life. He knows which ones end well and which ones don't.

Who else, then, should be our guide? If we ask him to, God will use his perfect knowledge to steer us in the way we should go. Able to see what we cannot, he will lead us along the paths that bring us ultimate fulfillment and joy. ✤

PRAYER

Dear God, we speak this prayer out loud to you even though we don't need to. You know our hearts. You know our thoughts. Help us understand that you know what is best for us. Amen.

day12

THE ALL-POWERFUL ONE

- How would you define power?
- How does God show his power?

"For no word from God will ever fail."   Luke 1:37

In the folktale "The Stonecutter," a stonecutter wishes to be rich because rich men are powerful. Then he wishes to be a prince because princes are even more powerful. But the sun is more powerful than a prince, so he wishes to become the sun. He notices that the clouds have the power to block the sun's rays, so he wishes for that instead. A raining cloud would be even more powerful, so he pours down rain, which destroys everything in sight except for a big rock. Finding that nothing could disturb the power of the rock, he wishes to be a rock. In the end, he realizes he is better off as a stonecutter. After all, nothing can chip away at the power of a rock—except a stonecutter.

The lesson we learn from this folktale is that people are to be content with who they are. But Christians take away an even more significant message. Who is more powerful than riches, royalty and nature? Our God. And our God has placed us in the exact time and place that we are in. He made us who we are, and he has created a plan for our lives. Christians have a great reason to be content because our power comes through God. ✤

PRAYER

Dear God, you are all-powerful. Nothing can happen without your permission. Nothing can stop what you put in motion. Thank you for helping us to recognize what a powerful God we serve. Amen.

day13

THE APPROACHABLE ONE

- Who intimidates you? What is it about that person that you find intimidating?
- What's the best way to make someone comfortable around you?

Come near to God and he will come near to you. Wash your hands, you sinners, and purify your hearts, you double-minded. JAMES 4:8

There's a scene in *The Wizard of Oz* in which Dorothy and her friends finally get to see the Wizard, and they're scared to death. They feel the heat from the fire shooting all around them. They hear the Wizard's booming voice. They see his giant head in front of them. And for a moment, they're almost too terrified to bring their requests to him.

Sometimes that's how we approach God—with fear and trembling. After all, he is perfect. He is the source of all power. He knows everything about us (even the really, really bad things). We should be scared of him.

Except that we don't need to be because God has made himself approachable. He makes himself available to us. In fact, he *invites* us to come near him. Because he loves us, we can have a relationship with him. ✤

PRAYER

Dear God, thank you for allowing us to come into your presence. Let us never lose sight of what a privilege it is to have a relationship with you. Amen.

day14

TRUE DEPENDABILITY

- Which of your friends is most dependable?
- How important is dependability in a relationship?

If we confess our sins, he is faithful and just and will forgive us our sins and purify us from all unrighteousness.   1 JOHN 1:9

You may have noticed that people are not always dependable. People make mistakes. People say one thing and then do another. People forget things. People break promises. Many people try to live good lives, but no one is perfect.

But God *is* perfect. God never has an "off" day. His rules are perfect. He is perfectly consistent. He's never in a bad mood. He will never say one thing and then do another.

He is faithful to his Word—and he's faithful to us. He was there when we needed him yesterday. He's there when we need him today. And he'll be there when we need him tomorrow. We can count on him to be exactly who he says he is and to do exactly what he says he will do.

Not only is he faithful, God is also just. He will punish all injustice. He will defend his people. Sometimes it may look as though people get away with sin. Sometimes it may seem as though bad people prosper while good people suffer. But ultimately, God will administer justice. ♣

PRAYER

Dear God, thank you for being faithful to us. Thank you for never making us wonder whether we can trust you. Help us show that same kind of dependability to other people. Amen.

OH GOODY!

- What does the word *good* mean?
- Name five things that are good. What makes them good?

Taste and see that the LORD is good; blessed is the one who takes refuge in him.

PSALM 34:8

The word *good* is a bit vague in our language. We use it to describe everything that's average in our lives. "How was your day today?" "Good." "How did you sleep last night?" "Good." "How was your peanut-butter-and-jelly sandwich?" "Good." So when we say, "God is good," what are we really saying?

The Hebrew word that is translated "good" in this verse meant pleasant, agreeable to the senses, excellent, valuable, kind and morally correct. It was a word packed with meaning, not an empty one!

God is difficult to describe. He is certainly not average. He is perfect. He is all the goodness we can imagine—and even more. Nothing about God is bad, evil or impure—everything about God is good.

And not only is God good, but he wants what's good for us. And there's nothing average about that either. God's idea of good may not mean easy or comfortable, but it will get us to where he wants us to be, which is right where we need to be. ❖

PRAYER

Dear God, we praise you for your goodness. Thank you for wanting what's good in our lives. Give us the vision to recognize the goodness of your plans. Amen.

PRAISE GOD!

- Can you think of a time when someone praised you? For what reasons might you praise other people?
- How do you praise God?

Praise the LORD, for the LORD is good; sing praise to his name, for that is pleasant.

PSALM 135:3

We know that God is good. All we need to do is look around to see that. But it's not enough for us to say, "God is good," and leave it at that. We need to do something about it. We need to respond. We need to tell him how we feel about his goodness. And then we need to share our response with others.

When you go to a restaurant and the server takes good care of you, what do you do? You leave a tip to show your appreciation. If you find an awesome vacation spot, what do you do? You tell everyone you know about it and give them a chance to enjoy it too. We also need to show our appreciation to God and share God with others.

God gets a lot of bad press in our world. People blame him for the bad things that happen. They accuse him of being unloving or uncaring. We can work to change people's perceptions. We can tell of his goodness and help people understand who he really is. ♣

PRAYER

Dear God, we praise you for your goodness. You could treat us any way you choose, and you choose to love us, even though we've done nothing to deserve it. Guide our words as we tell others about your goodness. Amen.

day17

GOD'S INTERPRETER

- Why do some people consider the Bible intimidating or hard to understand?
- What do you do when you read something you don't understand in the Bible?

What we have received is not the spirit of the world, but the Spirit who is from God, so that we may understand what God has freely given us.   1 CORINTHIANS 2:12

Are you comfortable with the Bible? Many people aren't. Some are intimidated by its size. Others get lost in all the old traditions and strange stories. Still others have a hard time understanding the actual words—even in modern translations. Because the Bible is not like any other book ever written, some people have a hard time getting into it.

God understands the limits of our human minds. He should—he created them. And he really wants us to understand what is in his Word. So he sends his Holy Spirit to act as an interpreter for us. The Holy Spirit takes the words of the Bible and translates them in a personal way so that we understand not only what they mean but also how we can use them in our lives.

The secret to understanding Scripture is to pray before and after you read it. Before you start to read, ask the Holy Spirit to clear your mind of any distractions. Ask him to help you focus on the words in front of you. After you read, ask him to help you find ways to use what you read in your daily life. ✤

PRAYER

Dear God, thank you for giving us your Holy Spirit to help us understand your Word. Give us the wisdom to understand Scripture and use it in our daily lives. Amen.

day18 january 18

THE ULTIMATE AUTHORITY

- Think of someone who has earned your respect. What makes that person worthy of your respect? If that person gave you an instruction, how would you respond? Explain.
- How would you respond if someone you didn't respect gave you an instruction? What would be the difference?

For everything that was written in the past was written to teach us, so that through the endurance taught in the Scriptures and the encouragement they provide we might have hope. ROMANS 15:4

The Bible contains a lot of really good advice—but it's not a self-help book. It's much more important than that. A self-help book may be a useful tool, but it's not absolutely necessary. The Bible is an integral part of our relationship with God.

The Bible is more like an instruction manual. It shows us how we are constructed and what we are designed for. It tells us very specifically what we must do in order to run at maximum capacity. The more closely we follow what the Bible says, the better chance we have of creating a life that resembles God's blueprint. Not only does the Bible give us instruction, the Scriptures are one means of grace by which the Holy Spirit works to transform our lives.

The Bible is also a law book. It is the final authory for what is right and wrong. The Bible, then, is the perfect yardstick for measuring the things that influence us. If an idea, teaching or piece of advice follows God's Word, we should consider it. If it doesn't, we should beware of it. It's that simple. ✤

PRAYER

Dear God, thank you for giving us the Bible as the authority to guide our lives. Help us keep a proper respect for your Word. Amen.

day19

TRUSTWORTHY

- Who do you trust? Why?
- What does it mean to be trustworthy?

The statutes you have laid down are righteous; they are fully trustworthy.

PSALM 119:138

For thousands of years, people have tried to prove the Bible wrong. They argue that its stories are fiction. They claim its teachings are narrow-minded and out-dated. Ultimately, though, their arguments don't stack up. After all this time, the Bible's reputation stands. The life principles it teaches are just as relevant today as they were a thousand years ago. Billions of people have built joyful, fulfilling lives on its words.

Like those people, we can trust God's Word enough to base our lives on it. James 1:22 says, "Do not merely listen to the word, and so deceive yourselves. Do what it says." It's one thing to *say* you trust the Bible; it's another thing to live as though you trust it. That's the kind of trust God is looking for—the living kind.

How do you know if you are living God's Word and not merely hearing it? The Holy Spirit will let you know. Ask God to help you take a good look at your life. Ask him to show you how trusting his Word is obvious in the way you live—as well as how your trust is not so obvious. ✤

PRAYER

Dear God, thank you for giving us something we can trust in our undependable world. Give us the wisdom and strength to keep trusting your Word, no matter what. Amen.

day20

THE SOURCE OF WISDOM

- How can you tell if someone is wise?
- What is the wisest thing anyone has ever said to you?

I have more insight than all my teachers, for I meditate on your statutes.   PSALM 119:99

In the Garden of Eden, the serpent—the devil—had a specific strategy for getting Adam and Eve to sin. Look at his words to Eve in Genesis 3:1: "Did God really say, 'You must not eat from any tree in the garden'?" Notice how he tries to make Eve question God's words.

Satan knew that whatever useful knowledge Adam and Eve possessed came from God. He knew that if he could plant doubts in their minds about God's words, he stood a good chance of making them sin. Unfortunately, his strategy worked. In fact, it worked so well that he still uses it today.

For us, the Bible is the source of wisdom. God's Word helps us distinguish right from wrong and equips us to make the best choices for our lives. Naturally, then, that is Satan's target. He tries to get us to doubt God's Word and underestimate its importance. He tries to convince us that it's boring or too hard to understand.

The way to defend yourself against Satan's attacks is to meditate on what the Bible says. If you fill your mind with God's wisdom, you will have the confidence to shoot down temptations and doubts. ❖

PRAYER

Dear God, thank you for giving us your wisdom in the pages of the Bible. Please bless our efforts to meditate on your Word and let it make a difference in our lives. Amen.

day21

PUT OFF YOUR OLD SELF

- What does it mean to "put off your old self"?
- How can you avoid temptation?

You were taught, with regard to your former way of life, to put off your old self, which is being corrupted by its deceitful desires.   EPHESIANS 4:22

When we invite Jesus into our lives, we repent of our sins and ask for God's forgiveness. To repent means not only to be sorry but also to turn completely away from sin. To repent means to turn our backs to sin and our faces to God.

The minute that we invited Jesus into our lives, we became a new creation. But this doesn't mean that our work (or his) is done. "Putting off your old self" is a continual process. We need to continue to turn away from sin and work to put evil out of our lives completely.

Sometimes this means that we need to break bad habits. Sometimes it means avoiding activities and situations that can lead us to temptation.

The Bible tells us that the devil prowls around like a roaring lion looking for someone to devour. Evil is very real, but Christians don't have to fall victim to it. By relying on God and resisting evil, we can have peace in our lives and rest in God's love. ❖

PRAYER

Dear God, thank you for saving us from sin. Please help us to put off our old selves every day. Please protect us from temptation and help us to serve only you. Amen.

WILLFUL SINS

- When has God helped you avoid sinning? What did you do instead of sinning?
- What is an example of a "willful sin"?

Keep your servant also from willful sins; may they not rule over me. Then I will be blameless, innocent of great transgression.   PSALM 19:13

Sometimes we sin without really planning to do so. For example, we might get angry with someone and think unkind thoughts. Before we know it, we've sinned. While we need forgiveness for these "accidental" sins, in this verse King David is referring to *willful* sins. These are sins that result from intentionally choosing to do wrong. King David is asking God to keep him from these willful sins because David knows that God can and will help him.

God doesn't want us to sin. If we ask God to give us strength against sin, he will help us. We can ask God to keep us from sin at any time. We can pray this prayer in the morning before we begin our day. We can pray it in the heat of the moment when we are trying to resist temptation. And we can pray it when we repent, after the fact. We can tell God that we are sorry for sinning willfully and ask him to help us to not do it again.

What matters is that we ask. God wants to help us avoid sin. ✤

PRAYER

Dear God, thank you for being willing to keep us from willful sin. Please help us to avoid sin and to rely on you for strength. Amen.

day23

FORGIVEN? FORGIVE!

- Why do you think it's important for believers to get along and love one another?
- How do you feel when someone forgives you?

Bear with each other and forgive one another if any of you has a grievance against someone. Forgive as the Lord forgave you. COLOSSIANS 3:13

It is important that believers get along with each other. People who do not know God may see his power in the way that believers love one another. This doesn't mean that we will never be hurt by another believer; Christians are not immune to sin. Even believers hurt each other's feelings, lie about others and take what doesn't belong to them. God tells us we still need to forgive others when they ask for our forgiveness.

We are to forgive as the Lord has forgiven us. No matter what someone does to us, it isn't as bad as the sins we've committed against God. And if we've repented and given our lives to Jesus, then we have been forgiven for all of it. The least we can do in return is to forgive others when they repent of their wrongs.

So when you are struggling to forgive someone for something they did to you, remember that God has already forgiven you for more. ✤

PRAYER

Dear God, please forgive us when we are reluctant to forgive. Thank you for forgiving us for our sins, and please help us to forgive others when they wrong us. Amen.

day24

DON'T KEEP TRACK

- Describe a situation in which you have had to forgive someone more than once. Did forgiving them get any easier?
- How many times do you think your parents have forgiven you for doing something wrong?

Then Peter came to Jesus and asked, "Lord, how many times shall I forgive my brother or sister who sins against me? Up to seven times?" Jesus answered, "I tell you, not seven times, but seventy-seven times."　　　MATTHEW 18:21–22

Peter may have been a bit frustrated when he asked Jesus how many times he had to forgive someone. Imagine his surprise when Jesus answered 77 times! Now, Jesus didn't mean that we're supposed to write down a tally mark whenever we forgive someone and then quit when we get to 77. In fact, we're not supposed to keep track at all. Jesus said this to show that there's no point in keeping track because we are to keep forgiving regardless of how many times we've forgiven in the past.

Jesus also illustrates this teaching with a parable. In the parable, a king forgives his servant of a debt. The servant then walks out, finds someone who owes him money, and demands repayment. Though this man had just been forgiven, he refuses to forgive someone else.

Sometimes we do the same thing. Though God has forgiven believers for all that we've done wrong, we sometimes forget that we too need to forgive. Even if it's over and over again. ♣

PRAYER

Dear God, thank you for forgiving us for our sins. Please help us to forgive others without keeping track. Amen.

day25

A CLEAN SLATE

- When God forgives you of your sins, what happens to those sins?
- What does it mean to have a clean slate?

"I will sprinkle clean water on you, and you will be clean; I will cleanse you from all your impurities and from all your idols."   EZEKIEL 36:25

The Bible says that "as far as the east is from the west, so far has [God] removed our transgressions from us" (Psalm 103:12). How far is that? As far as far can be. The distance between us and our sins cannot be measured—it is that great. When God forgives us of our sins, he wipes the slate clean. We become pure again, as when we were created.

This means that once we've confessed our sins and been forgiven, we don't have to feel guilty about our mistakes anymore. We don't have to carry around the weight of our sin. God has made us clean. He has rescued us from our sin. He has set us free.

This opens us up to strive for bigger and better things. Once we confess our sins, God gets them out of the way for us. We don't have to deal with them anymore; we can focus on learning about God, serving others and glorifying God. ✤

PRAYER

Dear God, thank you for your forgiveness. Thank you for giving us a new chance every time we need one. Help us to use these chances to honor you. Amen.

day26

DIFFICULT BUT WELL WORTH IT

- Why is it important for you to forgive others?
- Who is affected when you refuse to forgive someone?

"For if you forgive other people when they sin against you, your heavenly Father will also forgive you. But if you do not forgive others their sins, your Father will not forgive your sins."
MATTHEW 6:14–15

Have you ever had a hard time forgiving someone who has wronged you? It can be difficult to do, but God commands it.

As Christians, we have been forgiven. Jesus has paid the price for our sins, and when we repent, God forgives us. Imagine if one day we asked for forgiveness and God turned us down. That would be tragic! It is also tragic when we refused to forgive someone else. Jesus gave his life so that we could be forgiven. The very least we can do is forgive others. Even though it may be hard to do sometimes, it doesn't compare to what Jesus went through, and we have the Holy Spirit to help us with this difficult task.

God has given us a model for the greatest forgiveness possible. He wants us to emulate his gift. If we do not forgive, we are making light of his gift. As we have been forgiven, so we should, with God's help, forgive. ✤

PRAYER

Dear God, thank you for your forgiveness. Thank you for suffering the cross on our behalf. Please give us the courage and strength to forgive others as you have forgiven us. Amen.

day27

NO MATTER HOW BIG

- Share a time when your parents forgave you for doing something wrong. How did their forgiveness affect your relationship with them?
- Why do you think God forgives us for our sins?

You, Lord, are forgiving and good, abounding in love to all who call to you. PSALM 86:5

Susan was only seven years old when she burned down her family's house. No one was hurt, but the family lost everything—their home, their car and all of their possessions.

It wasn't an accident. Susan was angry at her mother, so she took a lighter and started a fire in the laundry hamper. She did not mean to burn the house down, but she did mean to sin. She knew that what she was doing was wrong.

Susan apologized to her mother, but she didn't think that her mother could ever forgive her. Then one day she overheard her mother telling a friend that she *had* forgiven Susan. Susan couldn't believe it. She asked her mother how she possibly could have forgiven her. Her mother wrapped her arms around Susan and said, "Because I love you. Of course I've forgiven you."

It is the same for the children of God. God loves us so much that he sent Jesus to die on a cross and pay the penalty for our sins. God loves us so much that he is willing to forgive us when we make mistakes. No matter how big those mistakes are, God's love is bigger. ✤

PRAYER

Dear God, thank you for your love. Thank you for your forgiveness. Help us to remember that you do love and forgive us. Amen.

day28

IF WE CONFESS

- What does it mean to confess your sins to God?
- What happens when you confess your sins to God?

If we claim to be without sin, we deceive ourselves and the truth is not in us. If we confess our sins, he is faithful and just and will forgive us our sins and purify us from all unrighteousness. 1 JOHN 1:8–9

When John was writing these verses, there were people claiming that they didn't sin. We know this can't be true. Everyone sins.

If we refuse to admit that we have sinned, that means that God's truth is not in us. In fact, God's truth cannot enter into us until we admit that we have sinned and that we need to be saved.

The Greek word that John used in this verse that is translated "confess" goes beyond admitting sins. We must also agree with God that we were wrong. This means that we need to confess our sins to God while agreeing that we need his forgiveness.

When we do this, when we sincerely confess our sins, he is faithful to forgive us. He will make us pure again. There is nothing that we could possibly do to separate ourselves from the love of God. ✤

PRAYER

Dear God, we confess that we have sinned. Please forgive us of our sins and purify us from all unrighteousness. Thank you for your faithfulness and your mercy. Amen.

day29

THE LIGHT OF THE WORLD

- What are some things you can do to show God's light to other people?
- Describe a time when someone did something kind for you. How did you respond?

"You are the light of the world. A town built on a hill cannot be hidden."

MATTHEW 5:14

Have you ever noticed that the scary scenes in movies always happen at night, in darkness? There's a reason that the "haunted house" rides at the fair never have any lights on. Darkness is scary!

Have you ever waited in the dark for the power to come back on? Didn't it feel wonderful when those lights popped back into action?

There's a reason Jesus told us we are the light of the world. Light is safe and good. In the light, we can see what's going on. We know what is true and what isn't. People who do not know God are living in darkness, but they can see the light when they look at Christians.

You may have a friend who is "waiting for the lights to come back on." And you might be the person who can help. You can show the light of God to people who are trapped in darkness. ✤

PRAYER

Dear God, please help us to live in such a way that other people see your light shining through us. Amen.

day30

DARKNESS INTO LIGHT

- How would life be different if you were blind?
- Why is it important to trust God?

"I will lead the blind by ways they have not known, along unfamiliar paths I will guide them; I will turn the darkness into light before them and make the rough places smooth. These are the things I will do; I will not forsake them."　　　ISAIAH 42:16

God will turn the darkness into light. Have you ever been in a situation that felt dark? Maybe you didn't know what to do next. Maybe you were scared, frustrated, anxious or angry. God was there with you. He uses the difficult situations in our own lives for our own good. God does turn the darkness into light. He also guides the blind "by ways they have not known." We may not feel like we're blind, but compared to what God sees, our sight is limited. If we will take his hand, he will guide us along paths that we didn't even know existed.

　God will never leave you or forsake you. He will calm the seas. He will make the rough places smooth. He will turn the darkness into light. All you have to do is accept that he can. All you have to do is trust him. ♣

PRAYER

God, help us to remember that you have more power than anything or anyone else in the universe. Thank you for promising to use that power to help us. Amen.

day31

THE ULTIMATE LIGHT SOURCE

- What words could you use to describe God?
- What is a stronghold?

The LORD is my light and my salvation — whom shall I fear? The LORD is the stronghold of my life — of whom shall I be afraid?   PSALM 27:1

God is light. God is truth and joy and safety. When we have God, our light and our salvation, we have nothing to fear. No one can compare to God. God is our stronghold, our place that we go to for comfort, safety, security and protection.

This doesn't mean that the world won't scare us. The enemy thrives on fear, and the world is a scary place. But Christians don't need to succumb to this fear. Christians don't have to be afraid of the dark. We have the ultimate light source behind us and in front of us. When we have the fortress of God to protect us, no other force stands a chance.

So when you do find yourself afraid, give your fears to God. Talk to him about what you're feeling and ask him to deliver you from fear. He is always there for you. ❖

PRAYER

Dear God, thank you for being our light and our salvation. Thank you for being our strength and protection. Please deliver us from fear. Amen.

day32

CHILDREN OF LIGHT

- What words would you use to describe darkness?
- What words would you use to describe light?

For you were once darkness, but now you are light in the Lord. Live as children of light.

EPHESIANS 5:8

Paul uses the extreme contrast between light and darkness to help us understand the extreme contrast between who we were before we knew God and who we are in God.

Most children are scared of the dark at some point. You may remember a time when you felt lost or trapped in the dark. You may also remember the joy, relief and love that you felt when your parent or caregiver arrived on the scene and flipped a light on.

This is a taste of the joy, relief and love that we experience when we invite God into our darkness to rescue us. And when we do, we become children of light.

This means that we don't go back into the darkness. Instead, we work to fight it. We work to love God, to love others and to avoid sin. We are no longer in darkness. We have been rescued. ✤

PRAYER

Dear God, thank you for rescuing us. Please help us to live like children of light. Amen.

JUST A KID

- Who did you look up to when you were younger?
- How would you react if you found out someone really looked up to *you*?

Don't let anyone look down on you because you are young, but set an example for the believers in speech, in conduct, in love, in faith and in purity.   1 TIMOTHY 4:12

Timothy was a very young man when the apostle Paul wrote to him. He was also a church leader. Timothy was afraid his youth would be a problem. He was afraid the people in the church would question his decisions or refuse to listen to him because he was "so young."

Paul saw Timothy as he really was—a godly, wise and humble young man who had a lot to offer his fellow believers. Paul told Timothy that he should not be ashamed of his age and that he should set an example for others. As far as Paul was concerned, age was just a number. It doesn't matter what year you were born; all that matters is what is in your heart.

That's a twist, isn't it? Usually young people are told to follow the example of older people. But young people are just as capable of being Christian role models as older people are. You don't need to be a certain age. You just have to be committed to Christ. ✤

PRAYER

Dear God, thank you for using people of all ages to do your work. Make us examples for other believers. Amen.

day34

RUN, RUN, RUN

- What are three things you would run away from?
- What makes people stay in bad situations when they should be running away from them as fast as they can?

Flee the evil desires of youth and pursue righteousness, faith, love and peace, along with those who call on the Lord out of a pure heart. 2 TIMOTHY 2:22

"Flee" is an unusual instruction for Christians. In other Bible verses, we find commands such as "stand firm" and "resist," words that call for courage and a fighting spirit. So what's different about this verse? The apostle Paul is talking about the evil desires *of youth.*

Here's where things get tricky. We'll face temptations our whole lives. That's part of living in a sinful world. But the temptations of youth are especially dangerous.

Part of the problem is immaturity. Young people don't have the life experience to understand why certain things are harmful or how they can lead to lifelong issues.

Another issue is that physical development can cause problems. When we're young, our hormones are raging, our adrenaline is flowing and our judgment is sometimes clouded. Trying to battle evil desires with those disadvantages is a bad idea. It's not a fair fight.

When you're young and face temptations, the wise thing to do is run. Don't give them a chance to become a problem. Rob them of their power. You'll be glad you did. ♣

PRAYER

Dear God, give us the wisdom to know when we should take a stand and when we should flee. Protect us from danger. Amen.

MAKING WORSHIP PERSONAL

- If you were in charge of a church worship service, what would it be like?
- What part of worship makes you feel closest to God? Why?

"I will praise you as long as I live, and in your name I will lift up my hands."

PSALM 63:4

A family-friendly church is one in which all members of the family are challenged, given opportunities for meaningful worship, and led to a closer relationship with the Lord.

Worship is too important to take lightly. That goes for kids as well as adults. If you're old enough to talk, you're old enough to worship. And if you're old enough to worship, you're old enough to take it seriously.

God created us to worship him. If we try to avoid worship or treat it like a chore, we're telling God we're not interested in him. If, on the other hand, we fully participate in worship opportunities—and even create some of our own—our relationship with God will deepen. ✤

PRAYER

Dear God, we praise you for who you are. We praise you for what you've done. We praise you for what you've promised to do in the future. We will worship you forever. Amen.

day36

REMEMBER ME?

- What is the first thing you learned about God?
- What aspect of God is still a mystery to you?

Remember your Creator in the days of your youth, before the days of trouble come and the years approach when you will say, "I find no pleasure in them."   ECCLESIASTES 12:1

How well do you know God? How much time do you spend thinking about him? How often do you and your friends talk about him? What keeps you from knowing him better?

Some young people make the mistake of thinking that God and his nature are adult topics, something to think about when they get older. The problem with that line of thinking is that there's a lot to learn about God. In fact, there's too much to learn in one lifetime. The longer you wait to start thinking seriously about him, the less time you'll have to enjoy him.

Start now, while you're young. Ask questions. Read books. Read *the* Book! Discover how God interacted with his people in the Old and New Testaments. Learn how he deals with people who oppose him. Investigate his promises and warnings. Study his creation. "Remember your Creator in the days of your youth." ♣

PRAYER

Dear God, forgive us for the times we've neglected to get to know you. Please help us learn more about you every day of our lives. Amen.

TO OBEY OR NOT TO OBEY

- How does your family compare to other families you know when it comes to rules and discipline?
- What happens in a family when obedience and discipline break down?

Children, obey your parents in everything, for this pleases the Lord.   Colossians 3:20

"Obey your parents." Do any three words make kids roll their eyes more? Maybe "Eat your peas" or "Do your homework." But "Obey your parents" certainly ranks high on the list.

Obeying means giving up your personal freedom—doing what your parents tell you to do instead of what you want to do. And for what? What do kids get out of it? God's pleasure, that's what. Imagine being able to make the Creator of the universe happy. Sons and daughters are given the opportunity to do that every time they're faced with a rule or instruction.

Remember too that children aren't the only ones who get called out by the apostle Paul. He also gives instructions to husbands, wives and parents. In God's plan for the family, every member has a responsibility. When we fulfill it, we put a smile on God's face. ✤

PRAYER

Dear God, thank you for showing us what a loving Father is like. Help us remember that when we're obedient to our parents, we please you. Amen.

THE ARGUMENT AGAINST ARGUING

- Have you ever had an argument with someone about God? If so, what happened?
- List three activities that you think are useless. What makes them useless?

But avoid foolish controversies and genealogies and arguments and quarrels about the law, because these are unprofitable and useless.   TITUS 3:9

We learn in Titus 1 that Titus had to deal with many rebellious people. These people talked a lot without saying much, especially those who were holding on to old Jewish laws, and they were starting a lot of arguments.

Paul warns against engaging argumentative people, not because these people are right or because they should be feared, but simply because arguing is a giant waste of time.

Even if you are completely correct, even if you are a skilled debater, even if you *know* you could prove the other person wrong, there is still no point. Arguing with someone like that almost never sways the other person to your point of view. And when you are arguing about God, there's a very good chance that the other person has no interest in the truth.

Instead, God wants us to proclaim the truth through our actions. Walk away from the opportunity to argue with someone and walk toward the opportunity to love someone else. This is how we prove God's truth to others. ❖

PRAYER

Dear God, help us to avoid foolish arguments. Help us to demonstrate your truth by the way we live. Amen.

A GENTLE WORD

- How do you respond to someone who speaks harshly to you?
- Do you know anyone who speaks gently?

A gentle answer turns away wrath, but a harsh word stirs up anger. PROVERBS 15:1

In this proverb, Solomon teaches us that God wants us to speak to people gently, using gentle words. Harsh words stir up anger, even when that's not our intention.

Think about how you feel when someone speaks harshly to you. You probably get angry and defensive. But if that same person spoke to you with gentle words, you probably wouldn't get angry.

We need to think before we speak. Sometimes we need to pray before we speak and ask God to give us the right words to say. This becomes especially difficult when someone is speaking harsh words to us. How does God want us to respond? He doesn't want us fighting fire with fire. He wants us to answer with gentle words, which will put out the fire.

Words have tremendous power, but we don't have to let them get us into trouble. We can use them to honor God. ✤

PRAYER

Dear God, thank you for trusting us with the power of words. Please help us to speak gently, using gentle words. Please help us to respond to people the way you want us to. Amen.

LEAVE THE DOG'S EARS ALONE!

- If two dogs were fighting in the street, would you jump between them to stop them?
- How do you know when it's wise to get between two people who are quarreling?

Like one who grabs a stray dog by the ears is someone who rushes into a quarrel not their own.   PROVERBS 26:17

Imagine seeing a stray dog by the side of the road. Then imagine walking up to it and grabbing it by its ears. Not a smart move!

This proverb uses a dogfight as a metaphor for other people's arguments. Getting involved in them is also not a smart move.

Police officers are often called to homes where two people are fighting. When the police officer tries to stand between them to stop the fight, he or she is in danger of being attacked by both of them.

Sometimes we think we need to help out by stepping into the middle of an argument, but this is a dangerous habit, according to the proverb. Instead of helping to solve the argument, we might just get hurt ourselves.

If we want to help someone who is caught in an argument, the best thing that we can do is to pray for them and advise them to take their problem to a person who is trained in counseling. ✤

PRAYER

Dear God, please help us to keep our noses out of other people's business and to recognize the difference between being helpful and being a busybody. We pray for our friends or family who are in disagreement and ask you to bring peace between them. Amen.

DON'T STIR THE POT!

- How do you feel when you are involved in an argument?
- How do you feel when you watch two of your friends argue?

Whoever loves a quarrel loves sin; whoever builds a high gate invites destruction.

PROVERBS 17:19

The exact interpretation of this proverb is debated. However, it is clear about one thing: Quarrels are not a positive part of anyone's life. The second part of the proverb is usually thought of as being related to arrogance or pride. People who are proud or boastful bring about quarrels by asserting their own opinion without listening to others. Arguments result. Such people "stir the pot," which is a way of saying "cause trouble." Proverbs tells us that this is a sin. We're not supposed to run around provoking people and getting everyone angry.

Some people struggle with this. Perhaps they enjoy the control and or attention of causing a rift between others. It's an adrenalin rush for them, and they find it exciting. Perhaps they are angry at someone and want to cause that person problems. Perhaps their root problem of pride doesn't allow them to have good relationships with others.

Stirring up trouble is not okay with God. If you struggle with this, you need to ask God for help. With God's help, you can figure out a better way to relate to others. ✤

PRAYER

Dear God, please help us remember that you want your children to live together in harmony. Please help us to love you and others. Amen.

day42

INCOMPREHENSIBLE LOVE

- What are some things that you know about but don't really understand?
- How much does Jesus love you?

And I pray that you, being rooted and established in love, may have power, together with all the Lord's holy people, to grasp how wide and long and high and deep is the love of Christ.   Ephesians 3:17–18

A child asked Jesus how much he loved her. He answered, "This much," and then he stretched out his arms and died on the cross.

You may have heard this before. It's a good way to think about how much Jesus loves you. He loves you so much that he left heaven and came to earth for you. He loves you so much that he suffered and died for you. And the Bible says that nothing you can do will separate you from the love of Jesus.

In these verses from Ephesians, Paul describes Jesus' love as being "wide and long and high and deep." The idea is that it is infinite—you will never come to the end of it. God loved you before he created you. He loves you right this minute. And he will love you for eternity.

We cannot possibly understand how much Jesus loves us. We don't have to. All we have to do is accept it. ✤

PRAYER

Dear God, thank you for your love. Please help us to accept it. Amen.

LOVE FORGIVES

- How do you know that your parent or caregiver loves you? How do they know that you love them?
- When someone hurts you, how do you forgive them?

Above all, love each other deeply, because love covers over a multitude of sins.

1 PETER 4:8

On Valentine's Day, we hear a lot about love. But the love that God has for us goes beyond cards and gifts. So does the love that Christians are supposed to have for one another.

One of the features of Christian love is that it covers a multitude of sins. This love gives us the ability to forgive others just as we have been forgiven.

Since we all do things that are wrong sometimes, we all need lots of forgiveness. We please God when we are ready to forgive one another often. That is what genuine, godly love looks like.

Are you holding a grudge against someone today? Take a good look at your heart and see if there are any offenses that you haven't forgiven. God wants you to forgive others, and he has given you the love to do it. It might not be easy, but with God's love, it is possible. ✣

PRAYER

Dear God, help us to have real love for one another, so that we can be understanding and forgiving. Please help us to be eager to forgive others. Amen.

day44 february 13

REAL LOVE

- What does it mean to be sincere?
- Have you ever been around someone who seemed to be faking kindness? How did that person make you feel?

Love must be sincere. Hate what is evil; cling to what is good. ROMANS 12:9

We throw the word *love* around a lot. Jeremy loves basketball. Jocelyn loves ice cream. We love our new shoes. We love that song. We use the word so often that it has lost a lot of its meaning. But when the Bible talks about love, it's talking about the real deal.

Real love must be sincere. There is nothing fake or hypocritical about it.

Real love means action. If you tell someone you love them, or if you think you *feel* love toward someone, but you won't help them when they are in need, then that is not real love.

Real love is never selfish. If you love someone because you might get something in return, then that is not love.

Real love can only come from God. God is the source of real love, and it is through God's love that we are able to show sincere love to one another. ❖

PRAYER

Dear God, thank you for your love. Please help us to do a good job of showing your love to one another. Amen.

LOVE THAT CANNOT FAIL

- How would you describe God's love?
- Why do you trust in God's love?

Love never fails. But where there are prophecies, they will cease; where there are tongues, they will be stilled; where there is knowledge, it will pass away.   1 CORINTHIANS 13:8

This verse comes at the end of the famous 1 Corinthians "love" chapter, the chapter that describes God's love. What a fitting conclusion for the description of love — it never fails. Everything else will cease, will be stilled, will pass away, but love never fails. Love is eternal. Love never ends.

Over and over in the Bible, God tells us to trust in his love. This can be hard sometimes. When we are struggling, we might wonder where God's love is. But we know that it is right there, all around us and in us. God will never leave us or forsake us. Just because we can't see him doesn't mean that he's not right there loving us with a love that will not quit.

We can depend on this love. We can lean on it, hope in it and act on it. Even when we don't understand life, we can count on the fact that God's love will never fail us. God is perfect. His love is perfect. ❖

PRAYER

Dear God, thank you for your love. Thank you that your love never ends. Please help us to trust in your love. Amen.

day46

YOUR MISSION: LOVE YOUR ENEMIES

- Why is it hard to pray for your enemy?
- What prayer could you pray for your enemy?

"You have heard that it was said, 'Love your neighbor and hate your enemy.' But I tell you, love your enemies and pray for those who persecute you."   MATTHEW 5:43–44

It is easy to love and pray for our friends and our family members. We want things to go well for them. We care about them and enjoy asking God to help them and give them what they need to be healthy and happy.

But it is much harder to pray for our enemies. When it comes to people we do not particularly like, or those who have hurt us in some way, we often secretly don't want things to work out for them.

Jesus knows that it isn't natural for us to feel affection for our enemies. That is why he is careful to make sure we understand what he expects of us. As Christians, we are supposed to love our enemies and pray for them. But the good news is that he doesn't expect us to do this on our own. He intends to help us. We just have to ask him. ✤

PRAYER

Dear God, please help us to love our enemies. Please remind us to pray for them. Amen.

WORTHY OF RESPECT

- How do you show your parents respect?
- Why are your parents worthy of respect?

"Each of you must respect your mother and father, and you must observe my Sabbaths. I am the LORD your God."   LEVITICUS 19:3

The Bible teaches us to respect our parents. God wants us to always treat our parents with kindness and consideration. We should remember that their ideas and thoughts matter. We should consider their feelings and how our actions will affect those feelings. And even if our parents disappoint us or make poor choices, we should remember that God wants us to honor them.

Sometimes we get caught up in the drama of life, and we are tempted to be disrespectful to the people in charge. If you find this happening to you, talk to God about it. He gave us this command, so he's going to help us keep it. And remember, parents have been children too, and they know how hard it can be to show the appropriate respect.

Sometimes it's helpful to consider a situation from your parents' point of view. Can you imagine what it must be like for them? Can you imagine being responsible for the welfare of another soul? Parents are under a tremendous amount of pressure. They carry an immense responsibility on their shoulders. We can support them with our respect. ✤

PRAYER

Dear God, thank you for our parents. Please help us to be respectful toward them because you have told us to honor them. Amen.

CAVE DANGER

- How can you show respect to those in authority?
- What happens when you show disrespect to people in authority?

He came to the sheep pens along the way; a cave was there, and Saul went in to relieve himself. David and his men were far back in the cave. The men said, "This is the day the LORD spoke of when he said to you, 'I will give your enemy into your hands for you to deal with as you wish.'" Then David crept up unnoticed and cut off a corner of Saul's robe . . . He said to his men, "The LORD forbid that I should do such a thing to my master, the LORD's anointed, or lay my hand on him; for he is the anointed of the LORD."

1 SAMUEL 24:3–4,6

King Saul, along with 3,000 of his men, was out looking for David in order to kill him. David was hiding in a cave—as God would have it, the same cave where King Saul decided to "relieve himself."

Can you imagine hiding in a cave and having the murderous king stroll in for a bathroom break? Well, David's friends urged David to kill Saul on the spot, but David didn't. Instead, David snuck up on Saul and cut off a corner of his robe.

David then explained to his men that he would not kill the man whom God had made king. Even though Saul wanted David dead, David spared him because God had placed Saul in authority over David.

We don't always like the people who are placed in authority over us. But we still need to recognize their authority and show them respect. ✤

PRAYER

Dear God, please help us to show respect to those people you have placed in positions of authority. Amen.

day49

BURNING BUSH RESPECT

- How do you show God respect?
- Why does God deserve your respect?

"Do not come any closer," God said. "Take off your sandals, for the place where you are standing is holy ground."   EXODUS 3:5

Imagine you are Moses on that bizarre day long ago. You're out tending to your father-in-law's sheep, minding your own business, when suddenly, you see a bush on fire. You go in for a closer look, and the voice from the bush identifies itself as the voice of God. Then God tells you to take off your sandals.

If God appeared to us in a burning bush, we would naturally show respect to him. But we are also to respect God when he doesn't show up in miraculous ways. In the course of our daily lives, we need to remember that we are still dealing with the same God who can speak from a burning bush. We should still show God the same awe, respect, humility and obedience that Moses showed God that day.

God is more than worthy of our respect. Considering his almighty power and the fact that he's the one who made us, respecting him is really the least we can do. ❖

PRAYER

Dear God, please help us to give you the respect you deserve. Amen.

day50

THAT MEANS EVERYONE

- How do you show respect to someone?
- How does it feel when someone shows you respect?

Show proper respect to everyone, love the family of believers, fear God, honor the emperor.
                                                                    1 PETER 2:17

Ethan acted like he was better than everyone else. He felt that he had it all together, that he knew everything he needed to know. He was disrespectful to his peers, their parents, his teachers and coaches, acting as if they couldn't teach him anything because they didn't go to church.

Unfortunately, these people associated Ethan's lack of respect with his claims of faith. Over time, Ethan did a lot of damage to God's name. From Ethan's behavior, people began to think that they were not good enough for God. Because of his conduct, people decided they wanted nothing to do with his God.

As Peter writes, believers are to show proper respect to everyone, including non-Christians. We don't have to agree with everything that people do, but we do need to show them respect. ✤

PRAYER

Dear God, please help us to show proper respect to everyone we meet. Amen.

day51

BIBLE VERSES AND BALL GAMES

- Quick: What does John 3:16 say?
- Why is that the best-known verse in the Bible?

For God so loved the world that he gave his one and only Son, that whoever believes in him shall not perish but have eternal life.   JOHN 3:16

When you go to sporting events or watch them on TV, you see people in the crowd holding up all kinds of signs. One of the most popular is the John 3:16 sign. That's all it says: "John 3:16." The idea is that people will be so curious to know what John 3:16 says that they'll investigate it for themselves.

Let's say that happens. Let's say someone who knows nothing about God's Word or Christianity finds a Bible and opens it to John 3:16. What would they find there that would get their attention?

"God so loved the world"? That seems pretty basic. "Gave his one and only Son"? That doesn't really tell much. "Shall not perish but have eternal life"? There's the sweet spot! The possibility of living forever is enough to make almost anyone look twice. After all, death is our enemy because it means "Game Over."

So a claim about eternal life is likely to stir some interest. Even better is a Christian who can personally explain how eternal life is possible and how to receive it. So if you're wondering how to talk to people you know about Christ, you might want to start with John 3:16. ♣

PRAYER

Dear God, thank you for sending your Son to die so that we can live forever. Give us the wisdom, courage and creativity to share the message of John 3:16 in a way that gets people's attention. Amen.

day52

IT'S A GIFT

- What's the most impressive thing you've ever accomplished by yourself?
- Why is it sometimes hard to ask for help or admit that you can't do something by yourself?

For it is by grace you have been saved, through faith—and this is not from yourselves, it is the gift of God—not by works, so that no one can boast.   EPHESIANS 2:8–9

The apostle Paul's words in Ephesians 2 go against everything we've been taught. Our country was built with the spirit of self-sufficiency. We're told that the first step to success is a can-do attitude. Riding on someone else's coattails is looked down on. We've been led to believe that if you want something done right, you have to do it yourself. And in many cases, that's true—just not when it comes to salvation.

There's nothing we can do to make up for our sinful nature. We can't be good enough or sorry enough to earn God's forgiveness. Only Jesus can pay the price that God demands for sin. Only he can give us eternal life.

On the one hand, that's a pretty humbling thought. We're useless when it comes to saving our own souls. We're completely in Jesus' debt. On the other hand, it gives us an appealing message to take to other people who may be interested in eternal life: *Don't drive yourself crazy trying to earn it; just believe in Jesus and receive God's gift.* ✤

PRAYER

Dear God, thank you for taking the pressure off of us. We could never be good enough to earn salvation. Help us find ways to share that freedom from sin with others. Amen.

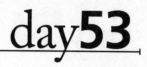

NO LIE

- What's the most embarrassing lie you ever got caught in?
- If you found out a friend lied to you, how would it affect your friendship?

In the hope of eternal life, which God, who does not lie, promised before the beginning of time. TITUS 1:2

What would you say if your best friend told you about an easier way to receive eternal life — one that didn't require you to believe in Jesus or live according to God's will? Would you be tempted to investigate it? What if your church pastor stood up on Sunday morning and announced that Bible scholars have found that Jesus *isn't* the only way to salvation anymore? Would you change your mind?

No matter how much respect you have for your best friend or your pastor, you would need to be cautious. Why? They're both human beings and capable of deception.

If you're going to trust your eternal life with someone, it should be someone who does not lie. And that's God. He's the source of all truth, which means there is no lie in him. When he offers eternal life, you can depend on it.

That's important to remember because there will be people who try to shake you out of your Christian faith. They'll give you dozens of reasons why other beliefs — or no beliefs at all — are better than Christianity. In the end, though, you have to ask yourself, "Who can I trust?" ♣

PRAYER

Dear God, thank you for the fact that we can trust everything you say. Help us always to recognize your truth in a world of lies. Amen.

HEIRS OF GOD

- What would you like to inherit someday?
- What's the best way to thank God for his gift of salvation?

He saved us through the washing of rebirth and renewal by the Holy Spirit, whom he poured out on us generously through Jesus Christ our Savior, so that, having been justified by his grace, we might become heirs having the hope of eternal life.   TITUS 3:5 – 7

The wording of this passage may make salvation seem like a car wash. We take our dirty, sinful selves to Jesus, and he gives us the deluxe treatment, scrubbing away all our guilt and shame until we shine like new. Actually, though, salvation is more like a complete overhaul. Jesus changes us from the inside out. We become completely different people.

And we have almost nothing to do with it. We can't renew or regenerate ourselves. All we can do is ask Jesus to do it for us. He's the only one who can.

Since the gift of salvation ultimately comes from God, our heavenly Father, that makes us his "heirs." Salvation is our inheritance. We're part of God's family, so we receive what he offers. But we've done nothing to earn it. We receive it because he wants us to have it.

Our inheritance gives us the hope of eternal life. Unlike heirs in human families, who often fight to get a bigger share of the inheritance, children of God are encouraged to share their wealth and invite others into the family. Who can you share your wealth with? ✤

PRAYER

Dear God, thank you for accepting us into your family and making us your heirs. Guide us as we invite others to share in your wealth. Amen.

day55

FAITHFUL FOLLOWERS WELCOME

- What's the hardest part about being a Christian in your school, neighborhood or workplace?
- What do you think heaven will be like? Explain.

"Not everyone who says to me, 'Lord, Lord,' will enter the kingdom of heaven, but only the one who does the will of my Father who is in heaven."   MATTHEW 7:21

God didn't create heaven as a club for people who say the right password. Many people think they can do a few good deeds and get into heaven. Their goal is to get into heaven by the skin of their teeth. They figure heaven is the reward for their efforts.

That's not how God figures it, though. It's not easy to follow God's will in this world. We have to resist sins that other people enjoy. We might have to put up with people making fun of us and accusing us of being narrow-minded and unloving. We sometimes live as foreigners in a place where other people feel at home.

God understands our difficulties. He's with us every step of the way. He knows what we go through. But he's here to help us. He rewards us with his presence, grace and forgiveness in this life, and we look forward to heaven in the next. When you think about it, that's an unbeatable deal. ✤

PRAYER

Dear God, thank you for giving us so much to look forward to. When things get rough on earth, remind us of what lies ahead. Amen.

day56

ONE WAY

- What's the most valuable gift you've ever given?
- What's the most valuable gift you've ever received?

Jesus said to her, "I am the resurrection and the life. The one who believes in me will live, even though they die." JOHN 11:25

People say that when you're given something, it means less to you than if you had worked to earn it. While there's certainly some truth to that theory, there are exceptions. For example, if your grandfather gave you a valuable family heirloom, you'd probably treasure the gift, even though you did nothing to earn it.

The same goes for eternal life. The salvation that leads to eternal life is a gift. We can do nothing to earn it; all we can do is accept it. That doesn't mean it was free, though. Our eternal life cost Jesus his earthly life. He gave himself to save us because no one else could. Our sin required a perfect sacrifice, and he's the only perfect person who ever lived.

That's why eternal life comes through Jesus and Jesus alone. Jesus is the resurrection and the life because death could not conquer him.

Anyone who wants eternal life must agree to Jesus' terms. But that's good news because all he asks is that we believe in his power—and his power alone—to save us. ✤

PRAYER

Dear God, thank you for sacrificing your Son for us. We put our faith in him alone to save us from sin and give us eternal life. Amen.

day57

THE POWER OF GIVING

- Who's the most generous person you know? Explain.
- How can we as a family be more generous?

When they arrived at the house of the LORD in Jerusalem, some of the heads of the families gave freewill offerings toward the rebuilding of the house of God on its site. According to their ability they gave to the treasury for this work 61,000 darics of gold, 5,000 minas of silver and 100 priestly garments.   EZRA 2:68–69

Jerusalem was conquered by the Babylonians in 587 BC. The entire city was destroyed, and its people were taken captive in Babylon. Seventy years later, the Israelites started moving back to their homeland to rebuild Jerusalem. Their first priority was the temple, the place where they worshiped God. The people wanted the rebuilt temple to be special, so they gave their money and materials freely.

God's people understood that generous giving honors God. But generosity isn't measured in donation totals. The person who gives the most money is not necessarily the most generous person. Generosity is measured in attitude and spirit.

One day Jesus was standing near the temple treasury, where people came to present their offerings. He watched several wealthy people put in large gifts. Behind them, a poor widow put in two very small coins. So whose gift did Jesus praise? The widow's because those two coins were all she had to live on. Her gift was a sacrifice (see Mark 12:41–44).

The woman understood that God could do more with her money than she could. And she knew he would take care of her, with or without the coins. That's the kind of giving spirit that honors God. That's the kind of spirit we should strive for. ❖

PRAYER

Dear God, thank you for the opportunity to honor you with our giving. Show us new ways we can use what we have for your sake. Amen.

day58

A GROUP EFFORT

- What's the best thing to share? Why?
- Is there such a thing as being too generous with your money or possessions? Explain.

All the believers were together and had everything in common. They sold property and possessions to give to anyone who had need.   ACTS 2:44–45

Ten days after Jesus ascended to heaven, his disciples gathered in Jerusalem with thousands of other Jewish people for the day of Pentecost. During the celebration, Peter stood up and preached an incredible sermon about Jesus. He told the crowd exactly who Jesus was and what he'd done. God used that sermon to bring 3,000 people to Christ.

Naturally there was a lot of excitement in that group. They'd given their lives to Jesus, but they wanted to do more. They were excited to show how much they loved him. So they put their money to use, taking care of their fellow believers' needs. Then they sold their houses and possessions, and they used that money to help each other too.

That's how the first church started—with a group of people helping one another and meeting each other's needs. God blessed their generosity with some of his own. He added to their numbers every day, and Christianity took root throughout the world.

How far should we go to help fellow Christians who are in need? What sacrifices could we make to care for others? What kind of giving are we capable of? ✤

PRAYER

Dear God, thank you for giving us a family in the body of Christ. Let us care for our brothers and sisters. Amen.

THE LOVE OF GOD IN US

- What does it look like to really care about people in need?
- What kind of giving would you like to see our family do?

If anyone has material possessions and sees a brother or sister in need but has no pity on them, how can the love of God be in that person?   1 JOHN 3:17

We are created in God's image. As believers, we've been adopted into God's family. We call God our heavenly Father. When people look at us, though, they may not always see the family resemblance. Instead, they may see our petty arguments and social drama. They may see our weaknesses and bad habits. They may see the times we give in to temptation. They may see the times we ignore others or treat them badly.

So who can blame them for questioning our connection to God?

The one thing no one can question, though, is a generous spirit, especially when God is the one who gets the credit. There are hundreds of ways to show that kind of spirit. For starters, we could get involved in a fundraiser, donate to a food pantry, help build a house, give money to those who need it, or share our lunch or school supplies.

People will notice a giving spirit—even if we do our best to keep it private. People respect real generosity. They can see God in it, whether they realize it or not. ✤

PRAYER

Dear God, thank you for your generous gifts to us. Bless our efforts to follow your example by giving generously to others. Amen.

day60

THE ONE WHO HAS EVERYTHING

- Who's the hardest person in your family to find a gift for? Explain.
- How can you tell if a gift has been given from the heart?

All who were willing, men and women alike, came and brought gold jewelry of all kinds: brooches, earrings, rings and ornaments. They all presented their gold as a wave offering to the LORD.   Exodus 35:22

What do you get for the One who has everything? Think about it. God created the universe. Everything on the earth is his. What could we possibly give him that would mean anything to him?

The answer: something sincere. Something meaningful to us. Something that requires work or sacrifice on our part. Something that shows him how much we love and honor him.

We can show God a generous spirit. We can honor him by using our resources for his work. The passage from Exodus 35 is a great example. God instructed the Israelites to build a tabernacle—a place where they could worship him. But he left it to those "who were willing" to donate the materials for it. The people of Israel jumped at the chance. They gave their most expensive jewelry, fabrics and building materials. They saw an opportunity to honor God, and they took advantage of it—whatever the cost.

What can we learn from the Israelites? What opportunities does our family have to honor God? How many similar opportunities have we missed in the past? How can we make sure we don't miss the next one? ✤

PRAYER

Dear God, we have nothing to give you that isn't already yours. Please accept our gifts and offerings for what they are and use them to accomplish your will. Amen.

day61

HOW TO BE A GOD-PLEASER

- Do you know anyone who is hard to please?
- How do you feel when you're around hard-to-please people?

And do not forget to do good and to share with others, for with such sacrifices God is pleased. HEBREWS 13:16

The Bible makes it clear that there aren't many ways we can please God. Isaiah 64:6 says our righteous acts—the things we do to make ourselves look like good people—are nothing more than "filthy rags" to God. What *does* please God, however, is when we help others who are in need.

What if, instead of making wish lists of the things we want to own, we started making wish lists of the things we want to *give*? We could get information from our church about people in our area who need Christmas gifts to give their kids, a new roof on their house or a dependable used car. We could research mission organizations about villages that need new wells for drinking water. We could use the money we'd usually spend on ourselves to help those people in need. More importantly, we could please God. ❖

PRAYER

Dear God, thank you for setting the ultimate example of sharing for us. Thank you for sharing your Son so that we may be forgiven for our sins. Amen.

day**62**

GIVE AND YOU WILL RECEIVE

- How does God reward his people?
- If you know God will reward you for helping others, how can you have a truly generous spirit?

"Truly I tell you, anyone who gives you a cup of water in my name because you belong to the Messiah will certainly not lose their reward."   MARK 9:41

God could have given us an eleventh commandment and *ordered* us to donate, say, 50 percent of everything we have to him. He could have made it a sin to give 49 percent or less. He could have decided to punish us when we are not generous with our possessions.

But that's not how he chooses to work. Instead, he poses it as an unbeatable opportunity. He asks, "Would you like to do me a favor?" Of course, the answer is yes. Who wouldn't want to do God a favor? And then he reveals what's really important to him: "Then take care of people who are in need."

When we lend a hand to someone in need—even if it's just offering a cup of water—we are helping God. His heart is with those who are overlooked and underprivileged. When we use what he has given us to help people, we touch God's heart. And he won't forget that.

God rewards people who look out for others—especially others in need. And his generosity puts ours to shame. If we commit ourselves to helping the needy, he will bless us in ways we can't imagine. ♣

PRAYER

Dear God, thank you for rewarding generosity. Let us focus on what we give rather than what we will receive. Keep your generous spirit alive in our hearts. Amen.

THE END OF PAIN

- Why does God allow good people to suffer?
- What can we do as a family to minister to people who are in pain?

And I heard a loud voice from the throne saying, "Look! God's dwelling place is now among the people, and he will dwell with them. They will be his people, and God himself will be with them and be their God. 'He will wipe every tear from their eyes. There will be no more death' or mourning or crying or pain, for the old order of things has passed away." REVELATION 21:3–4

The world is full of pain, but some people seem to experience more than their share. If you know someone who suffers from chronic pain, you know how hard it can be.

As followers of Jesus, we have two jobs when it comes to pain. First, we have a responsibility to help those who are suffering. In Matthew 25, Jesus said that whatever we do for people who are sick, we're actually doing for him. What can we as a family do to help hurting people in our community?

Second, we have a responsibility to tell others about the place where there will be no pain. If you're serious about helping others who are hurting, sooner or later you will be asked, "Why doesn't God do something about it?" or "Why does God allow pain to happen?"

People who are in pain — or who have loved ones who are in pain — are looking for hope. The words of the apostle John in Revelation 21:3–4 offer that hope. People who otherwise may not be interested in hearing about heaven may stop to listen if you tell them about God's promise to wipe out pain forever. ✤

PRAYER

Dear God, thank you for giving us the hope that one day there will be no pain. Until then, use us to comfort and help people who are suffering. Amen.

CHRISTIANS HELPING CHRISTIANS

- Who in your church can you help this week? What can you do?
- What do you suppose non-Christians think when they see Christians supporting one another?

Therefore encourage one another with these words. 1 THESSALONIANS 4:18

If becoming a Christian meant a person would never experience pain again during their life on earth, Christianity would be about ten thousand times more popular than it is now. But Christianity offers no such guarantee.

What our faith does offer, though, is support and encouragement. The Bible makes it clear that believers are all brothers and sisters in Christ. And when someone is hurting, who better is there to have near than family?

Of course, those bonds don't form overnight. They take time. The more time we spend with other believers—at church, at work, at school, in the neighborhood, at Bible study—the stronger our connection becomes. The better we get to know people, the more we become invested in their lives. We rejoice when they rejoice. We hurt when they hurt. And we feel motivated to come alongside them in the midst of their hurting.

If you know a Christian who is hurting, you can be an answer to prayer in that person's life. You can encourage your friend in the faith, help out with things that need to be done, pray with him or her and provide an all-important listening ear. ✤

PRAYER

Dear God, thank you for surrounding us with fellow believers to comfort us when we're hurting. Bless our efforts to help other Christians who are hurting so that we may show the world what it means to follow you. Amen.

A FRIEND TO COMFORT

- If you were in pain, which friend (or friends) would you want by your side? Why?
- Which friend would you definitely not want around when you're in pain? Why?

When they saw him from a distance, they could hardly recognize him; they began to weep aloud, and they tore their robes and sprinkled dust on their heads. Then they sat on the ground with him for seven days and seven nights. No one said a word to him, because they saw how great his suffering was.　　　　　　　　　　Job 2:12–13

After Job lost his family and possessions, three of his friends came to comfort him. We can learn a lot—good and bad—from their example. The first thing Job's friends did right was to visit Job in person. They didn't send a card wishing him well. They didn't let their discomfort or awkwardness keep them away. They went to grieve with him.

They also gave Job the space he needed to grieve. Job 2:13 says Job's friends sat in silence for seven days and seven nights. They saw how badly Job was hurting, and they were content to grieve quietly with him. They gave him time to process his thoughts and feelings. They didn't try to force a conversation.

That's not to say Job's friends did everything right. In their arrogance, they were convinced they knew the reason for his suffering. They believed Job was being punished for sin and kept urging him to repent. They were wrong, and as a result, they added to his misery.

Let's learn from the example of Job's friends. Each of us will have opportunities to help friends who are hurting. The way we respond to those opportunities will say a lot about us and about the God we serve. ✤

PRAYER

Dear God, make us aware of the people around us who need our help. Give us the strength and wisdom to comfort those who are hurting. Amen.

AN AMAZING TRUTH

- How does it make you feel to know that the Creator of the universe cares about you personally?
- When specifically have you experienced God's love?

Know therefore that the LORD your God is God; he is the faithful God, keeping his covenant of love to a thousand generations of those who love him and keep his commandments.
DEUTERONOMY 7:9

God is the Creator and Sustainer of the universe. He oversees everything from the tiniest atomic particles to the largest supernovas in space. He reigns supreme from his throne in heaven, superior to all his creation. He is perfect and holy and completely removed from anything imperfect or sinful.

There is no logical reason to assume that God, who is so powerful and so righteous, should care about the personal pain and struggles of one imperfect human creature on one average-sized planet in a universe of billions of galaxies. Yet that's exactly what God does.

He cares about you—specifically. He knows everything about you and cares about every part. He cares because he loves every one of us. And he is faithful to us. When we are hurting, we can count on him to comfort us.

Deuteronomy 7:9 tells us God has made a covenant of love with "those who love him and keep his commandments." God cares for us as a loving father cares for his children. He will not always make our pain go away, but he will never make us face it alone. This is a promise we can hold on to. ✤

PRAYER

Dear God, it seems too good to be true that you, in all your power and glory, should care about us. Yet you do, and we praise you for it. Remind us of your love and your presence when we are in pain. Amen.

day67

WHERE IS GOD WHEN WE SUFFER?

- Why do people suffer?
- What does God do about it?

But no one says, "Where is God my Maker, who gives songs in the night?"   JOB 35:10

Of all the people in the Bible, no one suffered more than Job. He had a lot to lose: seven sons, three daughters, 7,000 sheep, 3,000 camels, 500 oxen, 500 donkeys, and servants galore. And one day he lost it all, every bit of it.

Job knew God was allowing him to suffer, but he couldn't understand why. He'd always lived righteously and had served God. Job had no way of knowing that Satan was trying to break him and that God was showing Satan he couldn't. That's why Job wondered aloud why God had abandoned him. He didn't realize God was right there with him, suffering alongside his beloved servant.

For God, watching Job suffer must have been a terrible preview of watching his own Son on the cross. As part of Jesus' sacrifice, he had to take on the sins of the entire world. For one horrific moment, Jesus *became* sin on the cross. And God, because he is holy and cannot look on sin, allowed the punishment and sacrifice for all sin to be completed before he brought his Son back into his presence.

God will not always make pain go away, but he will always comfort you in the midst of it. He will not abandon you, just as he did not abandon Job. ✤

PRAYER

Dear God, you know everything that happens to us and every emotion we feel. Remind us of your love when our pain makes it difficult for us remember. Thank you for your loving concern. Amen.

day68

NO POTTY MOUTH ZONE

- Why do your parents teach you to be careful with what you say?
- What would it be like to go without talking for a week?

Nor should there be obscenity, foolish talk or coarse joking, which are out of place, but rather thanksgiving.   EPHESIANS 5:4

It can be easy for us to forget the power of words. But don't forget that God spoke the heavens and the earth into being!

Words are so powerful. We use words to communicate our thoughts and feelings. We use words to express who we are. We learn about God and life through words. We talk to God in words. Can you even imagine a world without words?

It's important for us to recognize and remember the power that words have. We can use our words to express love or to hurt people. We can use our words to make the world a better place or to damage it. We can use our words to honor God or dishonor him. It's up to us.

There is no room in a Christian's vocabulary for cursing or rudeness. Each of our words has power. Choose wisely. ♣

PRAYER

Dear God, thank you for the gift of words. Please help us to hold our tongues rather than engaging in rude and foolish talk. Help us to speak words of gratitude. Amen.

day69

SEASONED WITH SALT

- Why do people salt their food?
- Why is it important for Christians to speak in a way that is honoring to God?

Let your conversation be always full of grace, seasoned with salt, so that you may know how to answer everyone.   COLOSSIANS 4:6

If our conversation is full of grace, it is Spirit-filled and pure, gentle and kind, beneficial to people and honoring to God. Salt not only adds flavor to food but also prevents food from spoiling. Our words should be graceful, nurturing anyone we talk to.

When we lead a Christian life, people will eventually ask us about our faith. Sometimes they ask out of curiosity. Sometimes they ask because God is calling them to himself. Sometimes they ask to challenge us and our beliefs. Whatever the reason, believers need to be ready to respond the way God wants us to.

Our speech reflects our relationship with God. People, both believers and non-believers, learn about God from our words. We have the opportunity to speak the truth rather than allowing the truth to be hidden. The choice is ours, but Paul tells us in this verse which option God wants us to choose. ❖

PRAYER

Dear God, thank you for allowing us to influence others with our conversations. Please help us to always be ready to influence those people who ask about you, as well as those who don't. Amen.

DON'T UNDERESTIMATE YOUR INFLUENCE

- How old does someone have to be before he or she can serve God?
- How does what you say and do influence others?

Don't let anyone look down on you because you are young, but set an example for the believers in speech, in conduct, in love, in faith and in purity. 1 TIMOTHY 4:12

This Bible verse is taken from a letter that the apostle Paul wrote to Timothy, who was serving as a pastor at the time. Timothy was young for a pastor, which is why Paul tells him not to let anyone look down on him because of his age.

People of all ages, especially young people, should take this verse to heart. No matter what age you are, you can set an example for believers. You can do this with the way that you talk, the way that you act, how you love others and how you exercise your faith.

If this feels like a lot of pressure, it is. God is your only judge, and you only have to worry about pleasing him. But this doesn't mean that other people are not watching you. Choose your words and your actions to glorify God. Setting a good example for others is simply a by-product of this process.

You never know how much influence your words and actions may have on someone else. Never underestimate your own influence. Think before you speak and before you act. And try to make decisions that will glorify God. ✤

PRAYER

Dear God, thank you for loving young believers just as much as older ones. Thank you for giving me opportunities to influence others for you. Please help me to choose the right words and actions so I can glorify you in all that I do and say. Amen.

WE ARE ONE

- Besides male and female and Jew and Gentile, what are some other categories people are divided into?
- Have you ever been put into a category you didn't like? Explain.

There is neither Jew nor Gentile, neither slave nor free, nor is there male and female, for you are all one in Christ Jesus. GALATIANS 3:28

People can be put into all kinds of categories: dog or cat lovers, American or European football fans, technology lovers or haters. Some divisions, like these, are harmless. Others, though, can cause a great deal of harm. If people use divisions to decide that some groups are more important than others, it's called discrimination. And it goes against God's view of his people.

The key to breaking down harmful barriers is to focus on the similarities and common ground we share. We all want friendship. We all want acceptance. We all want to find a place in this world. We all want to be safe from bullying, name-calling and stereotyping. We all want to be known for who we really are and not for who people *think* we are. Most importantly, we all are loved by God.

If you feel separated from someone by race or cultural background or family income level, think about the connection you have in God's eyes and build from there. Don't pretend differences don't exist. Our differences are what make friendships interesting. Learning to bridge gaps with people can open our eyes to the world around us. ❖

PRAYER

Dear God, thank you for treating all people equally. Let us remember your example in the way we treat others. Amen.

day72

US AND THEM

- When you hear the phrase "us and them," who do you picture as "us"?
- What's the best way to get to know someone who doesn't seem to have much in common with you?

"Do not pervert justice; do not show partiality to the poor or favoritism to the great, but judge your neighbor fairly."   LEVITICUS 19:15

How often are you included in or excluded from a group based on who you are? Whether they are boys and girls, rich and poor, popular and unpopular, we all fall into "us and them" categories.

The best way to break down the barriers of "us" and "them" is to get to know "them." The natural tendency of most people is to surround themselves with people who are like them—from similar economic backgrounds, with similar upbringings and similar positions in society.

But if we're serious about learning to judge our neighbors fairly, we need to overrule our natural tendency. We need to expand our circle of friends. If friendship isn't possible, then we at least need to expand the circle of people we know. We need to break down the barriers that keep us apart. We need to step out of our comfort zones to "see how the other half lives."

God doesn't judge us based on a group we may or may not belong to. To him, there's no "us and them," no rich and poor, no powerful and weak. There are only individuals to be loved and judged based on who—not what—they are. If we're serious about pleasing God, we need to see people as God sees them. ❖

PRAYER

Dear God, never let us forget that you are the ultimate Judge. Give us the wisdom to see people as you see them. Amen.

WELCOME, ONE AND ALL

- How does your church make room for different people? How does it fail to do that?
- How can our family show hospitality to all members of our community?

My brothers and sisters, believers in our glorious Lord Jesus Christ must not show favoritism.
JAMES 2:1

In this passage, James is talking to church members. He's talking about how people tend to treat the rich differently than they treat the poor. It's bad enough when that kind of discrimination goes on among unbelievers; but when it goes on in the church, it's inexcusable.

God doesn't discriminate against people based on how much they're worth or how they're dressed. And if *he* doesn't discriminate, his people have absolutely no reason to do so.

Not all discrimination is obvious, though. Sometimes it's not even intentional. Sometimes it's just a matter of people staying in their comfort zones, hanging around the people they know or with whom they have things in common. They discriminate by not talking to new or "different" people.

But if discrimination is keeping people from feeling comfortable in a house of worship—a place where members claim to love and obey God—something is seriously wrong. We need to step out of our comfort zones and welcome people we don't know—people who may be quite different from us.

Whether it's in a kids' Sunday school class or an adult Bible study, we need to represent our church in a way that pleases God and makes everyone feel welcome. ✤

PRAYER

Dear God, give us welcoming hearts for all people. Help us create a church environment in which everyone feels welcomed and loved. Amen.

IF YOU'RE NOT PART OF THE SOLUTION,
YOU'RE PART OF THE PROBLEM

- When was the last time you said (or thought), "That's not fair"? What were the circumstances?
- If you could change one thing about our society, what would it be? Why?

"So I will come to put you on trial. I will be quick to testify against sorcerers, adulterers and perjurers, against those who defraud laborers of their wages, who oppress the widows and the fatherless, and deprive the foreigners among you of justice, but do not fear me," says the LORD *Almighty.*   MALACHI 3:5

God's commands in Malachi 3:5 seem pretty easy to follow. Don't cheat people out of what they're owed. Don't be cruel to people in need. Don't take advantage of people who deserve justice.

Seems pretty simple, doesn't it? As long as we don't try to hurt other people, we don't have to worry about violating God's commands, right?

Actually, it's not that simple. In our society, the odds are often stacked against people in need. Our culture rewards success, wealth and popularity. People who have achieved those things are often given positions of power and authority. And they tend to look out for their own—the people who support them and are similar to them.

The poor and disadvantaged tend to fall through the cracks. Their needs are overlooked. The injustices they suffer aren't considered important. If we stand by silently and allow that to happen, we're contributing to the problem—and we're guilty of doing the things God warned about.

As God's people, it is our responsibility to reach out to the poor and disadvantaged, to make sure their needs are met. Our mandate is to love them as God loves them. ❖

PRAYER

Dear God, thank you for loving all people, especially the poor and disadvantaged. Use us to show your love to people in need. Amen.

THE HAVES AND HAVE-NOTS

- Can you tell if people are rich, powerful or popular just by looking at them? If so, how?
- In what ways are rich, powerful or popular people treated differently from other people?

"Do not show partiality in judging; hear both small and great alike. Do not be afraid of anyone, for judgment belongs to God. Bring me any case too hard for you, and I will hear it."   DEUTERONOMY 1:17

Sometimes people are divided into two categories: the "haves" and the "have-nots." The haves are usually the ones who are on top in our culture. They have money, power, respect and popularity.

The have-nots . . . have not. They aren't wealthy or powerful. They're often overlooked and ignored. Through no fault of their own, they're treated differently from the haves. It's not fair, but it's the way things are in our society.

If we're not careful, we may contribute to the unfairness. We may be tempted to make up our minds about haves and have-nots based on the way *other* people treat them. We may buy into the lie that people who have money and popularity deserve respect and power. We may be fooled into believing that have-nots deserve less respect and power.

That's not how God sees things. God looks at individuals. He judges them based on their actions, not their status. A person's money, popularity and respect mean nothing to him. He focuses on what's important: the person's heart. We should follow his example. We may not be able to see inside people's hearts, but we can listen to the things they say and watch the way they treat others. We can make our judgments based on things that *really* matter. ✤

PRAYER

Dear God, thank you for setting the example for us in the way we treat people. Show us how to look past wealth and popularity when we deal with others. Amen.

day76

EQUAL OPPORTUNITIES

- Do you have a favorite friend? What makes that person your favorite?
- When is it bad to show favoritism?

Then Peter began to speak: "I now realize how true it is that God does not show favoritism."
ACTS 10:34

In the first century AD, Jewish people looked down on non-Jews, known as Gentiles. They wanted nothing to do with people they considered unclean. Even Jewish Christians like Peter felt that way. The problem was that God wanted *everyone* to hear about his Son—including the Gentiles. And he wanted Peter and the other Jewish Christians to take the message to them.

Peter had a very hard time obeying God's command. It went against everything he'd been taught. But when he got a message that Cornelius, a devout Gentile man, was looking for him, Peter saw that God was doing something special. Peter swallowed his pride and his prejudice and went to see Cornelius. He told Cornelius and his friends and family about Jesus.

Peter was stunned when God sent his Holy Spirit to enter the Gentiles. That meant the message of Christ wasn't just for Jewish people. It was for everyone. Anyone could be saved, regardless of race. And that's the way it has been ever since.

God does not discriminate among his people. He loves everyone, and he expects those of us who call him Father to have the same attitude. ✤

PRAYER

Dear God, thank you for loving people of all races. Please help us follow your example. Amen.

NO FAVORITES WITH GOD

- Do you know any teacher's pets or people who get treated better than everyone else?
- What happens in a group where some are treated better than others?

Anyone who does wrong will be repaid for their wrongs, and there is no favoritism.

COLOSSIANS 3:25

Moses was the man God called to lead the Israelites out of slavery. He stood in front of Pharaoh, the king of Egypt, and told him to let the Israelites go. He raised his arms in front of the Red Sea while God parted the waters. He met with God one-on-one on Mount Sinai to receive the Ten Commandments. He led the Israelites across the wilderness for 40 years. He brought them to the edge of the promised land. Moses was one of the greatest leaders—and one of the most faithful men of God—who ever lived.

One day, however, while the Israelites were wandering in the wilderness, complaining that they were about to die of thirst, God instructed Moses to speak to a rock so that it would produce water. In frustration, Moses struck the rock with his staff instead.

God responded immediately. For his disobedience, for hitting the rock instead of speaking to it, Moses was forbidden to enter the promised land, something he'd dreamed about for 40 years. That's a harsh consequence.

If God didn't play favorites with Moses, he won't play favorites with anyone. God doesn't discriminate when he punishes sin. He holds everyone equally accountable. ✤

PRAYER

Dear God, thank you for correcting us when we do something wrong and for not showing favoritism when you do it. Help us follow your example and treat everyone with equal kindness and love. Amen.

FOR YOUR OWN GOOD

- What gives you hope?
- Have you ever experienced an unpleasant situation that eventually led to a positive outcome? Explain.

And we know that in all things God works for the good of those who love him, who have been called according to his purpose. ROMANS 8:28

God is in control. He is in control of the planets as they circle the sun, and he is in control of the small details in our lives. This doesn't mean that he will always interfere on a supernatural level. But it does mean that he is always paying attention, that he always cares about what's happening in our lives, and that he is always working on us and for us.

Paul writes in this verse that God is always working for the good of those who love him. That's us. God uses whatever happens in the lives of believers for their own good. Through the circumstances in our lives, he teaches us, shapes us and helps us.

This is a great verse to remember when we have a bad day. Even when circumstances are hard, we who love God can rest in the knowledge that he is taking care of us and that he wants what is good for us. This should always give us hope. ❖

PRAYER

Dear God, thank you for using the things in our lives to help us. Thank you for giving your children a reason to have hope. Please help us to remember this hope every day. Amen.

HOPE FOR THE NEEDY

- Is there someone in your life who is in need of hope? Describe a way that you could share hope with that person.
- What does it mean to be totally dependent on God?

But God will never forget the needy; the hope of the afflicted will never perish.

PSALM 9:18

When we hear the term "needy," we probably think of the neediest people in our world, those who are hungry, homeless or victims of disaster. The word "afflicted" refers to people who are suffering from circumstances such as violence, sickness or poverty.

We all know of people who are needy and afflicted. And though this verse probably makes us think of others, at some point we too have been or will be needy or afflicted. What David is really talking about here are people who are completely dependent on God to meet their needs.

And God does not forget these people. He never will. People who are suffering because of circumstances in this life have every reason to hope in God. He promises to honor that hope and to take care of and meet the needs of those who love him.

When we are needy and afflicted, we can have hope in our God who will never forget us. And when we encounter others who are needy and afflicted, we can share this hope with them. ✤

PRAYER

Dear God, thank you for giving hope to the needy and afflicted. Thank you for giving hope to those who believe in you. Please help us to remember this hope and give us opportunities to share it with others. Amen.

day80

HOPE OUT LOUD

- What is something that you are confident about?
- What does it mean to be treacherous?

No one who hopes in you will ever be put to shame, but shame will come on those who are treacherous without cause.   PSALM 25:3

The Bible teaches us in many places and with many different illustrations that God will be faithful to those who faithfully hope in him. This verse tells us that God will not allow shame to come to us.

Sometimes it is difficult to have hope. It can be especially difficult to hope out loud. Sometimes, others are threatened by our hope because they have none, and they work to hurt those who are hopeful. These people are being "treacherous," which means they are faithless, deceitful and untrustworthy.

That's why this verse becomes so important to believers. We need to know that God will not forget us. He will not allow us to be shamed for our hope. When we put our hope in God, we will be victorious.

This should give us tremendous confidence. Believers should not be afraid to hope. We should hope boldly—out loud—because we know that God is real, and our hope in him is real. ✤

PRAYER

Dear God, thank you for giving us hope. Thank you for protecting those who hope in you. Let our hope in you give us confidence each day. Amen.

RESURRECTION POWER

- Which of God's miracles do you think is the most impressive?
- What is your favorite part of the Easter story?

By his power God raised the Lord from the dead, and he will raise us also.

1 Corinthians 6:14

Jesus, the Son of God, died on the cross to save us. This is the sad part of the story. But the entire basis of our faith—the reason for our hope and the joy in our salvation—lies in this: Jesus didn't stay dead. He didn't stay buried. Jesus rose from the dead.

No matter what we are dealing with in this life, we are still dealing with the same God. The God who created the galaxies, who created DNA, who created our souls, is the same God who raised Jesus from the dead. He has the power of resurrection. He has the power to bring the dead to life. He has the power to save us, and he will. Just like he raised Jesus, he will raise us, giving us new life.

No matter what circumstance or struggle is bringing you down, you can hope in the fact that God will bring you back from the dead, and you will live forever with him in peace, love and glory. ✤

PRAYER

Dear God, thank you for showing us your resurrection power. When we are discouraged, please remind us of this power and give us hope. Amen.

day82

THE POINT TO ALL OF THIS

- How would you have reacted if you had been the one to find Jesus' empty tomb?
- Share a time when you've felt God working in your life. What was your reaction to his presence and power?

If only for this life we have hope in Christ, we are of all people most to be pitied.

1 CORINTHIANS 15:19

Paul wrote the above verse to the Corinthians because some of them were struggling with the idea of resurrection. They were finding it difficult to believe. Their former religious and life experiences did not support the idea that Jesus could have walked out of his tomb.

We might be able to relate to this. With all that we know about science today, it can be easy for us to have doubts about Jesus' resurrection. In human terms, it just doesn't make sense. It just doesn't seem possible.

Paul wrote to the Corinthians and basically said, "Look, if Jesus wasn't resurrected, then there's no point to any of this." Our entire faith depends on the fact that Jesus did not stay dead. He was resurrected. He ascended into heaven. He is alive today. And those who love, serve and believe in him will also be resurrected and join him in heaven.

The hope of Christians lies completely in the risen Savior. Thankfully, we know that Jesus is alive because we feel his Spirit working in our hearts and in our lives. We know that there is a point to all of this. And that point is Jesus. ♣

PRAYER

Dear God, thank you for the resurrection. Thank you that our Savior is alive and well and working within us right now. Thank you for the hope that Jesus gives us. Amen.

EVERY BODY NEEDS A HEAD

- Why do we call the church the "body" of Christ?
- What does it mean to be the head of something?

And he is the head of the body, the church; he is the beginning and the firstborn from among the dead, so that in everything he might have the supremacy. COLOSSIANS 1:18

The church is the body of Christ. *We* are the body of Christ. Each one of us is a part of this body. But Jesus is the head. Jesus is the brains of the operation.

This means that Jesus is in charge. We are to follow him. We are to do what he says. We are to submit to his authority. He knows way more about what we need to do than we do.

If we start placing something or someone else in charge, we will no longer be accomplishing God's work. If we put a pastor or leader ahead of Christ, the body will not work. If money becomes more important than Jesus, the body will not work. Even things that seem essential and beneficial, like music or church programs or community service—none of these things are more important than Jesus.

It's his body. We are representing him here on earth. We need to remember that he is the head of the church and serve accordingly. ✤

PRAYER

Dear God, please help us to accept Jesus as the head of the church. Thank you for giving him to us. Amen.

day84

MEMBERS OF HIS HOUSEHOLD

- What happens if you pull one stone out of a stone wall?
- Why does the Bible call Jesus the cornerstone?

Consequently, you are no longer foreigners and strangers, but fellow citizens with God's people and also members of his household, built on the foundation of the apostles and prophets, with Christ Jesus himself as the chief cornerstone . . . And in him you too are being built together to become a dwelling in which God lives by his Spirit.

EPHESIANS 2:19–20,22

God's church—the body of believers, not the building—is built on the foundation of the apostles and prophets of the Bible. And Jesus is the cornerstone. Traditionally, the cornerstone is the first stone laid in construction. It is also the most important stone—the one guides the placement of all the others.

We are a part of this metaphorical building—we are a part of the church. As God's children, we are members of God's household, and we form his church.

This gives us a lot of responsibility. We have been assembled to become a dwelling for the Holy Spirit. We must think and act like we are important members of this church. If we run off on our own agendas, we do a lot of damage to the structure and integrity of God's church. If we love ourselves more than we love others, we hurt the church, the entire body of believers in this world. ✤

PRAYER

Dear God, thank you for letting us become members of your household. Please help us to remember that we are part of your church. Amen.

day85

ESPECIALLY THE BELIEVERS

- Why do we call the people we go to church with "our church family"?
- How can we show love for other Christians?

Therefore, as we have opportunity, let us do good to all people, especially to those who belong to the family of believers. GALATIANS 6:10

In this verse from Galatians, Paul writes that believers are supposed to "do good to all people." This means that we are to show God's love to everyone we encounter. The verse then says, "especially to those who belong to the family of believers."

This doesn't mean that we are supposed to show care only for Christians, but it does mean that we are to recognize that the church is a family of believers. We are supposed to function as a family, supporting one another, helping one another and loving one another.

When we function as a family, we as individuals are better able to serve and help people outside of this family of believers. We make each other stronger and better equipped to "do good to all people." But the goodness needs to start at home, with the family, so that we will be strong enough to take that goodness out into the world. ❖

PRAYER

Dear God, thank you for your instructions. Please help us to remember to take care of one another and to function like a family of believers. Amen.

day86

ONE BODY — MANY PARTS

- What do you want to be when you grow up?
- Can you think of ways that people in our church serve as Jesus' hands? Jesus' feet? Jesus' ears?

Just as a body, though one, has many parts, but all its many parts form one body, so it is with Christ. For we were all baptized by one Spirit so as to form one body—whether Jews or Gentiles, slave or free—and we were all given the one Spirit to drink.

1 CORINTHIANS 12:12–13

There's a reason the Bible calls the church the body of Christ. We, Christ's followers on earth, work very much like a human body.

Imagine how many cells are in the human body, each one of them busy doing its own unique job. A liver cell cannot possibly do the job of a kidney cell, but when each cell does its own job well, the body stays healthy and is productive.

Now imagine how many believers there are on earth. The doctor in Toronto cannot possibly do the job of the missionary in Thailand, but when each believer does his or her own job well, the body of Christ stays healthy and is productive.

God will show us what our role in the body of Christ is. If you haven't figured it out yet, don't worry. If you are working to live according to God's will, he will make his will known to you. And you can take joy in your role because you were created for this. ✢

PRAYER

Dear God, thank you for creating each of us to have a unique job in the body of Christ. Please help us discover what you would have us do. Amen.

INTO HIS HOUSE WITH JOY

- Why is it important to go to church?
- How would your life be different if you couldn't go to church?

I rejoiced with those who said to me, "Let us go to the house of the LORD." PSALM 122:1

Sometimes it's a struggle to get ourselves up and going for church. But God wants us to go into his house with joy. This doesn't mean that we will always be excited when the alarm clock goes off. But it does mean that we need to work to prepare our hearts and minds for what God has in store for us.

God wants us to gather together with other believers. He wants us to study the Bible, to hear the Word, to sing praises together and to bless others. All of this should happen in church. If you find yourself dragging, ask God to replace your lack of enthusiasm with his joy.

Many believers in this world are being persecuted for gathering together. Some people are even being killed. That's how important it is to gather. For those of us who have easy access to a church, it can be easy to take it for granted. But we shouldn't.

If you find yourself bored with church, ask God what you could do to make it more exciting. If you find church a difficult place to be due to problems with fellow believers, pray that God will heal those relationships and restore your joy. ✤

PRAYER

Dear God, thank you that we can gather together in your name. Please help us to have nothing but joy in our hearts as we step into your house. Amen.

day88

ONE LAST SUPPER

- What do you think the mood was like during the Last Supper?
- Why were the disciples so confused about what Jesus told them?

Then Jesus told them, "This very night you will all fall away on account of me, for it is written: 'I will strike the shepherd, and the sheep of the flock will be scattered.'"

MATTHEW 26:31

On the night he was arrested, Jesus shared one last meal with his disciples. While they were eating, Jesus broke the bad news to them. That very night, he said, he was going to be betrayed by one of the men at the table. He was going to be arrested, put on trial and killed.

With words the disciples wouldn't understand until later, Jesus explained that the bread represented his body, which was going to be broken soon. The wine represented his blood, which was going to be poured out for his followers.

The disciples were stunned. Peter vowed that he would never leave Jesus, just hours before he and the rest of the disciples went into hiding. As if the horror of his coming crucifixion wasn't enough, Jesus had to endure being deserted and betrayed by his closest friends.

When we go through tough times, to whom do we turn for comfort and support? Our friends and loved ones. But when Jesus faced the worst crisis anyone has ever faced, he did it alone. And he did it for us. ♣

PRAYER

Dear God, thank you for the faithful friends you've brought into our lives. As we think about how Jesus' friends deserted him, give us the strength to stay faithful to you and to our friends when they need us. Amen.

THE PLOT TO KILL JESUS

- Why did the Jewish leaders need one of Jesus' closest friends to betray him?
- What do you think Judas Iscariot was like? Explain.

Then one of the Twelve—the one called Judas Iscariot—went to the chief priests and asked, "What are you willing to give me if I deliver him over to you?" So they counted out for him thirty pieces of silver.   MATTHEW 26:14–15

The Jewish religious leaders had been trying to get rid of Jesus for a long time. But they were afraid of how his followers would react. So they waited for just the right opportunity. And Judas Iscariot, one of Jesus' disciples, gave it to them. He came to them and agreed to betray Jesus for 30 pieces of silver. He led Jesus' enemies straight to him and watched while they arrested him and led him away to be crucified.

Soon afterward, Judas had a change of heart and tried to give the money back. But it was too late. Matthew 27:5 reveals the sad end of his story: "So Judas threw the money into the temple and left. Then he went away and hanged himself."

Judas may have thought he was the one responsible for Jesus' arrest. But he just played a role in God's plan. Jesus came to earth to die for our sins. Those plans were set when Adam and Eve ate the forbidden fruit in the Garden of Eden (see Genesis 3).

Judas didn't cause Jesus' death. We did. All of us. Our sin made it necessary for him to come to earth, live a sinless life and die as a sacrifice for us. ✤

PRAYER

Dear God, forgive us for sin, the sin that made it necessary to sacrifice your Son in such a terrible way. Thank you for the forgiveness and salvation that we receive because of him. Amen.

day90

IN THE GARDEN

- Why were Jesus' disciples so unreliable?
- If you had been in the Garden of Gethsemane with Jesus that night, what would you have done when the soldiers came to arrest him?

He went away a second time and prayed, "My Father, if it is not possible for this cup to be taken away unless I drink it, may your will be done." MATTHEW 26:42

With the weight of the world pressing down on him in the hours before his arrest, Jesus asked his closest friends—Peter, James and John—to accompany him to the Garden of Gethsemane. Jesus wanted to spend some time talking to his Father, and he asked his friends to keep watch while he prayed. Unfortunately, they couldn't keep their eyes open.

The stress on Jesus was almost unbearable. He fell facedown to pray. He prayed so fervently that his sweat was like drops of blood. He asked God to take the cup from him. He prayed until he was ready to face what lay ahead. Then he allowed himself to be arrested and taken to trial.

In his time of torment, Jesus gave us a model of prayer that we can use when life feels as though it's crashing down around us. He poured out his agony to his heavenly Father. He asked God to remove the situation he was about to face. Then he ended with the words, "May your will be done."

No matter how extreme our situation may seem, the best strategy is always to pray for God's will to be done. ✤

PRAYER

Dear God, thank you for your Son's example of faithfulness. Help us respond by praying and seeking your will when we face difficult situations. Amen.

day91

THE SON OF GOD ON TRIAL

- Why couldn't the Jewish religious leaders recognize the truth about Jesus?
- Why can't people today recognize the truth about Jesus?

"You have said so," Jesus replied. "But I say to all of you: From now on you will see the Son of Man sitting at the right hand of the Mighty One and coming on the clouds of heaven."
MATTHEW 26:64

After Jesus was arrested, he was brought before Caiaphas, the Jewish high priest, and the teachers of the Law. They were the ones people turned to for spiritual guidance before Jesus came. And they hated Jesus for exposing them as hypocrites. More than anyone else, they wanted Jesus dead.

They pretended to have a trial, but it was rigged. The only witnesses they could find were false ones. So the high priest asked Jesus point-blank if he was the Messiah, the Son of God. When Jesus said that he was, the high priest accused him of blasphemy and sent him to the Roman governor named Pilate to be executed.

The high priest and his associates were the religious leaders of Israel. They spent their lives looking forward to the Messiah's coming. Yet when the Messiah was standing right in front of them, they didn't recognize him. After all of Jesus' miracles and teachings, he was just a blasphemer in their eyes.

In order to recognize Jesus for who he really is, you have to have faith. The Jewish leaders of Israel didn't have it. It's amazing what people can overlook even when there's so much evidence to support it. Keep that in mind when you talk to your unbelieving friends and family members. ✤

PRAYER

Dear God, thank you for opening our eyes to the truth about your Son. Use us to help open other people's eyes to him. Amen.

day92

TAKE ME TO PILATE

- Why did the Jewish religious leaders hate Jesus so much?
- Why did Pilate allow him to be crucified if he knew Jesus was innocent?

When Pilate saw that he was getting nowhere, but that instead an uproar was starting, he took water and washed his hands in front of the crowd. "I am innocent of this man's blood," he said. "It is your responsibility!" MATTHEW 27:24

The Jewish religious leaders were the ones who wanted Jesus dead. But they didn't have the authority to execute him. At that time, Israel was part of the Roman Empire. Only a Roman official could sentence Jesus to death.

Pilate was the Roman governor of that region, so Jesus was taken to him. The Jewish leaders explained why they wanted him dead, but Pilate wasn't convinced. He took the matter to a crowd of Jews. He offered to let one prisoner go, and they could choose: Jesus or Barabbas, a criminal. The crowd, influenced by the religious leaders, chose Barabbas and demanded that Pilate execute Jesus.

To prevent a riot, Pilate agreed. But he washed his hands first in front of the crowd to show that he was innocent of Jesus' death. He didn't want Jesus' blood on his hands.

Even people who don't believe Jesus is the Savior or Son of God recognize something special in him. Pilate recognized his innocence. Other people recognize that he was a great teacher or a caring leader. This Easter season, let's think about what we can do to help our friends and loved ones recognize the truth about Jesus. ❖

PRAYER

Dear God, your Son made an impression on everyone he encountered. Give us the wisdom, courage and creativity to help others understand why he continues to make an impression. Amen.

day93

THE DARKEST DAY

- How do you feel when you hear the crucifixion story?
- Why did Jesus have to suffer so much?

And when Jesus had cried out again in a loud voice, he gave up his spirit.

MATTHEW 27:50

After Jesus was sentenced to death, Pilate's soldiers beat him viciously. They made a crown of thorns and put it on his head while they mocked him and spat on him. They struck him over the head with a wooden staff. They whipped him until his back was raw and bloody. They made him carry his cross until he collapsed from exhaustion and pain.

At the execution site, they laid him on rough wooden beams. They drove a nail through each of his wrists and one through his feet to attach him to the cross. His suffering was terrible. The only innocent person who ever lived took on himself the sins of the entire world. His misery continued for hours until he finally gave up his life.

For many people, the crucifixion story is hard to read or listen to. What makes it even harder is the fact that it's our fault. Jesus had to suffer and die because of *us*. Before we can celebrate his resurrection, we have to own up to our role in the crucifixion. Jesus came to earth to save *us*. For that, we can never be thankful enough. ✤

PRAYER

Dear God, forgive us for the sins that caused your Son so much pain and suffering. Thank you for loving us enough to save us from those sins. Let us never forget what our salvation cost. Amen.

day94

VAINLY THEY SEAL THE DEAD

- How do you think the disciples were feeling the day after Jesus' death? Be specific.
- If you had been one of Jesus' disciples, what would it have taken for you to believe that he had risen from the dead?

"Don't be alarmed," he said. "You are looking for Jesus the Nazarene, who was crucified. He has risen! He is not here. See the place where they laid him."   MARK 16:6

The day after Jesus' crucifixion—which was Saturday, the Jewish Sabbath—may have been the darkest day in human history. The light of the world had been extinguished. The great Teacher was silenced. The Messiah was dead, and with him all hope for eternal life. At least, that's the way it appeared.

When Sunday dawned, however, there came strange and exciting news from Jesus' gravesite. The stone had been rolled away. The burial clothes were lying on the ground. The tomb was empty.

A group of women who had come to anoint Jesus' body with spices were the first to discover the amazing truth. An angel in the tomb told them Jesus had risen. They ran to tell Peter and the rest of the disciples, so they could share in the joy. Some were skeptical at first. Then it dawned on them that this had been Jesus' plan and purpose all along.

When Jesus rose from the grave that Sunday morning, he defeated death once and for all. Anyone who believes in him will have eternal life. That is the reason we celebrate Easter. ❖

PRAYER

Dear God, you have the power over death. You raised Jesus so that we may have eternal life with you. Thank you for your awesome love and sacrifice. We love you. Amen.

day95

GOD SPEAKS

- How does God speak through the Bible?
- If someone claims to speak for God, how do you decide whether to believe that person?

In the past God spoke to our ancestors through the prophets at many times and in various ways, but in these last days he has spoken to us by his Son, whom he appointed heir of all things, and through whom also he made the universe. HEBREWS 1:1–2

In the past, God spoke to people through his prophets. When the Israelites or other people did evil in his sight, God sent specially selected men and women to warn them about his coming judgment. Sometimes the people listened and repented. Other times they ignored the prophets and suffered the consequences.

God also spoke through angels. When he had a special message to convey, he used angels to deliver it in person. Abraham, Daniel and Jesus' mother, Mary, all received messages from angels. Mary's message foretold Jesus' birth.

When God sent Jesus, he gave humankind its clearest and best messenger. Jesus is better than prophets and angels because he doesn't speak *for* God; he speaks *as* God. John 1:1 tells us Jesus *is* the Word. Every word he speaks is from the mouth of God. If we live according to Jesus' words—if we think of ourselves and treat others as he instructs—we will please God.

We are blessed because we don't have to rely on prophets or angels to receive the voice of God. All we have to do is pick up the Bible and read Jesus' words. ✤

PRAYER

Dear God, we have done nothing to earn your love and concern. Yet you speak to us through your Son and through your Word. Thank you for communicating with us. We would be lost without you. Amen.

day96

LOVE IS PATIENT

- Can you share a time when you were patient with someone?
- Can you share a time when your parents were patient with you?

Love is patient, love is kind. It does not envy, it does not boast, it is not proud.

1 CORINTHIANS 13:4

People told Janice that she was nuts to take on a foster child, but her biological children were grown up and her husband had died, so Janice felt she had the resources and time to care for a child.

But Denise was no ordinary child. She was angry all the time. She was disrespectful to Janice, refused to follow Janice's rules, and complained constantly. Janice invited Denise to go to church with her and to read the Bible with her, but Denise just made fun of her, calling her a "Jesus freak."

When people asked Janice how she put up with it, she would just smile and say, "Love is patient, love is kind."

Then one day, Denise herself asked Janice, "Why do you put up with me? I don't deserve your love."

Janice answered, "I wonder the same thing about God. I don't deserve his love, but he never gives up on me."

That day, Denise and Janice began to study the Bible together. Eventually, Denise even joined Janice in church. Life wasn't perfect—Denise still struggled, but Janice remained patient. And through Janice's patience, Denise learned about real love. ❖

PRAYER

Dear God, thank you for being patient with your children. Please help us to love others and be patient with them. Amen.

day97

FORBEARANCE FRUIT

- Why do you think the Bible refers to good qualities as "fruit"?
- Can you think of a time when you were wronged, but you gave it to God instead of acting on it yourself?

But the fruit of the Spirit is love, joy, peace, forbearance, kindness, goodness, faithfulness.

GALATIANS 5:22

The Greek word that is translated "forbearance" in this verse also means patience, endurance, perseverance and restraint.

When the Bible talks about forbearance or patience, it's talking about the supernatural ability to trust in God completely, even when we don't understand what is happening in life. Being patient means that when things don't go our way, we remain in control of our reactions, and that we don't drive ourselves and others crazy trying to make things go our way. We are being patient when we peacefully endure unpleasant situations because we know that God is in control, that God has a plan.

People cannot be patient on their own. Being patient requires the power of the Holy Spirit. Therefore, patience is evidence of the Holy Spirit working in our lives. When you feel yourself becoming more patient, you know that God is working within you and that you are changing for the better. You are becoming more fruitful for God! ✤

PRAYER

Dear God, thank you for being in control. Thank you that we can lean on you when things get rough. Please help us to have forbearance and patience. Amen.

day98

PATIENCE VS. PRIDE

- What does it mean to patient?
- What does it mean to be prideful?

The end of a matter is better than its beginning, and patience is better than pride.

ECCLESIASTES 7:8

Two girls wanted to join their church's worship team, but their pastor said, "Not yet. Keep practicing, and when you're a little older, you can audition."

One of the girls got mad. She decided that she was "too good" for the worship team. She told everyone who would listen how talented she was and that someone on the worship team must have something against her.

The other girl was patient. Every day, she practiced the piano, and every night prayed, "God, when the time is right, please make it happen."

Less than a year later the second girl was invited to audition for the team, and because of her hard work and good attitude, she was welcomed aboard. Her patience, her hard work and her faith that God would lead the way was rewarded.

When the Bible talks about pride, it's talking about an arrogance that leaves no room for God. When we are proud, we think we don't need God. We think we are smarter than God and more important than other people.

Humility, on the other hand, brings patience. When we are humble, we submit to God's will for our lives. We know we can't do it alone, and we trust God and know that he will take care of us in his own time. ♣

> ### PRAYER

Dear God, please forgive us when we are prideful; please replace our pride with patience. Amen.

day99

WHY PRAY?

- What are some things that you have been praying about recently?
- Why does God want you to pray?

Be pleased to save me, LORD; come quickly, LORD, to help me.   PSALM 40:13

God loves to answer the prayers of his people. Many times in the Bible, he tells us to pray to him, to ask him for things and to call out to him. He even tells us that there are some things that we do not have simply because we have not asked him for them.

God wants us to pray to him because he enjoys helping us. He cares for us deeply and knows that our lives are full of hard things—we get sad or hurt or sick or just plain confused about what to do next. Praying for help is good for us because it causes us to slow down and pay attention to God.

God also enjoys helping us because it makes his power obvious to other people. When other people see what God can do, they may also slow down and pay attention to him. Our friends and family members may be interested to know more about our faith when they see us following God. ✤

PRAYER

Dear God, thank you for being so willing to help us. Please let other people see your power through our prayers. Amen.

day100

WHY DO YOU WANT WHAT YOU WANT?

- Can you share a time when you asked God for something, but he did not give it to you?
- What are some reasons why God might not give you what you ask for?

When you ask, you do not receive, because you ask with wrong motives, that you may spend what you get on your pleasures.   JAMES 4:3

Sometimes God does not give us what we ask for. According to this verse from James, this may happen because we are not asking for the right reasons. Have you ever stopped to think about why you want what you want? God is interested in the "whys" behind our requests.

When our motives are purely selfish, meaning that we only want something for our own pleasure, God may not give us what we want. He wants us to be concerned with things bigger than our own desires, such as how what we are asking for might affect other people, or whether it is something that will help us love God more, or if it might come between God and ourselves.

The next time you ask God for something think about why you want it. And if necessary, ask God to change your motives so that they honor him. ♣

PRAYER

Dear God, please forgive us for our selfish motives. Please help us care about what matters to you. Amen.

day101

TAKING GOD AT HIS WORD

- What does it mean to doubt something?
- What are some things that you are absolutely sure about?

But when you ask, you must believe and not doubt, because the one who doubts is like a wave of the sea, blown and tossed by the wind. JAMES 1:6

This verse was written by Jesus' brother James. Can you imagine how much James knew about Jesus?

James tells us in this verse that when we ask God for what he has promised to give us, we should not doubt that he can do so. This makes sense. Doubting God's promises is a lot like calling him a liar.

Just before this verse, James wrote that if any of us lacks wisdom, all we have to do is ask for it, and God will give it to us. God has promised many things in Scripture. He has promised that he will give us everything we need, that everything will work out for our good, and that we will make it to heaven. And so much more!

When you pray, believe that God is true to his word. Believe that he is going to do what he says he will do. ♣

PRAYER

Dear God, please help us believe what you have promised. Please give us confidence in what the Bible says. Amen.

day102

NEVER, EVER, EVER!

- How does a person who loves money behave?
- How does a content person behave?

Keep your lives free from the love of money and be content with what you have, because God has said, "Never will I leave you; never will I forsake you." HEBREWS 13:5

Contentment is an important part of the Christian walk. Contentment shows that we trust God to provide for us, that we know God is in control and that we are happy to live within God's will for our lives.

A big part of contentment is knowing and believing that God will never leave us or forsake us. If we spend some time with this thought, that God is with us always, it becomes difficult to be discontent. We have God—what more could we want?

Still, we live in the world, and the world is always preaching discontent. The enemy always wants us to want more, more, more—more stuff, more money, more activities—because he knows that this "stuff" will separate us from God.

Hebrews tells us to keep our lives free from the love of money. The best way to do this is to focus on the fact that no matter what, God will never, ever leave us. No matter what, God has our back with his almighty power, a power to which earthly wealth cannot compare. ✤

> **PRAYER**

Dear God, thank you for providing for us. Thank you for never leaving us or forsaking us. Please help us to be content with what we have and to keep our lives free from the love of money. Amen.

SO SHOULD WE

- How do you feel when you do something generous?
- How do you feel when someone shares with you?

They devoted themselves to the apostles' teaching and to fellowship, to the breaking of bread and to prayer . . . All the believers were together and had everything in common. They sold property and possessions to give to anyone who had need. ACTS 2:42,44–45

These verses from Acts describe the way that Christians lived in the early church. They devoted themselves to learning about God and each other. They spent time together and shared what they had. And even more impressively, if one of them didn't have enough, the others would sell what they had to provide for the person in need.

There's no reason to think that God doesn't want Christians of today to behave in the same way. When one of our brothers or sisters in Christ is in need, we should help. We should share our resources—time, money, belongings, talents, energy—to help those who need help.

The body of Christ is designed to work together. If we ignore a brother or sister's need, we are ignoring Jesus, and we are weakening the body of Christ. The early church had it rough. They faced significant persecution. But they worked together, and they stayed strong. So should we. ✤

PRAYER

Dear God, thank you for the model of the early church. Open our eyes to the needs of our brothers and sisters and make us willing and able to help. Amen.

day104

DON'T FALL FOR IT!

- How do you feel about money?
- How do you think God feels about money?

Now the overseer is to be above reproach . . . not given to drunkenness, not violent but gentle, not quarrelsome, not a lover of money.   1 TIMOTHY 3:2−3

In these verses from Timothy, Paul is describing how leaders of the church should behave: They should not become drunk, violent or quarrelsome or love money.

Many Christians struggle with this money part. The world tries to teach us that money is everything, that money makes us happy and that money makes all our problems go away. These are all lies from the enemy. We can have all the money in the world and still go to hell.

When we love money, we live for money, not God. Luke 16 tells us that we cannot serve both God and money, that we will end up loving one and hating the other (see v. 13). If loving money means hating God, then we should definitely make sure we do not love money.

This does not mean that we should get rid of our money. In most places in the world, money is necessary. We work hard to earn money, and money allows us to provide for ourselves and our families. But we are not supposed to love money. We are supposed to love God. Money is just a tool we use to serve him. ❖

PRAYER

Dear God, please help us to recognize money for what it is: a tool that we use to serve you during our lives on earth. Please help us to love you, not money; keep us from falling for the world's lies. Amen.

day105

SOME ADVICE ON ASKING FOR ADVICE

- What are some things people ask advice about?
- When you need advice, who do you ask?

Blessed is the one who does not walk in step with the wicked or stand in the way that sinners take or sit in the company of mockers. PSALM 1:1

Violet really wanted to go to a concert with some friends. Her parents had already told her she couldn't go because the concert was too far away and it was on a school night.

Violet's friends offered her lots of advice on the subject. One thought she should just sneak out and go with them anyway—that her parents would never know. Another wasn't so sure about that plan, but thought maybe Violet should ask her dad again when her mom wasn't around because he was more likely to say yes.

Kaitlyn, who always thought things through and prayed about her decisions carefully, said that Violet should listen to her parents.

The friends kept talking, and eventually they looked up the band's website. They found out that the band would be coming to another nearby city in a few months, and this time the concert would be on a Saturday. Kaitlyn offered to wait until then to go with Violet if her parents approved.

When we need advice, it's important to go to a source that can be trusted. Fellow Christians are especially good to talk with, since we can trust that their motivation to serve the Lord is the same as ours. Others may not have our best interests as Christians in mind and may give us advice that could cause us to stumble in our walk with God. ❖

PRAYER

Dear God, when we need advice, help us to seek it in the right places. Give us wisdom to tell the difference between good and bad advice. Amen.

day106

THE DISCERNING GET GUIDANCE

- Do you consider yourself to be a wise person? Why or why not?
- What are some of the steps you take when you make a decision?

Let the wise listen and add to their learning, and let the discerning get guidance.

PROVERBS 1:5

One of the biggest decisions we have to make in life is what to do after high school. And because this decision is such a difficult one, schools have guidance counselors. Schools don't expect students to make these decisions on their own.

We face many difficult decisions in life, but God doesn't expect us to make them on our own either. In this verse from Proverbs, King Solomon tells us that discerning people should get guidance.

This means that if we are smart, we will ask for guidance from other people who love God. Don't underestimate the experience of your friends and family. There's a good chance that someone you know has had to make a decision similar to the one you are facing.

You might consider asking your parents, grandparents, siblings, friends, teachers, pastors, coaches—anyone who loves God and will want to help you grow in your faith. Two (or three or four) heads really are better than one. You don't have to make difficult decisions alone. ✤

PRAYER

Dear God, please give us the courage to ask for advice when we need it. Lead us to people who will give us wise guidance. Thank you for the good advisers in our lives. Amen.

day**107**

THE ULTIMATE SOURCE OF ADVICE

- How does God give advice?
- Who is the wisest person you know?

You guide me with your counsel, and afterward you will take me into glory.

PSALM 73:24

What if you knew someone who was unbelievably wise, with the ability to give perfect advice, exactly right for each and every individual? What if this someone could see into the future and base the advice on what was truly best for you? Wouldn't you go to great lengths to get that advice?

You do know this someone. You have access to this kind of advice.

God's wisdom is beyond our understanding. He knows exactly what we need at any given time. He knows exactly which decision we should make, every time. He knows the future, and he knows what is best for us.

First John 2:27 tells us that the Holy Spirit is the only teacher we need. Of course, it is always smart to ask other believers for advice, especially when it's difficult to find the answers to our questions in the Bible. But the answers are there. In the end, God is the ultimate source of advice. And we can ask him for it at any time. ✤

> **PRAYER**

Dear God, thank you for giving us the Holy Spirit and the Bible. We pray we will remember that you are the ultimate source of advice. Amen.

day108

THROUGH MANY ADVISERS

- Who helps the president make decisions?
- When you need advice, do you ask just one person or several? Why?

For lack of guidance a nation falls, but victory is won through many advisers.

PROVERBS 11:14

The president of a country does not make decisions alone. He or she has a cabinet of experts. In the United States, we have the secretary of state, the secretary of education, the secretary of defense, the attorney general, and the list goes on. Why all the help? It just seems kind of silly—and maybe even dangerous—to leave such major decisions to a single, flawed human being.

And we are all flawed, even you. So when you need to make a major decision, Proverbs tells you that you would be wise to seek advice from many advisers. This doesn't mean you should distribute a survey, but it does mean to consider asking several "experts" for advice. The nature of your decision will influence who you need to ask, but make sure that you ask people who share your commitment to Christ.

This type of advice helps governments to be successful. It helps organizations, businesses and schools to be successful. And it will help you to be successful too. ✤

PRAYER

Dear God, thank you for the wisdom of your Word. Please help us to be successful and to ask advice from the right people. Amen.

IF YOU WANT TO BE WISE

- Share a time when you ignored someone's advice. Why did you?
- Share a time when you followed someone's advice and were glad that you did. What was the outcome?

The way of fools seems right to them, but the wise listen to advice.   PROVERBS 12:15

Sometimes people ask for advice simply because they want their own ideas to be validated. Sometimes people will continue to ask for advice from different people until they find someone who tells them what they want to hear. This is foolishness.

God blesses us with other people to help us. We shouldn't waste other people's time asking for advice if we are not going to seriously consider what they say.

If we ask just one person for advice, and they give us advice that doesn't seem Biblical, then of course we should ask someone else for advice. But if multiple God-loving people tell us the same thing, then we should listen up. People put time and thought into their advice. And if these people are trying to honor God with the advice that they give, then there is a good chance that God stands behind their advice.

If you want to be wise and make good decisions, decisions that will bless you, then listen to Proverbs 12:15. Listen to the people who give you advice, and listen to God. ❖

PRAYER

Dear God, thank you for blessing us with people to help us in our lives. Please give us the wisdom and courage to listen to good advice, even if it's not what we want to hear. Amen.

day110

ASK THE ELDERS

- Share a time when an older person gave you some good advice. What was it?
- Think of an older person you look up to. What makes you respect him or her?

Then King Rehoboam consulted the elders who had served his father Solomon during his lifetime. "How would you advise me to answer these people?" he asked . . . But Rehoboam rejected the advice the elders gave him and consulted the young men who had grown up with him and were serving him . . . The young men who had grown up with him replied, "These people have said to you, 'Your father put a heavy yoke on us, but make our yoke lighter.' Now tell them, 'My little finger is thicker than my father's waist.'"

1 KINGS 12:6,8,10

When King Rehoboam became king of Israel, the people asked him to make some changes. He consulted the elders, who gave him wise advice that he ignored. He asked his friends, who gave him bad advice that he followed. He treated the people badly, and this foolish decision led to a revolt that divided the nation of Israel.

It is tempting to ask advice from our friends, people our age. It feels natural because these people think like us—they understand us. And therein lies the problem. Why ask people for advice if they aren't any wiser than we are?

The truth is that people who are older than us are often wiser. They have lived longer. They have more experience. They have served God longer. They can often give really great advice. If you have access to the wisdom of "the elders," then you would be foolish to pass it up. You can still ask your friends for advice, but ask your grandparents or other adults too. ✤

> **PRAYER**

Dear God, thank you for the older people we know and love. Please remind us to ask for advice when we need it. Amen.

day111

ENVYING THE WRONG PEOPLE

- Describe a time when you saw someone "getting away with" their sin. How did this make you feel?
- Why do you think God gave us his commandments?

Do not fret because of those who are evil or be envious of those who do wrong.

PSALM 37:1

In this psalm, King David tells us not to be jealous of people who sin. David writes later in the psalm that "their day is coming" (v. 13), meaning that we will all be judged one day, and that God will judge these evil people in due time. Thankfully, we don't have to worry about what other people are doing. God will take care of that.

There is also a more immediate reason why we shouldn't envy those who do wrong. You see, God's commandments are not arbitrary. God gave each and every one of his commandments to protect us. When we sin, we hurt ourselves, others and God. When we don't sin, we protect ourselves from pain and suffering.

If you are tempted to envy someone whose sin seems to be making their lives better or more fun, and they appear to suffer no consequences, realize that their fun is short-lived. No one really ever "gets away with" anything. ✣

PRAYER

Dear God, thank you for giving us your commandments. Give us joy in keeping them, and keep us from foolish envy of people who sin. Amen.

day112

PUT ENVY BEHIND YOU

- How might your life be different if you didn't know God? How would you behave?
- Describe a time when you were envious of someone. Why did you envy them?

At one time we too were foolish, disobedient, deceived and enslaved by all kinds of passions and pleasures. We lived in malice and envy, being hated and hating one another.

TITUS 3:3

In this verse, the apostle Paul refers to what life is like before people come to know God. He essentially means, "Don't forget that at one time, we didn't know anything about God either."

Before people make the decision to live for Jesus, they are slaves to sin and envy. Once we decide to live for Jesus, however, we are changed by the Holy Spirit. The Holy Spirit helps us to live in obedience to God's Word, and changes the way we look at our lives. We don't need to envy others anymore.

The truth is that envy has no place in a Christian's life. What do we have to be envious of? God has given us more than we could ever deserve. As Christians, we know that God has a plan for our lives and that he will be there with us through it all. We should be focused on living out God's plan for our lives, not envying what is happening in someone else's life. ✤

PRAYER

Dear God, please forgive us when we envy others. Thank you for providing everything we need. Set our eyes on you rather than what others have. Amen.

day113

WATCH YOUR STEP!

- What do you think of when you hear the word "prosperity"?
- Describe a time when you saw someone rewarded for bad behavior. How did that make you feel?

But as for me, my feet had almost slipped; I had nearly lost my foothold. For I envied the arrogant when I saw the prosperity of the wicked.   PSALM 73:2–3

It's easy to be jealous of someone else's wealth. It can make us angry to know that someone has acquired wealth through wickedness. We might wonder why, when we work so hard to live the way God wants us to, we still struggle, while other people ignore God and prosper.

Sometimes in this life, it seems that a person can be rewarded for bad behavior. But if you could spend a few minutes in this person's shoes, you would soon find out that it's not all that pleasant.

As the psalmist Asaph writes later in Psalm 73, the rewards of wickedness are fleeting, while the rewards of godly living are eternal (see vv. 18–19,24). A life without God is scary and lonely, so don't be envious of the prosperity of wicked people. Their prosperity is short-lived. As a child of God, you possess a different kind of wealth, a wealth that will last forever. ❖

PRAYER

Dear God, thank you for meeting our needs today. Thank you for giving us a wealth that will last forever. Please help us to not envy the prosperity of wicked people, and please forgive us when we do. Amen.

day114

ROTTEN BONES? NO THANK YOU!

- How does being envious affect a person?
- What does it mean to be at peace?

A heart at peace gives life to the body, but envy rots the bones.   PROVERBS 14:30

Envy rots our bones? That's horrible! Now, envy probably won't literally rot your bones, but King Solomon chose these words to convey just how much damage envy can do to a person. Envy causes pain and suffering. Envy can eat away at our spiritual life.

But there's good news too. A heart at peace gives life. And as believers, our hearts can be at peace. We know the answers to life's big questions: We know why we are here; we know what our greatest purpose is; and we know what will happen when we die. Having knowledge of and trusting in God's truth will give us a heart at peace.

A heart at peace has no need to envy anyone. We know that we have everything we really need. We know that we have no need to envy anyone else because God has a perfect plan especially designed for us. We don't need to let envy get in our way. ❖

PRAYER

Dear God, thank you for freeing your believers from envy. When we are tempted to feel envious, please fill our hearts with your peace instead. Amen.

WARNING: POISON ENVY

- Describe a time when not getting something you wanted made you angry. How long did you stay angry?
- When you feel jealous of someone, what other emotions do you feel towards them?

"Resentment kills a fool, and envy slays the simple." JOB 5:2

When you feel resentment, you feel anger and ill will towards someone else because things haven't gone as you wished. When you feel envy, you want something that someone else has. These two emotions often go hand in hand. We often feel resentment because we don't have something that someone else has.

The Bible teaches us that both of these emotions are dangerous. In fact, if a person who is having these emotions doesn't deal with them, resentment and envy can destroy their life.

People can spend their whole lives being jealous of others. Instead of seeking God, instead of serving others, instead of enjoying life, they spend their time and energy wanting what others have. This only brings pain to them.

As children of God, we don't have to suffer from resentment or envy. When we experience these emotions, we need to talk them over with God and get at the root of the problem before they take over our lives. ✤

PRAYER

Dear God, forgive us when we feel resentment or envy. Thank you for all that you have given us; help us to enjoy life to the fullest. Protect us from the temptation of jealousy and the trap of resentment. Amen.

day116

BY HIS GRACE

- Have you ever gotten something good that you didn't deserve?
- How would you explain God's grace to someone who knows nothing about it?

For it is by grace you have been saved, through faith — and this is not from yourselves, it is the gift of God — not by works, so that no one can boast.   EPHESIANS 2:8–9

Some people use an acronym to help them remember what the word *grace* means: **G**od's **R**iches **A**t **C**hrist's **E**xpense. As acronyms go, it's not bad, but it doesn't tell the whole story.

We need grace because our sin separates us from God. We can do nothing to earn God's forgiveness; only a perfect sacrifice will do. The only perfect sacrifice is Jesus, God's Son. So even though we've done nothing to earn it, God gives us the gift of salvation. That's grace.

If we've received God's grace and put our faith in Christ to save us, we have three responsibilities. The first is to thank God as often as possible for what he's done for us. He never gets tired of being praised and worshiped, so we should never get tired of showing him how grateful we are. The second is to lovingly obey God through the help of the Holy Spirit.

Our third responsibility is to make sure other people know about God's grace. The best strategy is to start with people we know and feel comfortable with. We can practice bringing it up in conversation little by little until we have the confidence to talk about it any place, any time. ❖

PRAYER

Dear God, we praise you for your grace. We know that we do not deserve your love. Thank you for giving us salvation through your Son. Guide our words as we tell others about your grace. Amen.

day117

SLOW TO ANGER

- What makes you angry?
- How do you react when you get *really* angry?

But you, Lord, are a compassionate and gracious God, slow to anger, abounding in love and faithfulness.
PSALM 86:15

If you want proof that God is slow to anger, you need only look at Sodom and Gomorrah in Genesis 18–19. When God told Abraham that he was going to destroy the wicked cities of Sodom and Gomorrah, Abraham had the nerve to ask him to reconsider. Abraham was afraid that righteous people in the cities would be destroyed along with the wicked. So he asked God if he would save the cities if 50 righteous people could be found in them. To his great relief, God agreed.

But then Abraham worried that he wouldn't be able to find 50 righteous people, so he tried to lower the number to 45. Once again, God agreed. So Abraham kept going: 40, 30, 20, 10. And each time, God agreed. Even though the people of Sodom and Gomorrah were extremely evil, God gave them every chance to repent and turn to him.

God doesn't make exceptions to his justice. And he doesn't look past sin—ever. But he is slow to punish sinners because he wants everyone to have a chance to turn to him. He shows his compassion before he shows his anger. ✤

PRAYER

Dear God, thank you for giving us every opportunity to repent and receive your forgiveness. Let us learn from your example, being quick to show compassion and grace and being slow to get angry. Amen.

THE GREAT HOPE

- Besides salvation, what are some other examples of God's grace that you've experienced?
- Why is it sometimes easy to overlook God's gifts? How can you keep from doing this?

Therefore, with minds that are alert and fully sober, set your hope on the grace to be brought to you when Jesus Christ is revealed at his coming.   1 PETER 1:13

God's ultimate work of grace will be revealed when the kingdom of God is realized in its fullness. But salvation is not the only form of grace we receive from God. We can find evidence of his grace in our lives every day.

Sometimes God gives physical things, such as much-needed college money or a dependable car. Other times he gives healing for ailments big and small. He gives direction when we're not sure which way to turn, and he gives comfort when we're hurting. He gives peace of mind when we're confused or stressed. Every one of those gifts is an example of his grace.

James 1:5 tells us that God gives wisdom generously to all. Lamentations 3:22–23 says, "His compassions never fail. They are new every morning." Every gift God gives is linked to his grace. We don't deserve anything he gives us. We've done nothing to earn it. Yet God loves to give, so we are the grateful recipients of his grace. We serve a generous, gracious God. And for that reason, we always have reason to hope—no matter what situation we're facing. ♣

PRAYER

Dear God, we see evidence of your generous grace everywhere. Thank you for loving us. Thank you for overwhelming us with gifts. Thank you for giving us hope. Amen.

day119

SALVATION THROUGH GRACE

- What do the words of the hymn "Amazing Grace" mean to you?
- What would you say to someone who claimed that he or she "deserved" to go to heaven?

In him we have redemption through his blood, the forgiveness of sins, in accordance with the riches of God's grace that he lavished on us.   EPHESIANS 1:7–8

You can't talk about God's grace without also talking about his justice and mercy. Justice means getting exactly what we deserve. Mercy means not getting the bad that we deserve. Grace means getting the good that we do not deserve.

Grace can never be earned. It can only be given. God gives us his grace because he loves us. There's no other explanation for it. Not only do we not deserve it, but we deserve the exact opposite of it.

If a prisoner on death row is executed for a crime, that's justice. If the prisoner is pardoned by the governor just before the execution, that's mercy. If the prisoner is set free and given a house to live in for the rest of their life, that's grace.

Let's make a commitment as a family to spend some time thinking, talking and praying about God's grace. Let's think about what God's grace cost him, namely, his Son. Let's talk about how his grace completely changes our future. After all, as sinners we had no hope of spending eternity in heaven. And let's pray to show God how grateful we are for his amazing grace. ✤

PRAYER

Dear God, we praise you for being perfectly just, as well as merciful and gracious. You have changed our lives and given us a future that we don't deserve. Let us never forget what your grace cost you. Thank you for loving us. Amen.

day120

NO CONDEMNATION

- What is condemnation?
- Why did Jesus die on the cross?

Therefore, there is now no condemnation for those who are in Christ Jesus, because through Christ Jesus the law of the Spirit who gives life has set you free from the law of sin and death. ROMANS 8:1–2

We are told that we are forgiven for our sins. But sometimes we don't really "feel" forgiven. We still carry some of that old guilt around.

As Christians, we don't have to do this. We don't have to be slaves to our guilt, to our condemnation, because Jesus has set us free from all that. He has given us new life. Jesus took the penalties of our sins on himself when he gave his life on the cross. If we allow ourselves to be consumed by sins that God has forgiven us for, we are essentially saying that Jesus' sacrifice wasn't big enough to cover our sins—and we know that this just isn't true.

If you hear a voice reminding you of the sins for which you've already been forgiven, know that this is not the voice of God. Your guilt is valuable to the enemy. But he can't do much if you are free. And you are free, free from the law of sin and death. Jesus Christ set you free two thousand years ago at Calvary. ❖

PRAYER

Dear God, thank you for Calvary. Thank you for forgiving us for our sins. Please set us free from guilt and condemnation. Amen.

ONE THING IN COMMON

- Why do you need Jesus?
- Who do you know who never sins?

For all have sinned and fall short of the glory of God. ROMANS 3:23

Different people struggle with different sins, but we all have one thing in common—we all sin. We have all sinned, which is why we all need Jesus. We all fall short of God's glory, no matter how hard we work to do good deeds, and no matter how well we behave ourselves.

The only way that we can atone for our sins, the only way that we can be forgiven, the only way we can be acceptable to God, is through Jesus Christ. We need to confess that we have sinned and fallen short, recognize and admit that we need God's forgiveness. And we need to accept that Jesus gave his life as a sacrifice for us so that we can be forgiven. Then we can accept God's gift of love and, in return, give our lives to him. In doing so, we honor God and are assured of spending the rest of eternity with him, in his glory. ✤

PRAYER

Dear Jesus, we know that we have sinned, and we know that we need you in our lives. Thank you for paying the penalty for our sins on the cross. Help us to live our lives in a way that honors you. Amen.

day122

THE SIN PROCESS

- How does sin start?
- Can you give an example of a situation that would likely lead to temptation?

Then, after desire has conceived, it gives birth to sin; and sin, when it is full-grown, gives birth to death.   JAMES 1:15

The Greek word that is translated "desire" in this verse means a craving or longing for something that is forbidden. Think of Eve in the garden with the forbidden fruit. What seemed like such a small temptation turned into disaster. This verse from James tells us that sin is not an accident that happens by chance but a process that begins with temptation.

We will all be tempted. If we do not fight against that temptation, it will give birth to sin, and sin gives birth to death. Obviously, this doesn't mean that everyone who sins will fall down dead immediately. While some sins do lead to physical death, more importantly, sin results in spiritual death.

And all of this starts with the smallest temptation. Recognizing the dangers of temptation can help us guard ourselves against it. If there is a particular person, place or situation that leads us to be tempted, we need to avoid it. ❖

PRAYER

Dear God, thank you for giving us your Word, which teaches us how to avoid sin. Please help us to avoid temptation today and every day. Amen.

THE PUNISHMENT FOR SIN

- Why does sin matter so much?
- Who do we hurt when we sin?

"Now go, lead the people to the place I spoke of, and my angel will go before you. However, when the time comes for me to punish, I will punish them for their sin."   EXODUS 32:34

In Exodus 32, while Moses was away talking to God, the Israelites built a golden calf—an idol—to worship. This was a horrific sin against God, who had just rescued them from slavery in Egypt, and Moses was irate when he found out. So was God.

Moses went to plead with God for mercy, offering his own life if God would spare the lives of his people. And God answered: I will punish them for their sin.

The Bible tells us many times that the punishment for sin is death. Sin is never something to be taken lightly. Still, as Christians, it can be easy for us to take for granted that our sins have been forgiven. It can be tempting to just give in to sin because "we're already forgiven, right?" We need to remember that God does punish sin. It's just that in our case, Jesus has already been punished. It's not that we're getting away with something; Jesus died for us.

When we are tempted to sin, we need to remember that the suffering that Jesus endured is nothing to take for granted. ❖

PRAYER

Dear God, thank you for the cross. Thank you for forgiving our sins. Please help us to remember the seriousness of sin. Amen.

day124

FREE AND FORGIVEN

- Have you ever had to confess a mistake to another person?
- Why do you need to confess your sins to God?

If we claim to be without sin, we deceive ourselves and the truth is not in us. If we confess our sins, he is faithful and just and will forgive us our sins and purify us from all unrighteousness. 1 JOHN 1:8–9

To confess means to admit to our sin and also to agree with God that we need forgiveness. When we genuinely confess our sins to God, he is faithful to forgive us. When we repent, he purifies us from our sins.

This doesn't mean that we need to keep a diary of every bad thought we think and every bad deed we do and then name them to God one by one. But it does mean that, as Christians, we need to continually acknowledge that we are sinners in need of God's saving grace.

When we do this, God makes us new. He wipes the slate clean and gives us a fresh start—every time. We do not need to return to our sinful habits. We do not need to be slaves to our sin. Through the blood of Jesus, God sets us free from our sin. We are free and forgiven. ✤

PRAYER

Dear God, thank you for freeing us from our slavery to sin. Thank you for making us new creations in you. Please help us to live like free people. Amen.

STATING THE OBVIOUS

- Why does worship sometimes seem stale and boring?
- What can you, or our whole family, do to make worship more exciting and alive?

Ascribe to the LORD, you heavenly beings, ascribe to the LORD glory and strength. Ascribe to the LORD the glory due his name; worship the LORD in the splendor of his holiness.

PSALM 29:1–2

In Revelation 4, the apostle John describes God's throne in heaven. He uses the image of precious stones to describe the one sitting on the throne, since God can't be seen directly. Surrounding God's throne are 24 other thrones with 24 elders sitting on them. Positioned around God's throne are four living creatures covered with eyes. "Day and night they never stop saying: '"Holy, holy, holy is the Lord God Almighty," who was, and is, and is to come'" (Revelation 4:8).

At the sound of their voices, the 24 elders fall down and worship him with these words: "You are worthy, our Lord and God, to receive glory and honor and power, for you created all things, and by your will they were created and have their being" (Revelation 4:11).

Why do the creatures and elders do it? They can't help themselves. Being in God's presence, seeing his perfection and holiness up close, is so awe-inspiring that they *have* to keep praising and worshiping him. The excitement we feel when we see something incredible is a small sample of what these worshipers feel all the time. What would it take for us to feel that same kind of excitement when we worship God? How can we become more awestruck when we praise him? ✜

PRAYER

Dear God, we join with the creatures and elders around your throne in worshiping you. We are awestruck by your holiness and your goodness. We will praise you forever in this life and the next. Amen.

day126

COURTESY OF JESUS CHRIST

- When do you feel most like worshiping God? Why?
- In what way is Jesus the bridge between God and us?

And by that will, we have been made holy through the sacrifice of the body of Jesus Christ once for all. HEBREWS 10:10

We can choose which church we want to attend. We can choose whom we sit next to. But we can't choose whether or not we're going to worship—not if we want to be truly fulfilled.

We were made to worship God—he created us for it. When we worship with all our heart, we are fulfilling our purpose and bringing ourselves as close to God as we will get in this lifetime. Without Jesus, though, our purpose would be unfulfilled.

We couldn't get anywhere near God's presence without Jesus. His sacrifice bridged the gap that our sin created. Without his death on the cross and his resurrection, we might not even know what our purpose was. We would just live our lives with a sense that something was missing—something big and important. No matter how much happiness or success we experienced, we would still be left unsatisfied.

Until we fulfill our created purpose of bringing praise and glory to God, we can never live fully. Without Jesus' sacrifice, that wouldn't be possible. ✤

PRAYER

Dear God, thank you for sending your Son to bridge the gap between us. Thank you for giving us the privilege of worshiping you. Amen.

PERPETUAL WORSHIP

- Is our church a good place for you to worship God the way you want? Explain.
- If you could worship anywhere, what setting would you choose? Why?

Therefore, since we are receiving a kingdom that cannot be shaken, let us be thankful, and so worship God acceptably with reverence and awe.   HEBREWS 12:28

Some people say a church is just about the worst place for a person to worship God. They point to the bad lighting, the early morning start time and any number of other distractions to prove their point. They argue that we can't "worship God acceptably with reverence and awe" in that kind of setting.

The big problem with that argument is that it suggests that worship takes place only when we are at church. And that's not how God intends it. Our church may not be perfect. No church is. But it gives us a chance to fellowship with other believers, learn about God's Word, give our offerings to God and use our gifts to serve others.

Worship, on the other hand, can be done anytime we see something that inspires us or makes us stare in awe. Worship can be done every time we think about what an incredible God we serve. Worship can be done anytime, anywhere and as often as we want. ❖

PRAYER

Dear God, let us never think of worship as a "church thing." Open our eyes to your incredible work so that we will be inspired to worship you everywhere. Amen.

GET CLOSER

- Where and when do you feel closest to God? Why?
- What would you say to a friend who asked how he or she could feel close to God?

Come near to God and he will come near to you. Wash your hands, you sinners, and purify your hearts, you double-minded.   JAMES 4:8

In the Garden of Eden, Adam and Eve enjoyed a personal relationship with God. It was such a close friendship that he would walk with them through the garden during the cool of the day.

We know what happened to that relationship, how sin messed it up. We also know how Jesus restored that relationship by taking the punishment for our sin and making it possible for us to be sinless in God's eyes. We can and should praise God for that.

But let's not forget that God's plan all along was for us to have a personal relationship with him. That really is what he wants. He's always ready to come near to us. All we have to do to make that happen is to come near to him.

We come near to God through worship. When we praise him and show him we understand how incredible he is, God comes near to us. He rewards our worship by giving us more to worship him for.

If you don't feel close to God, try spending some time in worship. Focus on him—who he is and what he's done. Give him the glory that he is due. ♣

PRAYER

Dear God, thank you for coming near to us. Your presence gives us courage, comfort and peace of mind. We will worship you forever. Amen.

day129

AN ENCOUNTER WITH THE HOLY GOD

- What's the first thing you would do if God appeared to you?
- What does it mean that God is holy?

"Do not come any closer," God said. "Take off your sandals, for the place where you are standing is holy ground." Then he said, "I am the God of your father, the God of Abraham, the God of Isaac and the God of Jacob." At this, Moses hid his face, because he was afraid to look at God.   EXODUS 3:5 – 6

Moses was born a Hebrew, but he was adopted and raised as an Egyptian. He grew up hearing about, and perhaps even worshiping, Egyptian gods. He knew little or nothing about the God of the Hebrews.

When he was 40 years old, Moses killed an Egyptian who was beating a Hebrew slave. He had to flee Egypt. He ran to the desert, where he started a new life as a shepherd.

One day while he was leading his flock across the desert, he saw a burning bush. When he stepped in for a closer look, a voice from the bush called his name. After 40-some years, God was reintroducing himself. He immediately told Moses not to come any closer and to remove his sandals because he was standing on holy ground.

The first thing God wanted Moses to know about him was that he is holy. Moses was able to have a conversation with God and eventually enjoy a personal relationship with him — but only after he honored God's holiness.

That's important to remember in our worship. Before we do anything else, we must honor God's holiness and praise him for it. ✤

PRAYER

Dear God, you are holy. Nothing sinful can exist in your presence. Thank you for making us sinless through the blood of your Son. Amen.

day130

HIS NAME IS JEALOUS

- Can jealousy ever be a good thing? Explain.
- What are some things that make people jealous?

Do not worship any other god, for the LORD, whose name is Jealous, is a jealous God.

EXODUS 34:14

In Exodus 34:14, God tells Moses that he is a jealous God. That seems kind of odd, doesn't it? What does God have to be jealous about?

Unfortunately, the Israelites, God's people, gave him plenty of reason to be jealous. When the Israelites mingled with foreigners, they often adopted their worship habits. And since most foreigners worshiped idols, the Israelites often became idol worshipers too, despite God's warnings.

Imagine God's reaction. *He* was the one who had rescued the Israelites from slavery in Egypt. *He* had parted the Red Sea so that they could walk across safely. *He* had protected them from dangerous enemies. *He* had provided them with all the food and water they needed in the desert. And every chance they got, the Israelites would bow down, give thanks and worship those *things* . . . little carved statues.

God loved the Israelites, and they ignored him. Of course he was jealous—not in a human, sinful way—as he watched his people give the love he deserved to gods that didn't even exist.

We need to make sure we don't follow the Israelites' example. We might not be tempted to bow down to little statues, but we need to make sure that we never make anything—not sports or friends or anything else—more important than God. ✤

PRAYER

Dear God, forgive us for the times when we put other things in our lives ahead of you. We do not want to make you jealous. We love you above everything else. Amen.

WHO IS APPROVED?

- On what do you base your self-esteem?
- Whose opinions matter most to you?

But, "Let the one who boasts boast in the Lord." For it is not the one who commends himself who is approved, but the one whom the Lord commends.

2 CORINTHIANS 10:17–18

It may feel good to brag, but in the end, it doesn't really matter what we, or anyone else for that matter, think of ourselves. What matters is what God thinks of us. Therefore, we should base our self-esteem on what God thinks.

Do we love God? Are we seeking him? Are we working to keep his commandments? Are we working to put others' needs ahead of our own? These are the questions we should be asking when questioning our own worth.

It's not about what our friends think. It's not about what the media tells us. It's not about what our teachers, coaches or pastors think. It's not even about what our parents think. It's about what God thinks. He asks us to love him and to love others. He asks us to seek him. If we are doing these things, we are approved, and we should have no shortage of self-esteem. Ever. ✤

PRAYER

Dear God, thank you for your Word, which teaches us how to please you. Thank you that our self-worth lies completely and safely in you. Amen.

day132

FEARFULLY AND WONDERFULLY MADE

- What makes you different from everyone else?
- What is your favorite thing about yourself?

For you created my inmost being; you knit me together in my mother's womb. I praise you because I am fearfully and wonderfully made; your works are wonderful, I know that full well.
PSALM 139:13–14

God made the heavens and the earth. Pretty impressive stuff. He made the majestic mountains, the immense oceans and the vast sky. He made the dancing honeybee, the dreamlike jellyfish and the colorful parrot. He made the comets, Saturn's rings and massive black holes. And he made you.

God's works are wonderful. You know that full well. So, why do you sometimes believe that one of his works isn't wonderful? Why do you sometimes believe that *you* are not wonderful? It's simply not true. You are fearfully and wonderfully made. You were not created by chance—you were *designed*. God knit you together in your mother's womb.

God would not create something that didn't matter. God would not waste his time or his power on something that wasn't wonderful. Don't ever doubt that you matter. You matter to God—you're his child. You are one of his many masterpieces. ❖

PRAYER

Dear God, please forgive us when we forget that we are fearfully and wonderfully made. Thank you for this life. Please give us confidence in who we are in you. Amen.

GOD SAYS YOU ARE

- According to television, movies or popular music, what makes people important?
- What do you think makes someone important?

For God so loved the world that he gave his one and only Son, that whoever believes in him shall not perish but have eternal life.   JOHN 3:16

This world can do a lot of damage to someone's self-esteem. The media are constantly telling us that we're not good enough because they want us to spend more money on trying to be better. They tell us that if we have the newest toy, the fastest car and the biggest house, people will love us.

If we look to the world for our self-esteem, we will be disappointed. But, as children of God, we can feel certain of our self-worth. The God of all creation loved us enough to send his only Son to die for us.

Even if you were the only person on earth, God still would have sent Jesus for you. That's how much he loves you. Don't ever allow the world to make you think you're not beautiful, not special, not worthwhile—God says you are. Trust in God and his love; remember how much he loves you. ✣

PRAYER

Dear God, thank you for Jesus. Thank you for sending him to earth to die for us. Please help us to remember your love when we are feeling down. Amen.

day134

ROOTED IN CHRIST

- What is one thing that you are good at?
- What is the difference between self-esteem and arrogance?

For by the grace given me I say to every one of you: Do not think of yourself more highly than you ought, but rather think of yourself with sober judgment, in accordance with the faith God has distributed to each of you. For just as each of us has one body with many members, and these members do not all have the same function, so in Christ we, though many, form one body, and each member belongs to all the others. ROMANS 12:3–5

God wants us to have a true understanding of our self-worth, but he doesn't want us to be arrogant. Arrogance will separate us from God. We are not to depend on ourselves. We are to depend on God. True self-esteem is rooted in sincere humility.

When we recognize our own weaknesses, we can draw on God's immeasurable strength. This strength becomes a part of who we are. And God's strength is a well that never runs dry.

In order to draw from this well, we must be rooted in Christ. We must get to know who we are in him. Just as our bodies are made up of many parts, we are one part of the body of Christ. We are a uniquely and intentionally designed part of the body of Christ.

There is a thrill in finding out who you are in Christ. There is excitement in discovering what God has in store for you. You probably can't even imagine what he has planned for you. But if you center your life on your relationship with him, you will soon find out. Prepare to be amazed. ❖

PRAYER

Dear God, thank you for the opportunity to have a personal relationship with your Son. Thank you for giving us unique gifts and talents. Please help us to use these gifts to serve you. Amen.

POWER SOURCE

- When you think of Jesus, what comes to mind first: his love or his power? Why?
- What are some of the most amazing things Jesus ever did?

For to us a child is born, to us a son is given, and the government will be on his shoulders. And he will be called Wonderful Counselor, Mighty God, Everlasting Father, Prince of Peace. ISAIAH 9:6

Someone once said Jesus is like Clark Kent and Superman at the same time. (In case you're wondering, Clark Kent is Superman's secret identity.) That's probably not the best description of Jesus, but it is understandable. Like Clark Kent, Jesus appeared to be mild-mannered and average. He was a patient teacher. He was good with children. He talked about love.

At the same time, he was the most powerful person ever to walk the earth. He went one-on-one with Satan himself and walked away with the victory. He drove demons out of people who were possessed. He commanded a raging storm to calm down, and it obeyed him. Superman never did anything like that! And Jesus didn't even need a cape.

Jesus is the Prince of Peace, but we shouldn't overlook his power. He was fully human and fully God, which means he possessed the power of the Creator of the universe.

That is our Savior and Lord, the one who watches over us and protects us. He is the Shepherd who takes care of his sheep. We can sleep well knowing all that power is on our side. ✤

PRAYER

Dear Lord, we praise you for your incredible power. You left no doubt that you are God. Thank you that we can depend on your power when we need it most. Amen.

RETURN ENGAGEMENT

- How do you picture Jesus' return?
- Is it something you're looking forward to? Explain.

We wait for the blessed hope—the appearing of the glory of our great God and Savior, Jesus Christ. TITUS 2:13

Some people have made a career of predicting when Jesus will come back. Way back in 1988, someone wrote a book called *88 Reasons Why the Rapture Will Be in 1988.* Obviously the author was off by more than a few years. More recently, a well-known radio preacher convinced his followers that Jesus would return on May 21, 2011. When that didn't happen, he recalculated and predicted Jesus would return on October 21, 2011. When that didn't happen, he apologized and gave up predicting.

Those kinds of assertions would be humorous if they hadn't deceived so many people. Several families sold everything they had and emptied their bank accounts and children's college funds to support the radio ministry because they figured they wouldn't be needing money.

The fact is, we don't know when Jesus will return. The Bible says we *won't* know (see Mark 13:32–34). Trying to figure it out is a waste of time. We should recognize that Christ could come back at any moment. But that shouldn't stop us from doing his work and living the earthly lives he calls us to. ✤

PRAYER

Dear God, we celebrate the fact that Jesus is coming again. We trust his promise and eagerly await his return. And while we wait, we will continue to do his work. Amen.

day137

FOREVER FAITHFUL

- When was the last time someone let you down? How did it make you feel?
- What are some ways you can make sure you don't let others down?

If we are faithless, he remains faithful, for he cannot disown himself.   2 TIMOTHY 2:13

People have a tendency to let others down. Maybe a friend gets a better offer and blows off your weekend plans. Or maybe a loved one promises to come to your game, but instead has to work late and misses it. That sting of disappointment can hurt.

Unfortunately, that's human nature. People are imperfect. Sooner or later, most people will let us down in one way or another. If we want someone who is faithful 100 percent of the time, we need to turn to Jesus. He will never leave us or forsake us. No matter how many times we let him down, he will always be there for us.

Jesus' faithfulness guarantees our salvation. We never have to wonder whether it's enough simply to believe in him. He promises that if we do, he will save us.

As followers of Jesus, we should do everything we can to follow his example. We can be examples of faithfulness to others. We can be the kind of people others rely on in tough times. We can show others what Jesus is like. ✤

PRAYER

Dear Jesus, we live in a world of disappointment, but we never have to worry about you letting us down. Thank you for being so faithful. Amen.

day138 may 18

THE WORD WAS GOD

- How would you respond to someone who said, "Jesus was a great teacher, but he was not God"?
- What does Jesus teach us about God?

In the beginning was the Word, and the Word was with God, and the Word was God.
JOHN 1:1

People who have grown up in the church have been taught that Jesus is God since they were little. To them, there's nothing unusual about the idea. To other people, though, it's one of the most radical and controversial claims imaginable.

Jewish people in particular have a very deep respect for God. They treat his name with such reverence that they won't even spell it out when they write it. They use G-d instead. Imagine the horror among Jewish leaders in New Testament times when a teacher named Jesus arrived on the scene claiming to be God.

Of course, they set out to prove that he wasn't God with the intent of punishing him for his blasphemy. The problem was, they couldn't disprove his claim. Every time they challenged him, he responded with wisdom that could only come from God.

Jesus didn't just *say* he was God. He proved it through his actions. He performed miracles that showed his power over God's creation—even over death. No one but God has that power.

Most of the Jewish leaders never believed Jesus during his lifetime. That's why they pushed so hard for his crucifixion. After he died and rose from the grave, though, many of them changed their minds. They discovered that Jesus is God. ♣

PRAYER

Dear God, before anything else existed, there was you—and your Word. Never let us forget how incredible it is that we can have a personal relationship with you, the eternal Creator of the universe. Amen.

THE GOOD SHEPHERD

- What are some things you know about sheep?
- What would it take to be a good shepherd?

"I am the good shepherd. The good shepherd lays down his life for the sheep." JOHN 10:11

Most people know the beginning of Psalm 23: "The LORD is my shepherd." Jesus confirmed that claim when he said, "I am the good shepherd." The question is, why did he choose such a description for himself?

At first glance, a shepherd seems like a tame analogy. What does a shepherd do but stand in the middle of a peaceful meadow, hold a stick with a curved end and watch a flock of sheep munch grass?

It turns out there's a lot more to shepherding than that. In 1 Samuel 17:34–35, David, who also was a shepherd, gives a brief job description: "When a lion or a bear came and carried off a sheep from the flock, I went after it, struck it and rescued the sheep from its mouth. When it turned on me, I seized it by its hair, struck it and killed it." Not only do shepherds have a deep concern for the safety of their sheep but they will risk—and even sacrifice—their own lives to keep the sheep safe.

As Christians, we are Jesus' sheep. He leads us to where we need to be, he watches over us and he protects us. He is the Good Shepherd. ✤

PRAYER

Dear God, thank you for sending Jesus, our Good Shepherd. We praise him for protecting us, searching for us and giving his life for us. Amen.

day140

WHAT'S SO BAD ABOUT BEING ANGRY?

- Can you share a time when you were really angry with someone?
- How do you think God feels about anger?

"But I tell you that anyone who is angry with a brother or sister will be subject to judgment. Again, anyone who says to a brother or sister, 'Raca,' is answerable to the court. And anyone who says, 'You fool!' will be in danger of the fire of hell." MATTHEW 5:22

"You shall not murder" is the sixth commandment. We all know that murder is wrong. But in this verse from Matthew, Jesus teaches that the sinful anger that causes us to call others names or say bad things about them is the same sinful anger that leads to murder. You don't need to have blood on your hands to be guilty of sinful anger.

If you feel yourself starting to get angry, take it to God immediately. Ask him to replace your anger with forgiveness, with love, with peace. We are commanded to love God and love our neighbors as ourselves—there is no room for sinful anger.

God looks at the heart. Yes, he sees the sin, but he also sees very clearly the motive behind the sin. God wants us to have clean hands *and* pure hearts. ❖

PRAYER

Dear God, please give us self-control; help us to not get angry with one another. Let the Holy Spirit purify our hearts. Amen.

NO FLYING OFF THE HANDLE!

- What does it mean to be quick-tempered?
- How do people react to an angry person?

Since an overseer manages God's household, he must be blameless — not overbearing, not quick-tempered, not given to drunkenness, not violent, not pursuing dishonest gain.

TITUS 1:7

Have you ever heard the phrase "fly off the handle"? It means to lose control of your emotions and act out in anger. Where does the phrase come from? Imagine an ax swinging through the air. Imagine the sharp, heavy, metal ax head flying off the handle and shooting off into the air, possibly hitting someone nearby. That's the basic problem with flying off the handle—there's a good chance someone is going to get hurt.

In this verse from Titus, Paul describes traits and behaviors that are unacceptable for leaders of the church. One of the traits he mentions is quick-temperedness. God doesn't want his church leaders flying off the handle.

The day may come when God wants you to lead others. Or maybe you're leading others right now. One of the best things you can do for God, for yourself and for the people you are leading is to work at controlling your temper. Work to lead with love and patience. Then you will be able to lead people closer to God. ✤

PRAYER

Dear God, please help us to be patient and understanding with people. We pray that you will strengthen and protect those who lead us. Amen.

ANGER VS. SELF-CONTROL

* Can you remember a time when you were quick to get angry?
* Can you remember a time when you were slow to get angry?

My dear brothers and sisters, take note of this: Everyone should be quick to listen, slow to speak and slow to become angry.   JAMES 1:19

James teaches us in this verse that we should be slow to become angry, "because human anger does not produce the righteousness that God desires" (James 1:20). God wants us to learn to control our anger. It's part of the transformation that we undergo as believers.

Galatians 5:23 tells us that a fruit of the Holy Spirit is self-control. We can't learn to control our anger in the moment that we're about to become angry. We need to first lay the foundation. We should commit to honoring God with our behavior and submit to the leading of the Holy Spirit. We need to spend time in the Word and in prayer. If we work at it, even those of us with strong tempers will be able to control our anger.

If the Bible says that God wants us to be slow to become angry, he will help make that happen. We just have to want it, work at it and let him help us. ✣

PRAYER

Dear God, thank you for being patient with us. Please give us the desire to tame our anger. Please help us to have self-control. Amen.

day143

DIDN'T JESUS GET ANGRY ONCE?

- Is there such a thing as good anger? If so, give an example.
- What makes God angry?

In the temple courts he found people selling cattle, sheep and doves, and others sitting at tables exchanging money. So he made a whip out of cords, and drove all from the temple courts, both sheep and cattle; he scattered the coins of the money changers and overturned their tables. To those who sold doves he said, "Get these out of here! Stop turning my Father's house into a market!" JOHN 2:14–16

There is such a thing as righteous anger. We see an example of it here in this passage from John. Jesus came to the temple in Jerusalem at Passover and found merchants and money changers charging high rates and taking advantage of people. In other words, they were exploiting God's house in an attempt to get rich.

Jesus was irate, with very good reason. And he drove all that sinful behavior out of the temple.

It's important for us to realize that Jesus did not lose control and react to the situation. Jesus responded to the situation with self-control and did what he had to do to make his point. Jesus was angry, yes, but it was a controlled anger that honored God. Jesus did not hurt anyone. In fact, his actions drew people nearer to him, not away from him.

There are things in this world that will make us angry. Evil and injustice in this world should make us angry, and God wants us to respond in a manner that glorifies him. ❖

PRAYER

Dear God, help us to know what attitudes and actions honor and glorify you. Amen.

DON'T FRET!

* What are some things you do when you get angry?
* Are you more likely to sin when you are angry? Why or why not?

Refrain from anger and turn from wrath; do not fret—it leads only to evil. PSALM 37:8

To "fret" means to worry, to be discontent, to be angry—basically, fretting is the opposite of being at peace. In this verse from psalms, King David tells us not to fret because fretting leads to evil. Worrying, discontentedness and anger all lead to evil actions. We might say that King David is telling us to calm down.

God wants us to be at peace. He doesn't want us uptight, with our fists and teeth clenched. If we work to keep ourselves from anger, if we work to turn away from it, we can protect ourselves from the temptation to worry. On the other hand, if we give in to the sinful expression of anger, then we will charge headlong into a situation where we may end up making ourselves miserable with stress.

God wants better for us. He doesn't want anger to lead us to sin. If we are angry, if we are fretting, we need to pray about that situation and consciously let God handle it. He will give us peace in whatever difficult circumstance we face. ✤

> **PRAYER**

Dear God, please help us to refrain from anger and turn from wrath. Please help us to not fret and to be at peace. Amen.

day145

NEVER GO TO BED ANGRY

- Share a time when you were angry about the way someone else was treated. How did you respond?
- Have you ever found yourself just a little bit angry and then felt that anger grow over time?

"In your anger do not sin": Do not let the sun go down while you are still angry, and do not give the devil a foothold. EPHESIANS 4:26–27

Have you ever heard of righteous indignation? This is the kind of anger that we feel toward injustice, cruelty or sin. It is the kind of anger that Jesus expressed in the temple when he flipped over the money changers' tables. If you are angry because of dishonor shown toward God or others, it is not sinful to express that anger, but it's still something to be careful about.

If we hold onto any type of anger for any length of time, it can eat away at us. God wants us to be at peace. He doesn't want us grinding our teeth in anger while we sleep.

The most dangerous part of righteous indignation, as well as any type of anger, is that it can give Satan a place in our lives. The verse says "do not give the devil a foothold." Do not give Satan any access to your heart or to your thoughts. This can and will lead to sin.

If you do experience righteous indignation, express it in appropriate words. Pray about it and talk about it with those you trust. Use it to galvanize you into action that will honor God. But don't hold onto it and dwell on. Don't let it lead you to sin. ❖

PRAYER

Dear God, thank you for giving us your Word to guide and protect us. Please help us to be angry in a righteous way about things that anger you as well. Amen.

day146

CALM, COOL AND COLLECTED

* Have you ever made a scene because you were angry? Describe that experience.
* Do you know someone who never seems to get upset? How would you describe that person?

Fools show their annoyance at once, but the prudent overlook an insult. PROVERBS 12:16

Think back to a time when you saw someone who was really angry. Maybe it was a coach on television. Or a kid on a playground. Or some guy on the street screaming at his girlfriend. Try to remember what that really looked like. Try to remember the impression that you got from that angry person.

You probably didn't think, "Wow, that person is really cool," or "That person is really smart," or "I wish I was as happy as that person." No, you probably didn't admire that person at all. You might have been troubled by their actions. You might have been scared of them. Maybe you vowed to yourself never to act like that.

When we let our anger drive us to lose control, we look like fools. When we overlook an insult, though, we look calm, cool and collected. When something annoys us, we don't have to react. We don't have to give anyone the satisfaction of making us lose our cool. We can honor God and save ourselves embarrassment by calmly walking away. ✤

PRAYER

Dear God, thank you for giving us the ability to control our emotions. Please help us to stay calm, cool and collected. Amen.

day**147**

THE LAP OF FOOLS

- Have you ever made an assumption that turned out to be wrong? Describe your experience.
- What does it mean to provoke someone?

Do not be quickly provoked in your spirit, for anger resides in the lap of fools.

ECCLESIASTES 7:9

While we are on this earth, we will never understand the big picture. We are not wise like God. We don't know the past. We don't know the future. And we don't know what is going on in someone else's heart.

When something happens that upsets you or makes you angry, don't assume you know what's happening behind the scenes. While you may well have been offended, and you may even have a legitimate reason to be angry, you still have an opportunity to honor God by slowing your reaction time, admitting that you don't have all the facts and acting graciously.

Anger resides in the lap of fools. Some people just wander around looking for reasons to be angry. They are easily offended and get a kind of satisfaction from it. You don't want to spend your time on this foolishness.

You want to be the person who takes a step back and acts with kindness. You want to be the person who doesn't make assumptions and who avoids unnecessary quarrels. ✤

PRAYER

Dear God, help us to be patient with others. Help us to not be quickly provoked in the spirit. Amen.

day148

FAMILY RESEMBLANCE

- Which family member do you look or act most like?
- When is it a good thing to resemble someone and when is it a bad thing?

Follow God's example, therefore, as dearly loved children.　　　　Ephesians 5:1

Like it or not, all kids get traits from their parents. Biological children inherit physical features such as hair color and body types. Adopted children or foster children inherit worldviews, attitudes and ways of speaking. If you look closely at yourself, you'll see plenty of evidence of the people who are raising you. In some cases, that's a good thing. In others, it's not so good.

But our parents aren't the only ones with whom we share similarities. The Bible says we're created in God's image. That means we're like him in many important ways. For example, our creativity is a reflection of him, the ultimate Creator.

We have the opportunity to be even *more* like him—in the way we act, the way we think, the way we treat others and the way we treat his Word. We can choose to play up our resemblance by following his instructions and staying close to him. Or we can separate ourselves by doing what we want to do.

The question is, when people look at your life, do you want them to see your heavenly Father? ✤

PRAYER

Dear God, thank you for creating us in your image. Thank you for making us your children. Never let us lose sight of what a privilege that is. Amen.

WELCOME TO THE FAMILY

- What's the best thing about having God as your heavenly Father?
- What's the most challenging thing about having God as your heavenly Father?

Yet to all who did receive him, to those who believed in his name, he gave the right to become children of God.   JOHN 1:12

Christians are children of God. That family connection brings with it a lot of responsibility. As God's children, we have to examine the way we act, the way we think, the way we treat others and the way we spend our time to make sure that everything we do brings glory to our Father.

Being a child of God also brings with it countless privileges. For example, we know for certain that we have a faithful companion who will never leave us. In Psalm 23:4, David wrote, "Even though I walk through the darkest valley, I will fear no evil, for you are with me." Like David, we have no need to fear with our heavenly Father by our side.

As children of God, we have the perfect guidance counselor. God created us, so he knows everything about us. He knows about skills and gifts we have that we aren't even aware of. And if we let him, he will lead us into situations where we can put our abilities to use.

Finally, as children of God, we have a place to live—forever. When our time on earth is over, God has a place for us in heaven—with him. ✣

PRAYER

Dear God, thank you for accepting us as your children. Let us always remember what a privilege it is to be able to call you Father. Amen.

day150

YOUR HONOR

* Where do you usually hear the word "honor"?
* How do you show honor to someone?

"Honor your father and your mother, so that you may live long in the land the LORD your God is giving you."   EXODUS 20:12

We could probably come up with at least 100 reasons why kids shouldn't always have to honor their parents. For example, some parents are untrustworthy. Some struggle with addictions. Some seem to care only about themselves. Some pursue unhealthy lifestyles. Some make incredibly bad decisions. Some abandon their children. The list could go on and on.

The problem is, none of those reasons overrule God's command. Regardless of their faults and personal issues, parents are to be honored. God's plan is for parents to give their children love, guidance, discipline and security, and for children to give their parents honor. The fact that parents don't hold up their end of the bargain doesn't excuse children from holding up theirs.

To honor our parents means to recognize their relationship with us, to treat them with respect, to love them unconditionally and to want what's best for them. If that's not safe to do in our own home, we can do it from a distance. But we can't ignore God's fifth commandment. All of us need to find ways to honor our parents. ❖

PRAYER

Dear God, thank you for telling us very clearly how we can obey you. Remind us to honor our parents every day, even when we don't feel like it or if it is hard to do. Amen.

day151

A GOOD HEAD START

- Name a skill that you developed at an early age. How did you develop it?
- What are some of the first things a child needs to understand about God? How do you communicate those truths to a child?

Start children off on the way they should go, and even when they are old they will not turn from it.   PROVERBS 22:6

The ancient philosopher Aristotle said, "Well begun is half done." When you apply that philosophy to parenting, you get Proverbs 22:6. Parents who begin training their children from an early age—and who back up that training with consistent love and discipline—will be well ahead of the curve in instilling lifelong spiritual disciplines in their kids.

No world-class athlete becomes a champion through natural ability alone. Practice is essential—the more, the better. Repetition is the key. The younger a competitor is when starting to develop proper form and technique, the better chance they have of making those skills second nature—and ultimately achieving success.

Of course, the competitor must be invested in the process, too. When it comes to developing spiritual maturity, the most successful parents and kids work as a team. The parents set the training agenda and closely monitor the progress being made. The kids honor their parents' authority and submit to the training—even when it seems difficult. The better parents and kids work together, the greater their chances are of impacting the world. ✤

PRAYER

Dear God, thank you for giving us parental wisdom in your Word. Help us as a family to exemplify the values and priorities that honor you. Amen.

day152

GENERATION TO GENERATION

- Do we talk about spiritual things enough in our family? Explain.
- What is one thing about God, the Bible or the Christian life that you don't understand?

These commandments that I give you today are to be on your hearts. Impress them on your children. Talk about them when you sit at home and when you walk along the road, when you lie down and when you get up. DEUTERONOMY 6:6–7

God expects children to honor their parents, which can be difficult sometimes. But he expects a lot from parents too. His command in Deuteronomy 6:7 is one of many that makes it challenging to be a father or mother. Parents are responsible for giving their children the spiritual training they need. What's more, God will judge parents based on how well they handle that responsibility.

The command in Deuteronomy is challenging for three reasons. First, we live in a very busy culture. Making time for spiritual training requires a lot of planning and work. Second, many parents feel unqualified to teach spiritual things because of their own lack of spiritual training. Third, many parents don't know what their kids are struggling with, spiritually speaking.

The first challenge can be solved by setting aside specific times every week to talk about spiritual things as a family; this could mean eliminating some things to make space in the schedule. The second problem can be addressed by a lot of studying and praying. The third can be addressed by open communication. Everyone in the family should be able to share questions or doubts about anything spiritual. If we're going to become the family God wants us to be, we need to work together. ❖

PRAYER

Dear God, thank you for making sure that your words will live on from generation to generation. Guide us in teaching and learning the truth about you and your Word. Amen.

day153

BELIEVE IS AN ACTION VERB

- How does your faith affect your life?
- What are some ways that you put your faith into action?

"The time has come," he said. "The kingdom of God has come near. Repent and believe the good news!"
MARK 1:15

At the very beginning of his ministry on earth, Jesus said, "The time has come." He had arrived. The world as people knew it was about to be changed forever, and they would need to take action. People needed to repent and believe the Good News.

But there's more to believing than lip service, isn't there? *Believe* is an action verb. Belief in Jesus has to affect the way that we live, or it's not sincere. Jesus asks us to repent and to believe in the gospel. This means that we need to accept him as our Savior and give our lives to him. It means we must submit to his will for our lives. It means we must follow his lead at all costs.

Worshiping Jesus should affect every aspect of our lives in every possible way. None of this is easy. None of this is simple. But when we do it, life changes for the better. We become healthier people, filled with joy, who make the world a better place. ✤

PRAYER

Dear God, thank you so much for your Son. Please help us to live out our beliefs. Please help us to make believe *an action verb. Amen.*

day154

NO EASY HILL TO CLIMB

- How do people know that you love God?
- Why did God give his people commandments?

"Obey the LORD your God and follow his commands and decrees that I give you today."

DEUTERONOMY 27:10

We don't have to guess how God wants us to behave. He hasn't hidden it from us, making it hard to know. All we have to do is open the Bible.

God gave Moses the commandments. God wanted his people to know how to act so that they would honor him and also so that they would be safe and healthy.

Today, we still demonstrate our faith by obeying these laws. This doesn't mean that we worship the laws, making them more important than they should be, because that would be disobeying the Ten Commandments themselves. But it does mean that we honor God when we act the way he wants us to.

Love is the fulfillment of the law. Remember: Above all else, we are to love God and love our neighbors as ourselves. No easy hill to climb. But the view from the top is unbeatable. ✤

PRAYER

Dear God, thank you for making it clear to us how you want us to live. Please help us to demonstrate our beliefs through obedience to your Word. Amen.

CREDITED AS RIGHTEOUS

- What does the word *righteous* mean?
- How can you achieve righteousness?

Abram believed the LORD, and he credited it to him as righteousness.   GENESIS 15:6

We cannot be righteous on our own. We cannot do enough good things or behave well enough to ever achieve righteousness—Isaiah wrote that all our righteous acts are like filthy rags compared to God's righteousness.

But despite our inadequateness, God has given us a way to be righteous. God called Abraham righteous, not because he did good things or was well-behaved, but because he *believed*. He believed with all his heart, all his soul and all his strength. And if we do the same, we too can be counted as righteous.

We don't have to be perfect. But we must agree with the Word of God. We also have to submit to the will of God and accept the sacrifice provided by the Son of God. And we too need to love our God with all our hearts, all our souls and all our strength. Then we too will be credited as righteous. ❖

PRAYER

Dear God, thank you for your grace and mercy. Please help us to love you with all that we are and all we have. Amen.

SPIRITUAL MILK

- Spiritually speaking, how "old" are you? How mature are you spiritually? When it comes to knowing God's Word, are you a newborn, a growing child, a confident teenager or a wise adult?
- How do you become more mature as a Christian?

Like newborn babies, crave pure spiritual milk, so that by it you may grow up in your salvation.   1 PETER 2:2

Accepting Christ as Savior is just the beginning of the Christian life. Once we are born again, we start the growing process. The key to that process is God's Word, which gives us nourishment. We can't grow without it.

Like all newborns, we start with milk. The apostle Peter says we should "crave" it. We start by digesting the basics of the faith—the well-known stories in Scripture and the general outline of Christian belief.

We must not stop there, however. In 1 Corinthians 3:2, the apostle Paul makes it clear that there is a difference between spiritual milk and spiritual solid food. If we don't progress to solid food—the more complex teachings in Scripture—we cannot continue growing as Christians.

God expects us to grow constantly. He wants us to learn about him and his nature. He wants us to know what he has done in the past. He wants us to know what he is going to do in the future. He wants us to crave the nourishment of his Word in the same way we crave food when we are hungry. He wants us to become spiritually mature. ✤

PRAYER

Dear God, thank you for feeding us through the words of Scripture. Help us continue to grow by reading and obeying your Word. Amen.

day157

THE NOT-SO-SECRET WEAPON

- Why is a spiritual battle especially dangerous?
- What can the Bible protect you from?

Take the helmet of salvation and the sword of the Spirit, which is the word of God.

EPHESIANS 6:17

In Ephesians 6:10–17, the apostle Paul warns believers that we are in a spiritual battle against the devil. Paul describes the battle gear we have available to us, our spiritual armor. All the equipment he lists is intended for defensive purposes—"the belt of truth," "the breastplate of righteousness," "the shield of faith," "the helmet of salvation"—except one. In verse 17, he tells us to "take . . . the sword of the Spirit, which is the word of God." The Bible is the weapon we use to battle anyone or anything that might lead us astray.

In Matthew 4:1–11, Jesus used the Word of God to defeat Satan during his temptation in the wilderness. Three times Satan tried to get Jesus to do wrong. Three times Jesus responded by quoting Scripture. The devil was helpless against God's Word. He left Jesus, completely defeated.

The more you know God's Word, the more dangerous you will be in battle. For example, if you know what the Bible says about lying, you can quote just the right passage the next time Satan tempts you to lie. You have an amazing weapon at your fingertips, just waiting to be used. Are you ready to master it? ✤

PRAYER

Dear God, thank you for giving us everything we need to protect ourselves as Christians. Teach us to use your Word in a way that honors you. Amen.

day158

GOD-BREATHED

- What do you think God's voice sounds like?
- If God were to speak directly to you today, what do you think he would say?

All Scripture is God-breathed and is useful for teaching, rebuking, correcting and training in righteousness.   2 TIMOTHY 3:16

God spoke to Jacob in a dream and promised to give him and his descendants the land in which he was staying (see Genesis 28:10–22). God spoke to Moses from a burning bush and instructed him to go back to Egypt to free the Israelites from slavery (see Exodus 3:1–22). God spoke to the prophet Elijah in a gentle whisper—after sending a windstorm, an earthquake and a fire. He eased Elijah's fears and gave him an important assignment (see 1 Kings 19:1–18).

Is it any wonder that all three men are remembered for their boldness, courage and faithfulness? They got their marching orders straight from the Lord's mouth. They never had to wonder whether they were doing the right thing. They had the words of God to guide them.

And so do we. In 2 Timothy 3:16, the apostle Paul tells us, "All Scripture is God-breathed." God spoke to the people who wrote it. The words of Scripture are God's words. Reading his words is like hearing his voice. If you're curious about what God wants from you, read the Bible. If you want to learn more about him, spend time in the Scriptures. If you'd like to use his wisdom to straighten out some things in your life, open his Word. ✤

PRAYER

Dear God, thank you for breathing the words of the Bible. Help us recognize that the words of Scripture come directly from you. Amen.

THE BOOK OF JUDGMENT

* How do you know when you've done something wrong?
* What does it mean that God's Word is "alive and active"?

For the word of God is alive and active. Sharper than any double-edged sword, it penetrates even to dividing soul and spirit, joints and marrow; it judges the thoughts and attitudes of the heart.   HEBREWS 4:12

If we tried hard enough, we could probably fool others into thinking we're good people—even if we really aren't. We could never fool God, though. He knows exactly how we think, feel and act. He knows how close or how far away we are from the standards he's given us in his Word.

For example, he tells us to love our neighbors as we love ourselves. He tells us our thoughts are just as important as our actions. He tells us to imitate Christ in all that we do. He tells us to honor him in every decision we make. Those are the standards he has set for us. If we obey the commands in his Word, we make him happy. If not, we make him unhappy.

If we want to face God's judgment with confidence, we need to know his Word. What does he say about dealing with difficult people? How about keeping a good reputation? The answers to these and hundreds of other important questions can be found in the pages of the Bible. If we learn our way around Scripture, we will discover how to please the only One whose approval ultimately matters. ♣

PRAYER

Dear God, we cannot fool you. The Bible gives us your words to live by, and you know whether we obey. Forgive us for the times when we don't follow your Word. Help us become obedient. Amen.

NOTHING BUT THE TRUTH

- If you read stories such as Noah's ark, God's parting the Red Sea or Jesus' resurrection in any other book but the Bible, what would you think of them?
- Why do you believe the Bible to be true?

For he vigorously refuted his Jewish opponents in public debate, proving from the Scriptures that Jesus was the Messiah.   ACTS 18:28

Apollos was one of the earliest Christian teachers. He traveled with the apostle Paul to help spread the Good News of Jesus. He also helped start churches in different cities where Jesus' followers could meet together.

Not everyone was happy with Apollos's work, though. The Roman government was afraid that Christians would band together and try to overthrow the government. The Jewish religious leaders were upset that Jesus' message was still spreading years after his death. They committed themselves to stopping the growth of Christianity.

One of the methods they used was to send out missionaries of their own to publicly challenge people like Apollos who preached the message of Jesus. The Jewish leaders believed if they could humiliate Jesus' followers in public, people would reject their message. When they tried that tactic with Apollos, however, it backfired. Using the Scriptures to prove his point, Apollos showed his accusers the truth about Jesus. He explained that Jesus is the Messiah the Jewish people were looking for.

Apollos didn't back down when people challenged him because he had the truth of God's Word on his side. When you know the truth, no lie can hurt you. ♣

PRAYER

Dear God, thank you for giving us the truth in your Word. When we face doubt or discouragement, remind us to go the Bible, where we will find the answers we need. Amen.

day161

TO COMPLETE, TO MAKE PERFECT

- What promises has God made to you through the Word?
- How do you know that God won't abandon you?

The LORD will vindicate me; your love, LORD, endures forever—do not abandon the works of your hands. PSALM 138:8

God promised David in 2 Samuel 7:16 that he would raise up one of David's descendants to establish his kingdom. God said, "Your house and your kingdom will endure forever before me; your throne will be established forever." And God did this through Jesus. God kept his word to David.

At the time David wrote Psalm 138, he didn't know yet *how* God would fulfill his promise, but he never lost faith that God would. King David made some mistakes, but he never doubted that God would keep his promises, that God would accomplish his will through David's life.

And like David wrote in this psalm, God will never turn away from us either. He will complete us and make us perfect. God is God—he would never start a project and then abandon it. He has a plan for us, and he's going to see it through to the end. God's love is an eternal love, a love that we cannot possibly understand, and yet it's ours for the taking. ❖

PRAYER

Dear God, thank you for your love and faithfulness to your children. Keep our faith strong. Amen.

BLESSED ASSURANCE

- How do you know that you're going to heaven?
- How do you know that God loves you?

"All those the Father gives me will come to me, and whoever comes to me I will never drive away. For I have come down from heaven not to do my will but to do the will of him who sent me. And this is the will of him who sent me, that I shall lose none of all those he has given me, but raise them up at the last day." JOHN 6:37–39

Sometimes, we make mistakes. Even though we love God, sometimes we make bad decisions that cause us to fear losing his love. Sometimes we fear that we will lose our salvation or that we won't go to heaven anymore. These verses from John tell us that none of these things could possibly happen.

If you are a believer, it's because God chose you. And because God chose you, Jesus said he will never let you go. Jesus left heaven and came to earth to give his life for *you*. He knew what he was doing. He knew who he was dying for. And he has promised that he will not lose you.

This is an amazing assurance of your salvation. You cannot lose Jesus' love. He promises, right here in these verses, that he will do the will of the Father. And loving *you* is the will of the Father. Jesus is with you every step of the way, until he raises you up on the last day. You will spend eternity with Jesus in heaven. Of that you can be sure. ✤

PRAYER

Dear God, thank you for choosing us. Thank you for assuring us of our salvation and for the gift of eternal life. Amen.

june 12 day163

WITH FREEDOM AND CONFIDENCE

- What gives you confidence?
- How do you approach God?

In him and through faith in him we may approach God with freedom and confidence.

EPHESIANS 3:12

Paul was in prison when he wrote the words "with freedom and confidence." Can you imagine what prompted those words? Can you imagine being in prison in the first place? And if you can, would you really be feeling free and confident?

The apostle Paul had tremendous faith. And this faith kept him strong. Even though he was in prison, he knew that he was serving God every second that he was behind bars, and his spirit was very much free.

Paul knew that at any moment, he could approach God. At any moment, he could ask God for help, praise God, worship God or just spend some quiet time with him. It is the same for us. If we too have a saving faith in Jesus, we too can approach God at any time with freedom and confidence.

Just as Paul didn't let prison walls get him down, we too can face the troubles in our lives. Be confident in Jesus. Take advantage of God's approachability. God is always there for you. ✤

PRAYER

Dear God, thank you for sending your Son Jesus Christ so that we can approach you through faith in him. Amen.

SHAKY LEGS

- Have you ever seen a young child toddling about? Describe what he or she looked like.
- On average, how many times do you ask God for help in a day?

The LORD makes firm the steps of the one who delights in him; though he may stumble, he will not fall, for the LORD upholds him with his hand. PSALM 37:23-24

You probably don't remember learning to walk, but you might want to ask your parents about it. It's usually quite a sight to watch a young child learn to use his or her own two feet. But you didn't do it on your own. There was always someone there to make sure you didn't take a tumble. There was always someone there to hold your hand.

In much the same way, we need to learn to walk spiritually. And we don't do this alone either. God is always watching. He knows every step we take, and he is always ready to catch us if we start to fall. He's always willing to hold us by the hands while we take our uncertain steps on shaky legs.

Sometimes we get stubborn, and we try to do it alone. We try to be sneaky. Or we get arrogant. Or maybe we even try to climb over the toddler gate. But all of this is silly. If we will just accept God's love and protection, we will be so much better off. We were not designed to walk through this life on our own. And we don't have to. ❖

PRAYER

Dear God, thank you for guiding us. Thank you for teaching us. Help us to rely on you and hold your hand when we need to. Amen.

day165

TO JERUSALEM AND BEYOND

- Which of your online friends lives the farthest away from you?
- How can you make someone new feel comfortable with you?

"But you will receive power when the Holy Spirit comes on you; and you will be my witnesses in Jerusalem, and in all Judea and Samaria, and to the ends of the earth."

ACTS 1:8

Jesus explained to his followers how they were to spread his message. They would start locally, in the city of Jerusalem. From there, they would move throughout the entire region of Judea. After that, it was on to Samaria, where the people were very different from the Jewish disciples. Beyond that, they would head to the ends of the earth.

On a smaller scale, the verse gives us a model of evangelism that we can follow. We start with the people closest to us: our family and friends. Since we already have a relationship with them, and since they probably already know about our faith, we don't have to worry about how to break the ice.

Once we've gotten comfortable sharing our faith with them, we can expand our circle a little to include casual acquaintances at work, at school, on the team, in the neighborhood. After that, we can expand again to include people who are different from us, people who don't share our views or background. Finally, we can expand our circle completely to include the entire earth.

If that sounds too ambitious, consider these two words: social media. We already have easy access to the world. We can support those who are already working in the world through encouragement, prayer and financial support as they bear witness in other places. And we can use our access to others in the world by being witnesses ourselves. Spreading the Good News of Jesus "to the ends of the earth" can be done. ✤

PRAYER

Dear God, thank you for trusting us with your message and giving us such an important assignment. Help us recognize the opportunities we have to share our faith. Amen.

BE PREPARED

- When was the last time something took you by surprise? How did you react?
- Have you ever been asked a question about your Christian beliefs that you couldn't answer? If so, what was it? How did you respond? How do you *wish* you'd responded?

But in your hearts revere Christ as Lord. Always be prepared to give an answer to everyone who asks you to give the reason for the hope that you have. But do this with gentleness and respect.   1 PETER 3:15

The Bible tells us to share the Good News about Jesus with others. But it doesn't tell us how they'll respond. It would be great if they all immediately dropped to their knees and believed that Jesus died for their sins. But that's not likely to happen.

What is likely to happen is that people will challenge us with statements or questions like these:

> "I'm a good person. Why do I need to accept Jesus to get into heaven?"
> "You believe what you want to believe, and I'll believe what I want to believe."
> "Why would I want to have a personal relationship with a God who allows so much suffering in the world?"
> "I can't stand church people. They're all hypocrites. Why would I want to become one?"
> "How do you know you're right? How do you know that Muslims or Hindus or Jews aren't right?"

The best way to deal with those challenges is to prepare. We need to spend time thinking about questions or arguments people might have. Then we need to talk about these challenges with other Christians and find answers in God's Word. Finally, we need to pray for wisdom and clear thinking. When we prepare ourselves the best we can, God will do the rest. ✤

PRAYER

Dear God, thank you for giving us resources to prepare for the questions we'll get asked about you and your Word. Give us the confidence and wisdom to give people the right answers. Amen.

SEED PLANTERS

- What's the best way to talk about your faith with someone you know?
- What's the worst way to talk about your faith with someone you know?

So neither the one who plants nor the one who waters is anything, but only God, who makes things grow. 1 CORINTHIANS 3:7

Back in the apostle Paul's day, the church had problems with people splitting into groups to follow popular teachers. Paul was one of those teachers, and so was Apollos. Christians would take pride in saying, "I follow Paul" or "I follow Apollos." When Paul heard what they were doing, he put a stop to it immediately (see 1 Corinthians 3:3–13).

He told them that he and Apollos were just messengers. All they did was plant the seeds of the gospel in people's minds. The Lord is the one who makes them grow, and that's why he's the only one people should follow.

If we want to please God in the way we share our faith with others, we need to remember our role. We're *not* the ones who lead people to Christ. We're *not* the ones who convert people to Christianity. We're the ones who start conversations about God or our beliefs. We're the ones who talk to people about our personal experiences with Jesus.

We're seed planters. What God does with those seeds is up to him. In fact, we may never see what happens to the seeds we plant. But that shouldn't stop us from planting them. God has given us a role in spreading his Word. We should be grateful for it and do the best we can. ✤

PRAYER

Dear God, thank you for giving us a small part in spreading your Word. We give you all the glory for what happens to the seeds we plant. Amen.

day168

THE RIPPLE EFFECT

- Who was the first person to explain the Christian faith to you in a way you could understand?
- What makes it difficult to share your faith with someone?

"Therefore go and make disciples of all nations, baptizing them in the name of the Father and of the Son and of the Holy Spirit, and teaching them to obey everything I have commanded you. And surely I am with you always, to the very end of the age."

MATTHEW 28:19–20

As amazing as it sounds, we don't necessarily have to travel far to spread the Good News of Jesus to "all nations." In fact, we can start with the people we see every day. Every time we talk to someone about Jesus, it's like a pebble being dropped into a pond. It causes only a tiny splash, but it creates a ripple that can travel to the ends of the pond.

Like that pebble, one conversation about Jesus may not seem like a big deal. But that single conversation could turn out to be the start of something far-reaching—especially with the Holy Spirit working behind the scenes.

The Holy Spirit has the power to:

> help us understand and communicate God's Word in meaningful ways;
> put us in the right place at the right time with the right words in our mouths;
> open people's eyes and hearts to our message.

If we step out and take risks by sharing our faith, the Holy Spirit will make sure it isn't done in vain. That doesn't mean every person we talk to will become a Christian. But it does mean that our efforts will never be wasted. Our words may spread seeds that are carried to all nations. ♣

PRAYER

Dear God, thank you for giving us a chance to be part of something so life changing. Guide our thoughts, attitudes and actions as we talk to others about you. Amen.

GOD'S MESSENGERS

* What's the most important thing people should know about the Lord?
* How can people see what God is like through you?

"You are my witnesses," declares the LORD, "and my servant whom I have chosen, so that you may know and believe me and understand that I am he. Before me no god was formed, nor will there be one after me. I, even I, am the LORD, and apart from me there is no savior."   ISAIAH 43:10–11

In the Old Testament, the people of Israel were God's witnesses or messengers. They were responsible for telling the world who God is and what he's done. Ever since Jesus came, though, that job has been given to Christians. We have a responsibility to tell others about who Jesus is and what he's done in our lives.

It's not an easy job. People aren't always eager to receive our message. In fact, many messengers have been killed for delivering it, including most of Jesus' disciples and the apostle Paul. The good news is that the Holy Spirit goes where the message goes. He will be with us, guiding our words and blessing our work. No messenger of God ever works alone.

As with anything we do, hard work is the secret to becoming a good messenger. First we need to learn the message. We do that by reading the Bible and talking with experienced Christians. Then comes the delivery. The more we practice what to say, the more confident we become in saying it. The more we talk to people, the more we discover how they respond and what questions or arguments they have. Experience is the key. ✤

PRAYER

Dear God, thank you for trusting us with your message. Bless our efforts to deliver it in the best way we know. Amen.

day170

CAN I GET A WITNESS?

- Have you ever had someone witness to you? If so, how did you respond?
- Have you ever witnessed to someone else? If so, what approach did you take? If not, why?

"You will be his witness to all people of what you have seen and heard."   ACTS 22:15

Paul is describing his commissioning by God to tell the Good News about Jesus. He told his audience that God instructed him to tell others what had happened to him.

To be Jesus' witnesses in the Roman Empire wasn't easy. The Romans didn't want Christianity to spread. They viewed it as a threat to their power. The Jews also were antagonistic towards this new faith, Christianity. Both groups persecuted Jesus' followers. In fact, Paul suffered many times for his choice to follow God and tell about Jesus.

Though the stakes are considerably lower today for most of us, witnessing is still difficult for many Christians. Fortunately, we don't have to do it alone. God has given us his Holy Spirit to empower us.

If you're not sure how to approach someone with the gospel message, ask God to work through his Holy Spirit to give you a sense of peace and confidence. Ask him to give you the right words to say. Ask him to help you keep a calm and loving demeanor, even if the person you are talking to isn't receptive. Ask him to help you answer questions to the best of your ability. Ask him to help you be an effective witness. ✤

PRAYER

Dear God, thank you for sending your Holy Spirit to assist us in spreading your Word. Give us the courage and wisdom to share the Good News of Jesus with others. Amen.

day171

THE NEW GUIDE

- If you could ask God one question about the direction of your life, what would it be?
- When was the last time you felt God's leading? Describe what it was like.

"But when he, the Spirit of truth, comes, he will guide you into all the truth. He will not speak on his own; he will speak only what he hears, and he will tell you what is yet to come." JOHN 16:13

Jesus' public ministry—the time he was baptized until the time he was crucified—lasted about three years. His disciples were with him for almost all that time. From the very beginning, Jesus made it clear to them that his time on earth was short. Sometimes they seemed to understand; other times they acted quite surprised by the news.

In John 16, we read that Jesus' time was almost up—and his disciples seemed to realize it. Naturally they were sad about losing their Teacher. They also were feeling a little lost. With Jesus gone, who would lead them? Jesus gave them their answer in verse 13. The Holy Spirit, or "Spirit of truth," would assist them after Jesus departed.

That was very good news for the disciples—and all followers of Jesus. The Holy Spirit isn't a flesh-and-blood being like Jesus. We don't have to vie for his time and attention along with millions of other followers. The Holy Spirit lives in each of us. He is always available to give us the guidance and direction we need.

When we have a question about our faith or when we have a doubt, we can ask the Holy Spirit to help us. What could be more convenient? ❖

PRAYER

Dear God, thank you for sending your Holy Spirit to guide us. Help us listen to his leading and follow his directions. Amen.

LIVING IN US

- How would you feel about having one of your parents with you every second of every day? Why?
- How is that different from having the Holy Spirit with you all the time?

And if the Spirit of him who raised Jesus from the dead is living in you, he who raised Christ from the dead will also give life to your mortal bodies because of his Spirit who lives in you.   ROMANS 8:11

This world can be a tough place for Christians. Jesus warns us of that in John 15:18–21: "If the world hates you, keep in mind that it hated me first. If you belonged to the world, it would love you as its own. As it is, you do not belong to the world, but I have chosen you out of the world. That is why the world hates you. Remember what I told you: 'A servant is not greater than his master.' If they persecuted me, they will persecute you also. If they obeyed my teaching, they will obey yours also. They will treat you this way because of my name, for they do not know the one who sent me."

God understands how difficult it is to be a Christian. So he sent his Holy Spirit to live in us and to give us strength, courage, patience, support, encouragement and anything else we need—just when we need it.

From within, the Holy Spirit inspires us to live in a way that honors God. He sees everything we do. He knows every choice we make. He knows everything we think. He encourages us to do the right thing—and lets us know when we don't. ✤

PRAYER

Dear God, thank you for sending your Holy Spirit to live in us. Please bless our efforts to live in a way that pleases you. Amen.

day173

EVERYDAY HOLINESS

- Why don't Christians stop sinning after they become saved?
- How can God accept you if you still sin?

He gave me the priestly duty of proclaiming the gospel of God, so that the Gentiles might become an offering acceptable to God, sanctified by the Holy Spirit. ROMANS 15:16

When we repent of our sins and give our lives to Christ, God forgives us of all our wrongdoings. But that's not the end of our struggle with sin. Instead, it's the beginning of our sanctification. To be sanctified is to be continually freer from sin and more and more like Christ in our lives. As followers of Jesus, our goal is to be more like him every day. That's not easy, since he was perfect.

In order to be like Jesus, every day we must do battle with sin. Our enemy, the devil, makes that battle as difficult as he can. He wants us to sin. That's why he does everything in his power to make sin seem inviting or easy or rewarding.

In order to stand up to such a powerful enemy, we need an even more powerful ally. That's where the Holy Spirit comes in. The Holy Spirit sanctifies us. He works in our lives to help us resist sin and become more like Jesus every day.

The Holy Spirit lets us know when we do wrong. He works through our consciences to show us the right thing to do. He helps us recognize the Lord's will. He helps us see God-pleasing alternatives in tempting situations. ✣

PRAYER

Dear God, thank you for giving us your Holy Spirit to sanctify us. Bless our efforts to be more like Jesus. Amen.

THE TEACHER

- When it comes to learning, what is the worst thing a teacher can do?
- What kind of teaching do you best respond to? Why?

"But the Advocate, the Holy Spirit, whom the Father will send in my name, will teach you all things and will remind you of everything I have said to you."   JOHN 14:26

Jesus does not always make life easy for his followers. That was as true two thousand years ago as it is today. Many times, instead of giving specific instructions, Jesus would speak in parables; he would tell stories to illustrate particular points. The problem was that a lot of people—including his own disciples at times—could not understand what he was saying.

Christians today still struggle to understand some of his teachings—not to mention a number of other Bible passages. Trying to discover their meanings on our own can be frustrating. Fortunately for us, God sent his Holy Spirit to help us with just that problem.

The Holy Spirit knows not just the meaning of every passage in the Bible; he also knows how each one can have meaning in our lives. And he stands ready to teach us what he knows—if only we'll ask.

When you study God's Word, remember that the Holy Spirit—God himself—is standing over your shoulder. If you come to a passage you don't understand, you can ask him to give you insight and clarity. He is happy to help you. If you really want to understand God's Word, the Holy Spirit will make it happen. ♣

PRAYER

Dear God, thank you for sending your Holy Spirit to teach us your truths. Help us apply your Word to our daily lives. Amen.

STANDING STRONG

- Do you feel more confident around your friends than you do when you're alone? Why or why not?
- Which of your friends do you think are spiritually strong?

"If we are thrown into the blazing furnace, the God we serve is able to deliver us from it, and he will deliver us from Your Majesty's hand. But even if he does not, we want you to know, Your Majesty, that we will not serve your gods or worship the image of gold you have set up."   DANIEL 3:17 – 18

Few people have faced the kind of danger Shadrach, Meshach and Abednego faced. The three godly Israelite friends had been taken captive after the Babylonians destroyed Jerusalem. In captivity, they maintained their faithfulness to God, and God blessed them for it. They became trusted advisers of Nebuchadnezzar, the king of Babylon.

The king's other advisers were jealous, so they concocted a scheme to use the Israelites' faithfulness against them. They convinced Nebuchadnezzar to erect a giant statue of himself and make a law that said anyone who didn't bow down to the statue would be thrown into a fiery furnace. They knew the Israelites would bow only to God.

Who knows how Shadrach, Meshach and Abednego would have reacted individually to such a life-threatening situation? What we do know is that *together* they refused to disobey God and bow down to the idol. So *together* they were thrown into the fiery furnace. And *together* they were miraculously protected from the flames by God.

Ecclesiastes 4:12 says, "Though one may be overpowered, two can defend themselves. A cord of three strands is not quickly broken." It's good to have Christian friends who will stand strong and encourage us to do right. ✤

PRAYER

Dear God, thank you for giving us friends who help keep us strong. Continue to give us the strength we need to obey you, regardless of the consequences. Amen.

day176 june 25

AS IRON SHARPENS IRON

- Why is it good to have friends who are Christians?
- When is conflict with a friend a good thing?

As iron sharpens iron, so one person sharpens another. PROVERBS 27:17

Though it may not be obvious at first glance, the words of Proverbs 27:17 describe friendship—specifically the friendship between two believers. The image the writer uses—iron sharpening iron—says a lot about how friendship works.

Sharpening a knife takes some skill and the right tools. A metal blade cannot be sharpened with cloth or wood. To sharpen a knife, we need something equally strong—a sharpener that is also metal. When the solid knife comes into contact with the equally solid sharpener, it creates friction. In the midst of that friction, the knife's dullness is shaved away.

So it is with Christian friends. When we have contact with people who are as solid as we are in their relationship with Christ, it has an effect on us. It sharpens us. It knocks away our dullness. It strengthens our relationship with Christ and with each other.

Sometimes the process involves friction. Sometimes other believers need to tell us things we don't want to hear about ourselves. They may shine light on areas we need to correct. But the ultimate result is worth it. A sharp Christian is a God-pleasing Christian. ✤

PRAYER

Dear God, thank you for the believers you have put in our lives to sharpen us. Help us be the type of Christians who sharpen others as well. Amen.

THE RIGHT FRIENDS

- Has a friend ever convinced you to do something you wouldn't have done otherwise? How did it happen? How do you feel about it now?
- Have you ever kept a friend from doing something wrong? If so, how? Why do you think you were able to do it?

One who has unreliable friends soon comes to ruin, but there is a friend who sticks closer than a brother.   PROVERBS 18:24

Proverbs 18:24 reminds us of a very important truth: Friends have a big influence on our lives. If you've ever gotten in trouble for goofing around with a friend at school, you understand.

If you take seriously the words of the proverb, you need to do three things. First, you need to examine the friends you have now and how much they influence you. If you notice yourself getting into trouble when you're with certain people, it may be time to find new friends.

Second, you need to surround yourself with friends who influence you in a good way. The first place to look for such friends is at church. Find out what your Sunday school class or youth group has to offer in the way of companions. You will also find Christians in your neighborhood, school and workplace, if you search hard enough.

Third, you need to be the kind of friend who influences other people in a good way. If you claim to follow Christ, you need to set a high standard for the way you talk and the way you act. Instead of being influenced by others, you need to be the one doing the influencing. ✤

PRAYER

Dear God, thank you for the friends you've brought into our lives. Please bless our efforts to be good influences on them. Amen.

DO NOT LIE

- Which of the Ten Commandments is easiest for you to keep? Explain.
- Which of the Ten Commandments do you think gets broken most often? Explain.

"Do not steal. Do not lie. Do not deceive one another."   LEVITICUS 19:11

God called the Israelites out of slavery in Egypt and led them across the wilderness to the promised land in order to create a new nation. This new nation would serve as a beacon to all the other nations of the world. It would show them what happens when an entire country faithfully worships and obeys him.

God knew exactly what laws and restrictions would be needed in order to create such a nation. He summarized them in the Ten Commandments. Among the ten laws that would be crucial to the new nation was this: "Do not lie."

God understands what lying does to interpersonal relationships. Without a commitment to truth, there cannot be trust. Without trust, there cannot be respect. Without respect, there cannot be genuine love. Without genuine love, there cannot be fellowship. Without fellowship, there cannot be community worship. Without community worship, there cannot be a relationship with God. Without a relationship with God, there could not be the new nation of Israel.

Telling the truth is just as important to God today as it was in the early days of Israel's history. We cannot have an intimate relationship with God until we commit ourselves to the truth. ❖

PRAYER

Dear God, forgive us for the times we have broken your commandment by lying. Give us the courage to speak the truth in love always. Amen.

THE TRUTH ABOUT LYING

- Describe a time when you really wanted to tell the truth but didn't. What happened? How did you feel afterward?
- Describe a time when you were tempted to lie but chose to tell the truth instead. What happened? How did you feel afterward?

Do not move your neighbor's boundary stone set up by your predecessors in the inheritance you receive in the land the LORD your God is giving you to possess.

DEUTERONOMY 19:14

Before the Israelites entered the promised land, Moses (who would not enter the land with them) gave them some final instructions. Among those instructions were rules regarding property lines. Moses warned the Israelites against the dishonest practice of moving boundary markers in order to steal land from a neighbor. He emphasized that there was no place for such dishonesty and selfishness in the promised land.

We may not have boundary issues today, but the temptation to be dishonest for our own gain is still very real. Depending on the circumstances, we may be tempted to lie to escape trouble or to avoid embarrassment or to make ourselves look good. Whatever the motive, dishonesty is a shortcut we should never take.

Whatever temporary benefit we get from avoiding the truth is wiped out by the damage we do to our relationship with the Lord. As Christians, we aren't called to seek our own good or to do what's best for us. We are called to honor God. Telling the truth, even when it makes our life difficult, honors him. If we tell the truth, he will bless us. If we don't, he will allow us to experience the consequences of our lies. ❖

PRAYER

Dear God, thank you for setting rules that help us honor you. Give us the courage and strength to follow those rules so that we may enjoy our relationship with you. Amen.

day180

GOD DETESTS LYING LIPS

- When was the last time you got caught in a lie? How did you feel?
- Why do you think God feels so strongly about lying?

The LORD detests lying lips, but he delights in people who are trustworthy.

PROVERBS 12:22

"The LORD detests." Those three words should get our attention. "Detests" is another word for "hates." And if God *hates* something, that should be our cue to stay as far from it as we possibly can.

Proverbs 12:22 tells us that God detests lying lips. You'll notice that he doesn't distinguish between different types of lying. It's all the same to him. There is no such thing as a "harmless, little white lie." As far as God is concerned, there is the truth and then there is everything else.

The reason God has such a strong reaction to lying is that he himself *is* truth. His Word is *the* truth. Every word that comes from him can be trusted. Every promise he makes will be fulfilled. If we can't depend on him, we can't depend on anyone or anything.

As the Lord's followers, we represent him in this world. That's why it's important for us to love and honor the truth as much as God does. If we can't be trusted in our everyday words, how can we be trusted when we tell others about Jesus? ✤

PRAYER

Dear God, thank you for telling us very clearly how you feel about lying. Help us keep that in mind the next time we are tempted to say something other than the truth. Amen.

MAKE EVERY EFFORT

- What is the difference between making an effort and laziness? How would you define "effort"?
- What do you do that takes a lot of effort?

For this very reason, make every effort to add to your faith goodness; and to goodness, knowledge; and to knowledge, self-control; and to self-control, perseverance; and to perseverance, godliness; and to godliness, mutual affection; and to mutual affection, love.

2 PETER 1:5–7

When Dalton showed up for his first baseball practice, he could not throw the ball. He could not catch the ball. And he didn't even come close to hitting the ball.

When we first begin to follow Jesus, it's a lot like showing up for that first baseball practice. We don't have the necessary skills.

Dalton chose to work at baseball. He practiced. When he made mistakes, he worked harder. And Dalton was transformed into a skilled baseball player.

There's a reason Peter used the words "make every effort" when he wrote these verses. If we are going to act like God wants us to act, it's going to take effort. We are going to have to work at it. We are going to have to practice.

When this verse talks about "mutual affection," it is talking about being kind to one another. We shouldn't expect this to always come easily. We need to work at it. God will help us, but it's still going to take effort on our part. And our effort will allow God to transform us into the people he wants us to be. ✤

PRAYER

Dear God, please help us to show kindness to one another. Please encourage us and give us the strength to make every effort for you. Amen.

day182

CHOOSE KINDNESS

- What are some choices that you make every day?
- What is it like to be around a person who likes to start arguments and pick fights?

And the Lord's servant must not be quarrelsome but must be kind to everyone, able to teach, not resentful.   2 TIMOTHY 2:24

When Paul writes that we should not be quarrelsome, he means that we should not be running around picking unnecessary fights. Instead, we should be kind to others. The Lord's servants—that's us!—are supposed to be peaceful. We are supposed to work to promote peace, not conflict.

Kindness is a choice. We need to choose to be kind. Our natural tendency might often be to argue instead of being kind, but this doesn't make it okay. In every encounter we have throughout the day, we have a choice: We can be kind or we can be unkind. We can choose to get along or we can pick a fight. God wants us to choose kindness.

What about when people are unkind to us? What about those times when people are quarrelsome? Even in those instances, we are to choose kindness. We can walk away from conflict. Kindness is always an option. ✤

PRAYER

Dear God, please help us to honor you by choosing kindness. Amen.

GOD'S REPRESENTATIVES

- How are Christians supposed to treat one another?
- What does it mean to be compassionate?

Be kind and compassionate to one another, forgiving each other, just as in Christ God forgave you.   EPHESIANS 4:32

Davon was having a tough time, so when he heard that some kids were starting a Bible club that would meet after school, he decided to check it out. Something inside him made him think that learning more about God might help him.

When Davon arrived to his first meeting, the others were discussing what to name their new club. They paused to offer Davon a warm welcome and got him a chair. Then, as soon as he sat down, they went back to their discussion—a discussion that Davon quickly realized was an argument.

Davon was surprised to find that these kids were not getting along at all. They were being rude and insulting each other. One even told another he was stupid. Davon stayed for the rest of the meeting, but he never went back.

As believers, we *must* be kind to one another. Even when we disagree. We are God's representatives here on earth. Our behavior sends a message to the world. When people watch us interacting with one another, they draw conclusions about what God is like. What do people see when they see you interacting with other believers? ✤

PRAYER

Dear God, please help us to be kind to other people. When we disagree with other Christians, inspire us to act with love and kindness in spite of our differences. Amen.

day184

BURNING COALS OF KINDNESS

- Share a time when someone was unkind to you. How did you respond?
- What does the phrase "melt your heart" mean?

Make sure that nobody pays back wrong for wrong, but always strive to do what is good for each other and for everyone else.   1 THESSALONIANS 5:15

This verse from 1 Thessalonians teaches us that we are not supposed to repay unkindness with unkindness. We are to do just the opposite — repay unkindness with kindness.

Proverbs 25:22 teaches us that showing kindness to our enemies is like piling burning coals on their heads. When someone is unkind to us and we respond with kindness, we completely confound them, opening their eyes to the gulf between the world's ways and God's ways. To respond like this is not human nature. It is not of this world.

When we respond to unkindness in a worldly way, repaying nastiness with more nastiness, we simply feed the cycle. Our unkindness never stops the other person from being unkind — it only kindles the fire. However, our kindness can potentially melt our enemies' hearts, introduce them to God and change their lives.

Only God can transform our enemies into friends, but we can help start the process by introducing our enemies to God's kindness. In Romans 12:20–21, Paul quotes the verse about the burning coals of kindness. Then he writes, "Overcome evil with good." Our only real defense against unkindness is God's love. ✤

PRAYER

Dear God, please help us to overcome evil with your good by repaying unkindness with kindness. Please give us a gentle spirit as we try to show your love to the world. Amen.

IN GOD WE TRUST

- Why does your country have laws?
- Of all the laws in your country or state, which do you find the most difficult to abide by?

Let everyone be subject to the governing authorities, for there is no authority except that which God has established. The authorities that exist have been established by God. Consequently, whoever rebels against the authority is rebelling against what God has instituted, and those who do so will bring judgment on themselves.   ROMANS 13:1–2

God is our first authority. Everything we think, do and say should be in line with what he wants us to think, do and say. At all times, we are supposed to obey God.

But because we live here in this world, we also have human leaders. These leaders create rules that we are expected to obey. As long as these laws do not ask us to sin, then God wants us to honor him by honoring them.

If we truly believe God is in control, then we know that he has placed us where we are, under the authority of that leadership, for a reason. Obeying our leaders and their laws helps us learn to trust God. It's also one way for us to demonstrate to others that we do trust God. ✣

PRAYER

Dear God, we pray for our leaders. Please give them strength and wisdom. Please also help us to honor you by obeying the laws that our leaders have created. Amen.

"YOU'RE NOT REALLY IN CHARGE HERE"

- Who was Pontius Pilate? Why was he an important Biblical figure?
- How would the world be different if Jesus had never been crucified?

Jesus answered, "You would have no power over me if it were not given to you from above. Therefore the one who handed me over to you is guilty of a greater sin."

JOHN 19:11

Imagine saying to your governor, "You're not really in charge here." That's essentially what Jesus said to Pontius Pilate, who was the governor of Judea when Jesus was crucified. Jesus basically said, "You wouldn't even be here if God hadn't placed you here."

This is true of government today as well. God gives government its authority. We don't always like it, but that's the way it is. Sometimes God brings certain people to positions of power. Other times, he allows people to hold authority, even when they don't serve him. But he is always aware of what is going on. God is always in control.

We may not always understand why governments do what they do. We may disagree with those in power, and we may wonder why God doesn't intervene to change things. But we need to remember that we don't know the whole story. We don't know all of God's plans for the world. God may be allowing certain things to happen so that his will may be fulfilled. In the case of Pilate, God didn't intervene. And as a result, millions of people have been saved by the blood of Jesus Christ. ✤

PRAYER

Dear God, we praise you for the fact that we can rest in the peace of knowing that you are in charge. Amen.

THE LIGHT OF THE WORLD

- How can Jesus be the light of the entire world?
- What would life be like without light?

"While I am in the world, I am the light of the world."   JOHN 9:5

In John chapter 9, Jesus and his disciples walk by a blind man. The disciples ask Jesus, "Why is this man blind?" And Jesus answers, "So that through him, I can show the world God's power." Jesus says, "I am the light of the world," and then he heals the blind man.

The world is a dark place because of sin. Jesus is light. He is the truth that illuminates everything. Jesus heals us just like he healed that blind man. In a spiritual sense, he touches our eyes, allowing us to see. And by healing us, Jesus shows the world God's power.

When we accept Jesus into our lives, we change. The light of Jesus begins to shine through us. The world can see this change and learns about God because of it. Jesus said, "While I am in the world, I am the light of the world." Jesus is no longer in the world as a human. But we are still here. It is now our job to be the light of the world by letting Jesus' light shine through us. ✤

PRAYER

Dear God, thank you for the light of Jesus. Thank you for opening our eyes to your truth. Please let Jesus' light shine through us for the whole world to see. Amen.

day188

A LIGHT ON MY PATH

- What would happen if you walked around all day wearing a blindfold?
- Why is it so comforting to have a flashlight when it is dark?

Your word is a lamp for my feet, a light on my path. PSALM 119:105

Have you ever tried to walk on a bumpy path without a flashlight? Have you ever walked around an unfamiliar, dark room, feeling the walls for a light switch? We are not designed to walk around in the dark. When we do, we often smash into things and end up with stubbed toes, bruised shins—or worse!

As believers, we don't have to stumble around in the dark. God gives us the Bible to shine a light on our path. The wisdom contained in the Bible helps us to make decisions, to know which paths to take in life and which paths to avoid. The Bible warns us of potential hazards and tells us where to turn for safety.

When we read and study the Bible, we are better able to avoid the bumps and bruises of stumbling in the dark. It is so important for believers to spend time in the Word each day. The more we read, the fewer stubbed toes and painful shins we will suffer. ❖

PRAYER

Dear God, thank you for caring about every decision we make. Please help us pay attention to the light you give us in the Bible, so we will make good decisions. Amen.

THE LIGHT SOURCE

- Why did God create light first?
- When are you thankful for light?

And God said, "Let there be light," and there was light.   GENESIS 1:3

Can you imagine the very beginning, when the world was formless, empty and dark? And then God spoke, "Let there be light." Can you even imagine what a difference there must have been? All of a sudden, there was light throughout the universe.

When we think about the world and thank God for all the good things in it, we don't usually begin by naming light as a good thing; we think of nature or other people as God's beautiful creations. How often do we thank God for the sun? For electricity? We take light for granted. It is such a part of our world that we can't even begin to think of life without it.

Not only did God create physical light for our world, he also created spiritual light. The Bible often uses the word *light* to represent God's truth and goodness. This spiritual light illuminates the darkness of our sinful state before we knew God. Without the light of God's salvation we would exist in the inky blackness of a world lost from God.

Let's take time to appreciate God's light, both physical and spiritual, to be in awe of it. Where would we be without God's light? ✤

PRAYER

Dear God, thank you for light. Prompt us to be grateful for it and remember what it means to our lives. Amen.

day190

THE LIGHT IN YOUR HEART

- How did your heart change when you gave your life to Jesus?
- What are some ways that you can share your light with others?

For God, who said, "Let light shine out of darkness," made his light shine in our hearts to give us the light of the knowledge of God's glory displayed in the face of Christ.

2 CORINTHIANS 4:6

The universe didn't exist. There was nothing but darkness. And God banished the darkness when he created light on that first day.

Our hearts were empty. There was nothing but darkness. And God banished the darkness when he shone his light into our hearts, when he showed us his glory through Jesus Christ.

The same God who created physical light to shine throughout the universe also created the supernatural light that shines in the hearts of Christians. We need to recognize the power of this light. We need to appreciate it so much that we can't help but share it with others. We share this light by loving others the way that Jesus loves us. We share this light by telling people the truth about what God can do.

Do you know someone who doesn't know Jesus? Pray for that person today. Ask God to shine his light into that person's heart too. ✤

PRAYER

Dear God, thank you for Jesus. Thank you for saving us. Please help us to share your light with others. Amen.

NO IDLE ZONE

- What are you working on for God right now? How could you get others involved in your work?
- Do you ever procrastinate? Describe a time when your parents have been patient with you while you procrastinated in getting work done.

And we urge you, brothers and sisters, warn those who are idle and disruptive, encourage the disheartened, help the weak, be patient with everyone.   1 THESSALONIANS 5:14

In this verse from Thessalonians, Paul is describing how Christians are to treat one another within the church.

One of his instructions is to "warn those who are idle." When a person is idle, he or she isn't doing anything, isn't accomplishing anything and isn't contributing anything to the body of Christ. Paul tells believers to encourage these individuals to work.

Notice that Paul ends the verse with the instructions, "be patient with everyone." He's not teaching us to run around barking orders at other believers and hollering at anyone we catch sitting still. We are no one's judge and jury. But we are brothers and sisters, and if we see a brother or sister in need of encouragement, we need to try to help that person find a fulfilling way to join in God's work. ✤

PRAYER

Dear God, show us ways to do your work. Help us to see the gifts in our brothers and sisters, and help us to encourage them to serve you. Amen.

day192

BIG REWARDS

- What work do you do? At home? In school? In church? In the community?
- Why is it dangerous to be lazy?

Lazy hands make for poverty, but diligent hands bring wealth. He who gathers crops in summer is a prudent son, but he who sleeps during harvest is a disgraceful son.

PROVERBS 10:4-5

God rewards hard work. God does not reward laziness. In fact, although poverty is not always caused by it, laziness can make a person poor.

These verses from Proverbs apply to people of all ages. No matter what age we are, God wants us to have a healthy work ethic. While a child may not leave the house every morning to go to the office, they still have a job to do. There is always work to be done at home, at school, in the community and in church.

God rewards all kinds of work in many different ways. One reward we get from hard work is a good habit. When we work hard, we develop good work habits, and these will serve us well for the rest of our lives. Solid work habits glorify God, allow us to provide for ourselves and our families, and help others. ❖

PRAYER

Dear God, please help us to be motivated to work hard for you. Please bless our efforts, whatever our work may be. Amen.

GO TO THE ANT

- Have you ever watched ants at work? Describe their behavior. What did you see?
- How do you feel after you've worked hard at something?

Go to the ant, you sluggard; consider its ways and be wise!... A little sleep, a little slumber, a little folding of the hands to rest—and poverty will come on you like a thief and scarcity like an armed man.   Proverbs 6:6,10–11

In these verses from Proverbs, King Solomon tells us to observe the ant. Why? Because ants are incredibly productive workers. They have a plan, they work well together, they work hard and they get the job done.

Solomon writes that a little sleep or rest will cause poverty to come on us like a thief. Now, Solomon did not mean that we're not supposed to go to bed at night. God wants us to be healthy and get the rest that we need. What Solomon did mean is that laziness leads to more laziness, and ultimately, it can ruin a person. We can't let laziness take over our lives.

We need to realize that God did not design us to sit around and accomplish nothing. God designed us to do work—*his* work. He designed us to work so that we can take care of ourselves and take care of others who need our help. ✤

PRAYER

Dear God, thank you for blessing us with the ability to work. Please help us to be faithful in our work and to avoid laziness. Amen.

A LION ATE MY HOMEWORK!

- Have you ever made up a silly excuse to get out of work? Share that experience.
- What do you think God wants us to do when we don't "feel" like working?

The sluggard says, "There's a lion outside! I'll be killed in the public square!"

PROVERBS 22:13

King Solomon makes a joke here at the lazy person's expense: "I can't go to work! I may be eaten by a lion before I ever get there!" We know this is ridiculous, but we have also likely heard equally ridiculous excuses come out of people who do not want to do their work.

The truth is that we make excuses to avoid admitting that we are being lazy. Lazy people make excuses because they are ashamed of their laziness. No one really *wants* to be lazy—laziness is just a sin that many people struggle with.

Instead of making excuses, when we are tempted to be lazy, we should ask God for help. He doesn't want us to be lazy, and he will help us get our work boots on.

We've all been lazy at some point. We all make mistakes. But we don't have to make excuses. Let's turn those excuses into prayers. ✤

PRAYER

Dear God, please help us to work hard and to find satisfaction in serving you. And if we do succumb to the temptation of laziness, remind us to come to you instead of making excuses. Amen.

WILLING TO WORK

- How would your life be different if you didn't have enough to eat?
- Why do you think God wants us to work hard to provide for ourselves?

For even when we were with you, we gave you this rule: "The one who is unwilling to work shall not eat."   2 THESSALONIANS 3:10

In most cases, people need to work in order to stay alive. Either people work to earn the money they need to buy food, or they work to grow and harvest their own food.

Paul is teaching the Thessalonians here that God does not want them eating if they are not willing to work for it. Notice that Paul chastised those who were "unwilling to work." Sometimes people are unable to find jobs or are physically unable to work. The key here is that we should be *willing* to work hard when we are able.

God designed us to work. He wants us to work to provide for ourselves. In these verses, Paul reminded the Thessalonians of his own example. Though he was an apostle, and he could have expected the people to provide for him, he worked for his food in order to set an example for them. We too, as believers, are to set an example for those around us. ✤

PRAYER

Dear God, thank you for the opportunity to glorify you in our work. Please help us to work hard and to provide for ourselves. Please help us to be an example to the world. Amen.

day196

DILIGENT HANDS

- How does it feel when you are forced to do something you don't want to do?
- What happens to people who are unwilling to work?

Diligent hands will rule, but laziness ends in forced labor.   PROVERBS 12:24

To be diligent means to take care with our work, and to stick to it. It means to pay close attention and do our very best. In this proverb, King Solomon teaches us that diligent work leads to a type of freedom. Those who work hard will end up in positions of authority. Those who work hard will have more choices in work and in life.

On the other hand, "laziness ends in forced labor." It is the word "forced" here that should alarm us. When people don't give their all, they may end up with fewer choices. They may have to do work that they don't want to do just to survive. Being lazy can make a person a slave to difficult circumstances and work that they hate.

God wants us to work hard. He wants us to do all our work as if we were doing it for him. ❖

PRAYER

Dear God, please help us to be diligent with our work, whatever it may be. Please protect us from laziness. Amen.

THE MINDSET OF CHRIST

- What does it mean to be humble? Describe someone you know who is humble in the way they deal with other people.
- What is one example of how Jesus acted humbly during his life on earth?

Do nothing out of selfish ambition or vain conceit. Rather, in humility value others above yourselves, not looking to your own interests but each of you to the interests of the others. In your relationships with one another, have the same mindset as Christ Jesus.

PHILIPPIANS 2:3–5

What was Jesus' mindset when he walked on this earth? Was he "all about Jesus"? Did he wear flashy clothes, ride the fastest donkey and eat the best foods? No, he didn't. Even though he very well could have, Jesus never "showed off" that he was God.

Even when people were doubting him, making fun of him and physically abusing him, Jesus remained humble. At any moment, he could have called down a million angels. He could have shown everyone who was boss. But he didn't.

Instead, he acted like a servant. He cared for others. He listened to them. He cured them. He washed their feet. And ultimately, he died on the cross for them.

We are to have the same mindset as Jesus when we deal with others. We are to become servants, putting others' needs ahead of our own. When we serve others, we are serving God; we are serving the humble King who gave his life for us on the cross. ✤

PRAYER

Dear God, thank you for Jesus' example. Give us humility when we deal with others. Please help us to love others more than we love ourselves and to put their needs ahead of our own. Amen.

day198

THE ONES I LOOK ON WITH FAVOR

- Has anyone ever told you that they were sorry, but you could tell that they didn't really mean it? How can you tell when someone is being insincere?
- What does it mean for God to look on someone "with favor"?

"Has not my hand made all these things, and so they came into being?" declares the LORD. "These are the ones I look on with favor: those who are humble and contrite in spirit, and who tremble at my word."   ISAIAH 66:2

In the verse previous to this one, God calls the earth his "footstool." This helps put things in perspective, doesn't it? We can try to be a big deal, but our entire world is a footstool to God.

If you ever catch yourself putting what you want ahead of what God wants, remember that he is the one who made you. It's hard to be arrogant when we remember that God made us. God made it all.

God does not want us to be show-offs. He wants us to be humble and to recognize that he is God. He wants us to be sorry for our sin. He wants us to respect the Bible and everything that it teaches us; he wants us to work to honor his commandments.

God loves all of us, but this verse tells us, "These are the ones I look on with favor: those who are humble." When we recognize God for the awesome and almighty Creator that he is, when we humble ourselves before him, we receive his favor. And this is a far greater blessing than anything our boasting could accomplish for us. ❖

PRAYER

Dear God, thank you for caring for the humble. Help us to be humble before you. Give us contrite hearts and respect for your Word. Amen.

day199

IF MY PEOPLE WILL HUMBLE THEMSELVES AND PRAY

- Give an example of a prayer that would not be humble.
- Think about the Lord's Prayer (see Matthew 6:9–13). Is this a prayer that a humble person would pray? Why or why not?

"If my people, who are called by my name, will humble themselves and pray and seek my face and turn from their wicked ways, then I will hear from heaven, and I will forgive their sin and will heal their land." 2 CHRONICLES 7:14

In this verse from 2 Chronicles, God offers Israel forgiveness and healing. But first, he asks for four things from the Israelites: that they be humble, that they pray, that they seek him and that they turn from their wicked ways.

Notice that the first step is humility. Before we can accomplish anything for God, we must be humble. We must recognize that we are servants of God and that we are put on this earth to glorify God, not ourselves.

The second step is to pray. God hears the prayers of the humble. When we are humble, we pray the way we were designed to pray. When we are humble, we approach God as if he really is the God of all creation. We ask God to meet our needs so that *he* may be glorified. We pray to God that *his* will may be done. And these are requests that he happily grants. ♣

PRAYER

Dear God, help us to be humble when we pray. Thank you for hearing the prayers of the humble. Amen.

day**200**

BE HUMBLE OR BE HUMBLED!

- How does being around an arrogant person make you feel?
- What does it mean to be exalted?

"I tell you that this man, rather than the other, went home justified before God. For all those who exalt themselves will be humbled, and those who humble themselves will be exalted."   LUKE 18:14

Let's set the stage for this verse from Luke. Jesus is sharing a parable with some people who were behaving arrogantly.

In the parable, two men go into the temple to pray. One is a Pharisee, and one is a tax collector.

The Pharisee prays, "God, thank you for making me better than everyone else, especially this tax collector. I am so awesome."

The tax collector stands begging God for mercy.

Jesus tells his listeners that it is the tax collector who went home justified. When we try to exalt ourselves, as the Pharisee does in this example, there is no room in our hearts for God. We are too full of ourselves, and God can't do anything with us.

However, when we are humble, God can and will use us. He will use us to accomplish his work, and we will be glorified. And this glory will last for eternity.

If we work for our own glory, we may find some, but it won't last long. We are all going to die and stand before God. What good will our arrogance be to us at that moment? We will most definitely be humbled then. We would do much better to humble ourselves now. ❖

PRAYER

Dear God, thank you for exalting the humble. Give us humility before you, serving only you, not ourselves and our vanity. Amen.

day201

IN THE PRESENCE OF THE LORD

- Describe a time when you felt God's presence in your life.
- What does it mean to humble yourself?

Humble yourselves before the Lord, and he will lift you up. JAMES 4:10

God tells us in Psalm 46:10 to "Be still, and know that I am God." Have you ever sat quietly and just let God be God? Have you ever paused, even in the midst of a busy day and just spent a moment with him? Have you ever tried to feel his presence, listen to his voice and open your heart and mind to him? When you do this, it is easy to be humble. When you look for God, it becomes easy to see how small you are.

If we don't spend this time before the Lord, it is easy to become prideful instead of humble. If we stay busy, always thinking about "me, me, me," and how we can make our lives better, we don't let God in. We forget who God is.

James tells us in this verse to humble ourselves before the Lord. This is not just a suggestion—it is a command. We need to take the time to recognize who God is, so we can better understand who we are in him. We are to come before him as humble servants, so that he can save us, use us and lift us up. ❖

PRAYER

Dear God, help us to come before you humbly. Remind us that you are God, and help us make room for your awesomeness in our lives. Amen.

DIVINE SLOWNESS

- Have you accepted Christ as Savior? If so, how old were you? What inspired you to make that decision?
- How does it make you feel to know that God is holding back his judgment for as long as possible to give everyone a chance to repent?

The Lord is not slow in keeping his promise, as some understand slowness. Instead he is patient with you, not wanting anyone to perish, but everyone to come to repentance.

2 PETER 3:9

When we talk about salvation, who will go to heaven and who won't, there's one question that occurs to nearly everyone: Why doesn't God just let everyone into heaven?

The simple answer is that everything about him is perfect, including his love, faithfulness, holiness and justice. His perfection can't be canceled or compromised.

God's perfect holiness means sin and sinners cannot exist in his presence. His perfect justice demands that all sin be punished by death. His perfect love caused him to sacrifice his Son to pay the entire debt for the world's sin. His perfect faithfulness allows anyone who believes in his Son to escape the punishment for sin and receive eternal life.

God's deepest desire is that everyone would repent and believe in his Son. He's done everything we could hope for to make that possible. We need to admit that we are sinners and ask Jesus to save us—that's what God requires of us.

So the question isn't, *Why doesn't God just let everyone into heaven?* The question is, *How can anyone think God hasn't done enough already to make that happen?* ✤

PRAYER

Dear God, thank you for being patient with your judgment and slow with your anger. We cannot imagine how many people have been saved and will be saved because of it. Amen.

REMOVING THE WEDGE

- How do you know when you need to repent?
- Why is repentance sometimes painful?

John said to the crowds coming out to be baptized by him, "You brood of vipers! Who warned you to flee from the coming wrath? Produce fruit in keeping with repentance. And do not begin to say to yourselves, 'We have Abraham as our father.' For I tell you that out of these stones God can raise up children for Abraham." LUKE 3:7–8

Imagine that your best friend betrayed you. Maybe he humiliated you in front of the whole class. Or maybe she spread a terrible rumor to ruin your reputation. Whatever the case, your friend did something he or she knew would hurt you or make you angry.

Now imagine that your friend tries to pretend as though nothing happened after betraying you. He expects you to treat him the same way you always did. Or she thinks it's no big deal. How would you react? Could you treat your friend as though nothing had happened between you? Or would you demand an apology before you went back to the way things used to be?

This is an illustration of repentance. When we sin, we betray God. We become guilty of the one thing he hates. This drives a wedge between us and him. We can't pretend nothing's wrong because something is. Until we admit it and ask for forgiveness, we can't hope for a close relationship with him.

Repentance paves the way for a relationship with God. We have to understand how disgusting our sin is to him. Better still, we have to be disgusted by it too. When we do repent, God will forgive us and welcome us as a friend. ✤

PRAYER

Dear God, let us never forget the importance of repentance and forgiveness. Thank you for listening to us every time we come to you with our sin. Thank you for always restoring our relationship. Amen.

R-E-P-E-N-T

- How is repentance different from an apology?
- Why is baptism associated with repentance?

Peter replied, "Repent and be baptized, every one of you, in the name of Jesus Christ for the forgiveness of your sins. And you will receive the gift of the Holy Spirit." ACTS 2:38

The word "repent" (or some form of it) is used over 100 times in the Bible. It's also used a lot in sermons and on cardboard signs people make when they think the end of the world is coming. There's a reason it's so prevalent. Repentance is the foundation of our faith.

Repentance is still a confusing concept for a lot of people however. For example, repenting is not the same as simply saying, "I'm sorry." It's much more involved than that. Repentance is a four-part process. First, we need to recognize that we have sinned. Second, we need to recognize the damage our sin has caused, especially in our relationship with God. Third, we need to ask God's forgiveness for our sin. Fourth, we need to turn away from sin and start following God.

Once we've repented, the Holy Spirit can begin his work in our lives by guiding us toward God-honoring choices. We make the decision to turn away from sin to follow God, but it's the Holy Spirit who shows us how. ✤

PRAYER

Dear God, we know we have sinned and don't deserve your salvation. But you give it when we repent. Guide us as we tell others about the importance of repentance. Amen.

day205

AND THE CROWD GOES WILD

- Where is the best place to attend a sporting event? Why?
- Why don't we celebrate spiritual accomplishments the way we celebrate athletic ones?

"I tell you that in the same way there will be more rejoicing in heaven over one sinner who repents than over ninety-nine righteous persons who do not need to repent." LUKE 15:7

Have you ever given a great performance? Maybe it was a flawless recital. Maybe it was the game-winning free throw or home run. Maybe it was a memorable scene in a play. Whatever the circumstances were, think about the audience's reaction. Try to relive the excitement and emotions of the moment.

Now imagine being able to create that kind of reaction among the citizens of heaven. According to Jesus' words in Luke 15:7, the heavens react with a loud cheer whenever a person repents and asks God for forgiveness. All of heaven gets so excited about another person's salvation that they shout for joy.

It's comforting to know that the cheer comes from heaven—from those who have already received God's salvation. They know what lies ahead for us because they're experiencing it. And they can't wait for us to experience it. ✤

PRAYER

Dear God, thank you for filling heaven with people who celebrate repentance. With your help, we would love to keep the cheers going by encouraging others to repent and believe. Amen.

SEVEN TIMES A DAY

- What circumstances might cause you to end a friendship?
- What could that friend do to get back into your good graces?

"Even if they sin against you seven times in a day and seven times come back to you saying 'I repent,' you must forgive them."   LUKE 17:4

Think about how many times we ask God for forgiveness. Better yet, think about how many times we *should* ask God for forgiveness. We mess up in countless ways every day. Yet every time we turn to God with sincere repentance, he forgives us and wipes our slates clean.

Of course, if we keep doing the same thing over and over again, there may be reason to doubt that we're actually repentant. But if we make a genuine effort to change each time we repent, God will forgive us.

How can we, then, deny forgiveness to people who have hurt us? Our standards can't be higher than God's. If he forgives us, we must forgive others. If the person keeps doing the same thing over and over to us, we might doubt whether he or she is actually repentant. We might have to put some boundaries in place in that relationship. But our responsibility as followers of Christ is to forgive. ✤

PRAYER

Dear God, thank you for not setting a limit on the number of times you will forgive us. Give us the patience and strength to forgive people who hurt us. Let us be examples of your forgiveness. Amen.

REPENT OR ELSE

* Why might God allow a tragedy to happen?
* What would you say to someone who claimed that tragedy is God's way of punishing people?

"I tell you, no! But unless you repent, you too will all perish. Or those eighteen who died when the tower in Siloam fell on them—do you think they were more guilty than all the others living in Jerusalem? I tell you, no! But unless you repent, you too will all perish."

LUKE 13:3–5

In Biblical times, people believed that tragedies happened only to those who were extremely sinful. They figured that people got what was coming to them. The worse the tragedy, the more sinful the victims were assumed to be.

In Luke 13:1, Jesus' followers told him about an incident at the temple in which several Galilean worshipers were killed while offering their sacrifices. Apparently Pilate, the Roman governor, ordered their execution, though the Bible doesn't say why. The people who told the story probably expected Jesus to denounce the dead Galileans for whatever sin brought such judgment on them.

Like most people who thought they could predict Jesus' response, those followers were surprised. Instead, Jesus referred to another incident in which a tower in Siloam fell and killed 18 people. He refuted the idea that the people killed in the temple or by the falling tower were any more sinful than the people who survived.

Jesus' message was this: Everyone has sinned. No sin is worse than another in God's eyes. Therefore, everyone deserves a tragic death both spiritually and physically, but if we turn from our sinfulness to Christ, we will ultimately live. No one can be good enough to earn salvation; it is a gift that we accept when we repent and entrust our lives to Christ. ✦

PRAYER

Dear God, give us the words and wisdom to tell people the truth about sin and repentance. Let your Holy Spirit work in people's lives in such a way that they are eager to hear about your Word. Amen.

NOTHING BUT THE BLOOD OF JESUS

- What's the funniest thing you've seen or heard in church?
- Why might some people have a hard time accepting that Jesus' blood is the only thing that can bring salvation?

For you know that it was not with perishable things such as silver or gold that you were redeemed from the empty way of life handed down to you from your ancestors, but with the precious blood of Christ, a lamb without blemish or defect.   1 PETER 1:18–19

Some people think of Christians as boring folks who obey a bunch of old laws and never have any fun. They don't know how much fun we can have in church, how much fun we can have together. Most churches work hard at creating fun programs, for both kids and adults: youth groups, concerts, cookouts, softball leagues . . . the list goes on and on.

But we always need to remember that it's not all fun and games. There's a reason that we are free to have so much joy, and that reason is the blood of Jesus. We must never take our salvation for granted.

We can be thankful for Jesus' sacrifice. We can be in awe of our heavenly Father who made it possible. We can celebrate what it means for us. But we can never treat it lightly or take it for granted. The cost was too high. Our salvation required the blood of Jesus Christ. He suffered and died to save us. We cannot forget that. ✤

PRAYER

Dear God, we praise you for the salvation that could only be obtained by Jesus' blood. Give us the wisdom and courage to challenge people who say there are other paths to you. Help us defend your truth. Amen.

IT'S PERSONAL

- What does it mean to have a personal relationship with God?
- When do you feel especially close to him? When do you feel distant?

"Now this is eternal life: that they know you, the only true God, and Jesus Christ, whom you have sent."
     JOHN 17:3

Before we're saved, we don't have a good relationship with God. In fact, we don't have a relationship with him at all. We may recognize him as the Creator of the universe, but that's hardly a relationship. At most, he's a distant figure we can never hope to know. If we feel anything toward him, it's most likely fear. After all, we've been told that he is our Judge, the one who will pass sentence on us when we die.

We're certainly in no hurry to meet him. If we talk about him at all, we usually use jokey, impersonal names like "the Big Guy" or "the Man Upstairs." We're content to do our thing and let God do his.

We continue that way until one of two things happens: We die, which is the worst possible outcome, or we accept God's offer of salvation. Jesus' sacrifice makes the connection possible. He removed the sin that kept us apart from God.

Thanks to Jesus, we can have a personal relationship with the Creator of the universe, our heavenly Father. We can talk to him every day and listen for his response. We can turn to him for advice, comfort, direction or anything else we need. ❖

PRAYER

Dear God, we are honored to have a relationship with you. Thank you for reaching down to us so that we might know you. Let us never take that privilege for granted. Amen.

THE NECESSARY STEP

- How easy is it to repent?
- How can you make repentance sound appealing when you share your faith with someone?

Peter replied, "Repent and be baptized, every one of you, in the name of Jesus Christ for the forgiveness of your sins. And you will receive the gift of the Holy Spirit." Acts 2:38

"Repent and be baptized." That sounds a like a pretty quick path to launching your Christian life, doesn't it? One, two, and you're on the way, right? Not so fast.

The baptism part is pretty straightforward—extremely meaningful and important, but straightforward. The repentance part, though, requires a little more effort—emotionally painful effort.

Repenting of our sins means taking a hard look at areas of our lives we may be uncomfortable with. To repent means to sort through the ugly incidents in our past. It means to face up to certain habits or addictions we would rather ignore. It means to expose to God everything we try to keep hidden from other people.

Repenting of our sins means seeing ourselves as God sees us, not as we would like to see ourselves. It means we recognize we're polluted with sin and helpless to save ourselves, a dangerous combination. It means we realize our only hope for salvation is Jesus. It means we ask God to forgive us for the mess we've made of our life.

That's repentance. And it's followed immediately by celebration because God promises that if we will repent, he will forgive. ✤

PRAYER

Dear God, thank you for not punishing us immediately for our sins. Thank you for giving us the opportunity to repent. Work in our hearts to let us know when more repentance is necessary. Amen.

UNEARNED

- Why can't you do anything to save yourself?
- Why are even "minor" sins, like lying or disobeying parents, punishable by death in God's eyes?

For the wages of sin is death, but the gift of God is eternal life in Christ Jesus our Lord.
ROMANS 6:23

Most of us are taught from an early age that effort earns reward. We get gold stars for bringing our Bibles to Sunday school. We win ribbons for creating science fair projects. We collect trophies for playing hard in sports. We earn merit badges for mastering scouting skills. We receive scholarships for good grades. We are paid money for doing our jobs.

Maybe that's why some people seem to assume that they can earn favor with God. They think that if they can get him to like them for their goodness, they can make their own way to salvation. If they work hard enough, they can win God's approval. So they get busy doing "good" things—volunteering at a soup kitchen, sponsoring a needy child, helping the homeless—to earn God's favor. The problem is, when God looks at unbelievers, all he sees is sin. According to Isaiah 64:6, "righteous acts are like filthy rags" to God. Our impressive works mean nothing to him.

The bottom line is that we cannot do anything to earn salvation. None of us is good enough. We can only repent, humbly accept God's gift and believe in his Son. ✤

PRAYER

Dear God, thank you for your generosity. We have hope for the future, not because of anything we did, but because of what you did through your Son. We will praise you for it forever. Amen.

day212

CONFESSION AND BELIEF

- What does it mean that Jesus is Lord of your life?
- Which is easier to do: believe that Jesus rose from the dead or declare him Lord of your life? Explain.

If you declare with your mouth, "Jesus is Lord," and believe in your heart that God raised him from the dead, you will be saved.   ROMANS 10:9

The apostle Paul says two things are necessary to be saved: believing that God raised Jesus from the dead and declaring that Jesus is Lord. As far as Jesus' resurrection goes, we have eyewitness reports from the New Testament to support our belief.

Over 500 people saw Jesus after he rose from the dead. They talked to him, ate with him and even touched his wounds. His resurrection is not a myth or legend. We have reason to believe God raised him from the dead.

Declaring that Jesus is Lord requires a little more work on our part. In order to declare Jesus Lord, we have to understand who he is. We don't have to pass a theology exam, but we do need to know what God's Word says about him.

He is the Son of God. He came to earth to live among us, fully God and fully human at the same time. He lived a sinless life, which made him a perfect sacrifice for us. He was crucified to pay the price for our sin. He conquered death and rose from the dead three days later.

To declare Jesus Lord means to put all your eggs in his basket, give your life to him and do as he instructs. ✣

PRAYER

Dear God, thank you for your Son, our Savior and Lord. We praise you for raising him from the dead so that we may have eternal life. Amen.

day213

BORN OF GOD

- How might a person's relationship with an earthly father affect his or her opinion of God?
- What are some of the perks of having God as our Father?

Yet to all who did receive him, to those who believed in his name, he gave the right to become children of God—children born not of natural descent, nor of human decision or a husband's will, but born of God. JOHN 1:12–13

The salvation that Jesus won for us with his sacrifice on the cross is not just a ticket to heaven when we die. Everyone who receives salvation also becomes a child of God. To get an idea of what that's like, take a look at the story of the lost son in Luke 15:11–32. That's where you'll discover what kind of father God is.

After spending his inheritance and living a selfish and hopeless life for years, a son returns home to his father, hoping for nothing more than a place to stay. The father sees him from a distance and comes running to greet his son joyfully. Their relationship is restored, and the father is ecstatic—just as God is when we are saved.

Like a loving and committed earthly father, God wants the best for his children. He protects us from harm. He encourages us to use our talents and abilities. He disciplines us when we need it.

Unlike even the best earthly father, though, God is all-knowing. His wisdom is perfect. His rules are perfect. And his plans for our lives are perfect. Everything he says is not only right, it's right for us. He created us; he knows what will ultimately fulfill us. ❖

PRAYER

Dear God, thank you for allowing us to call you our heavenly Father. Guide us in our daily lives. Give us your wisdom. May we listen to your instructions as a young child listens to a father. Amen.

day214

THE LOST SHEEP

- How would you respond to someone who said, "If there is a God, he's too busy to care about our lives"?
- How do you know God cares about you personally?

"What do you think? If a man owns a hundred sheep, and one of them wanders away, will he not leave the ninety-nine on the hills and go to look for the one that wandered off?"

MATTHEW 18:12

If you had 100 sheep, and one of them wandered off, would you search for it? If you look at the sheep as one big flock, you probably wouldn't. The loss of one from a flock that big would be barely noticeable. Holding on to 99 percent of your sheep probably makes you a decent shepherd. You would probably be proud to put that on your résumé.

But Jesus isn't just a *decent* shepherd; he is the *Good* Shepherd. And he doesn't look at his sheep as one big flock; he sees them as individuals. When one wanders off, it's not just a tiny fraction of the group; it's a specific sheep that he knows and cares about. So he drops everything to go find the lost sheep and bring it home.

We should be glad that the Good Shepherd cares so much because each of us was once that lost sheep. Jesus made it his priority to find us and save us.

Now that we're part of the flock, we should adopt the attitude of our Shepherd. We should make it a priority to help bring other lost "sheep" to Christ. What can we do as a family to share the good news of Christ with others? ✣

PRAYER

Dear God, thank you for not being content with 99 sheep. Thank you for caring enough to search for us when we're lost and bring us back to you. Amen.

day215

THE WAY, THE TRUTH AND THE LIFE

- True or false: It doesn't matter what you believe about God, as long as you believe something. Explain your answer.
- How would you explain John 14:6 to a Muslim or a Buddhist?

Jesus answered, "I am the way and the truth and the life. No one comes to the Father except through me."   JOHN 14:6

Jesus' words in John14:6 are what separate Christianity from every other religion in the world. For that reason, they're also probably some of the most controversial sentences in all Scripture.

Few people like to be told that there's only one way to do something. The natural response is to disagree and offer several alternatives. That's certainly what happens when talk turns to religion. When Jesus says, "No one comes to the Father except through me," many people say, "Oh, yeah? What about Islam and Buddhism and Hinduism?" They don't like the idea of one group of people having exclusive rights to heaven. And they especially don't like the idea of one group believing that they are right and everyone else is wrong. That's why spiritual discussions often turn into heated debates or shouting matches.

As Christians, we should be aware of people's feelings about this topic, but we should never back away from the truth of John 14:6. We should learn to present the truth in a way that invites discussion instead of argument. And we should always be prepared to explain why Jesus, and Jesus alone, is the way to salvation. ❖

PRAYER

Dear God, we praise you for giving us what no one else could—salvation. You alone are the path to heaven. No one comes to the Father except through Jesus. Please help us to share this truth with others. Amen.

day216

GOD'S FAVORITE SON

- How can you spot a proud father, whether it's at a preschool play or a high school band concert?
- How do you picture the relationship between God the Father and Jesus the Son?

This is good, and pleases God our Savior, who wants all people to be saved and to come to a knowledge of the truth. 1 TIMOTHY 2:3–4

People who don't understand God sometimes try to portray him as a villain who sends innocent people to hell just because they don't believe exactly what he tells them to believe. But the apostle Paul's words in 1 Timothy 2 give us a more accurate picture. God wants all people to be saved because he loves all people. He wants us to spend eternity with him.

Beyond that, though, he wants us to understand the truth about his Son. Don't forget, God is a proud Father—and for good reason. His Son is perfect. When Jesus was baptized, God made his voice known from heaven: "This is my Son, whom I love; with him I am well pleased" (Matthew 3:17).

God knows exactly what it cost Jesus to come to earth, live as one of us, suffer at our hands and die for our sins. He is perfectly proud of his Son, and he wants everyone on earth to know exactly what he did.

That's our cue. When we talk about the greatest things that have ever happened to us, Jesus' sacrifice should be at the top of our list. Any time we have a chance to tell someone how incredible Jesus is, we should do it. ♣

PRAYER

Dear God, we praise you for sending your only Son to die for us. Give us the words to tell others what he has done. Guide us as we spread the news of his sacrifice. Amen.

FROM THE BEGINNING

- What are you supposed to do if you're in a building that's on fire? What if a tornado is headed your way? How often do you practice those drills?
- What can we learn about God from the fact that he had a plan for salvation in place as soon as Adam and Eve sinned?

"And I will put enmity between you and the woman, and between your offspring and hers; he will crush your head, and you will strike his heel." GENESIS 3:15

In schools and in many office buildings, people practice contingency plans for what they will do in the event of an emergency. They practice clearing the building during fire drills. They practice gathering in a safe area for tornado drills or intruder alerts. They hope they will never have to face the worst-case scenario, but if they do, they will be ready.

In Genesis 3:15, we see evidence that God had a contingency plan in place for his human creation. While he was cursing the serpent (Satan) for deceiving Eve, God revealed that one day Eve's offspring—Jesus—would crush Satan's head. What's amazing is that he was referring to Jesus' crucifixion. Yet his conversation was taking place in the Garden of Eden, immediately after Adam and Eve sinned.

That means God already had a contingency plan in place. God knew the risks of giving people free will, the ability to choose good or evil. He knew we would sin, and he planned how he would save us after we made that fateful choice. It's always been God's intention to deliver us from the death and destruction that we brought on ourselves. ✤

PRAYER

Dear God, we praise you for being all-knowing and for creating a way for us to be saved even after we disobeyed. Thank you for your incredible love. Amen.

day218

THE CORNERSTONE

- How do you think most people picture Jesus? How do you picture him?
- How would you explain Isaiah 53:2, which predicted that there would be "nothing in his appearance that we should desire him"?

Jesus is "'the stone you builders rejected, which has become the cornerstone.' Salvation is found in no one else, for there is no other name under heaven given to mankind by which we must be saved."
ACTS 4:11–12

After Jesus' death, resurrection and ascension to heaven, his disciples got busy spreading his Word. And people responded in a big way. Thousands came to Christ because of the disciples' ministry. That didn't make the Jewish leaders happy. They assumed they had heard the last of Jesus when they had him crucified.

The high priest and other rulers ordered Peter and John, two of Jesus' disciples, to be arrested and brought to them for preaching about the resurrection. Peter took advantage of the opportunity to remind the Jewish leaders of their mistake. Jesus, the stone they had rejected, had become the cornerstone of salvation—and of a new faith that would change the world.

The Jewish leaders were part of a long line of people who underestimated or misunderstood Jesus. One of his would-be disciples mocked him because of his hometown (see John 1:46). The people of his hometown rejected his teachings because he was just a carpenter's son (see Matthew 13:53–57). The problem was, Jesus didn't look or act like people thought the Messiah would look and act. He didn't live up to their expectations.

People still question him today. As his followers, we should be prepared to open their eyes to the truth about our Savior. ♣

PRAYER

Dear God, thank you for blessing us in unexpected ways. Your ways are higher than our ways. Teach us to trust you even when we are deceived. Amen.

ATTENTION: COMPLAINT DEPARTMENT

* Who do you complain to?
* How do you feel when someone complains to you?

I cry aloud to the LORD; I lift up my voice to the LORD for mercy. I pour out before him my complaint; before him I tell my trouble.   PSALM 142:1–2

When King David wrote this psalm, he was running for his life. Saul wanted David dead, and at the time that he wrote these words, David was hiding in a cave. David had something to complain about!

But notice who David complained to. He cried aloud to *God*. He didn't complain to his boss, co-workers, teachers or friends. He lifted his voice up to the Lord. He told God his troubles.

He didn't have to choose God. He had other people in the cave with him. He could have written his complaints down and sent them to someone else. He could have gone somewhere else to hide, somewhere with lots of people to complain to. But he didn't. Because he knew he didn't need to.

The truth is that complaining to anyone but God doesn't do any good. It's fine to go to friends and family for support in tough times, but God doesn't want us to spend all our time complaining to others. He wants us to bring our troubles to him. He's God—he can handle our complaints. ♣

PRAYER

Dear God, thank you for caring about our problems. Please remind us to bring our troubles to you. Amen.

day220

GRUMBLERS AND FAULTFINDERS

* Why do you think people complain?
* How do you feel when you complain?

These people are grumblers and faultfinders; they follow their own evil desires; they boast about themselves and flatter others for their own advantage. JUDE 16

The people to whom Jude is referring in this verse were not just unpleasant people. They were out to destroy God's church. We believers do not want to be compared to them!

The truth is that people who complain are usually doing so because they want their own way. As believers, we are not supposed to want our own way—we are supposed to want God's way. When we find ourselves complaining, we need to ask ourselves what is making us want to complain. We'll probably find that, on some level, we feel we are not getting our own way. And we'll probably realize that this is a good thing. God knows more about what we need than we do. If God's way doesn't match up with our way, we shouldn't grumble or try to find fault with God's plan. Instead, we should take a deep breath and pray about whatever is bothering us.

Remember that grumbling, faultfinding and complaining do nothing to glorify God. And these activities don't make us look very good either. ♣

PRAYER

Dear God, please forgive us when we grumble and complain. Please help us to want to do things your way, not our way. Next time we are tempted to complain, please remind us to pray instead. Amen.

NO GRUMPIES ALLOWED

- When you are told to do something that you don't really want to do, how do you respond?
- How can you avoid grumbling about doing what you don't want to do?

Do everything without grumbling or arguing.   PHILIPPIANS 2:14

Christians are usually busy people—they are busy at home, at work and in church, trying to do God's work and help as many people as possible. With all this busyness and all this work, it can be tempting to do a little grumbling about all we have going on.

But God doesn't want Christians grumbling to, or at, one another. God loves a cheerful giver, a person who gives of his or her time, energy and effort willingly and joyfully. When we grumble, we bring others down, and we make it harder for other people to do what they need to do for God. God wants us to support one another and bring joy to every situation.

God doesn't want Christians arguing either. He doesn't want us arguing with one another, with authorities or with him. When we are given a task to do, God wants us to do it with smiles on our faces. God wants us to be the lights of the world. ✤

PRAYER

Dear God, please help us to think before we speak and to not complain or argue. Please help us to do everything like we are doing it for you, with smiles on our faces. Amen.

day**222**

THE THRONE OF GRACE

- What would happen if you tried to call the president or leader of your country?
- What does it mean to do something with confidence?

For we do not have a high priest who is unable to empathize with our weaknesses, but we have one who has been tempted in every way, just as we are—yet he did not sin. Let us then approach God's throne of grace with confidence, so that we may receive mercy and find grace to help us in our time of need. HEBREWS 4:15–16

Have you ever felt like you were in a spot so tough that no one could possibly understand? Remember that Jesus was repeatedly tempted by Satan. Talk about a tough spot! Jesus knows what temptation feels like, and he wants us to conquer temptation and send Satan packing. And we are invited to call on Jesus for help when we are tempted.

Imagine you need help from someone powerful, so you attempt to call the president. Obviously, it wouldn't happen. It was equally impossible, at the time that Hebrews was written, to simply approach the throne of the king.

But this is not the case with our King Jesus. We are invited to approach his throne with confidence. He will not turn us away. Instead, he will bestow on us mercy and grace to help us in our time of need. Why would we want to try and defeat temptation on our own when we can call on the King for help? ❖

> **PRAYER**

Dear God, thank you that we can approach your throne for help whenever we need to. Please help us to remember this and to approach your throne with confidence. Amen.

day223

RESIST THE TEMPTATION

- Who tempts us to sin?
- What does the phrase "evil desire" mean?

When tempted, no one should say, "God is tempting me." For God cannot be tempted by evil, nor does he tempt anyone; but each person is tempted when they are dragged away by their own evil desire and enticed.   JAMES 1:13–14

You are in the department store. You really need a new set of headphones. You don't have any money. It would be so easy to just put those new headphones in your coat pocket and walk out of the store. Is God tempting you to steal something? Certainly not!

God does not want us to sin, and he will never tempt us to sin. We are tempted by our own desires, not by God. Remember that we have a sinful nature. Even though we have been reborn in Christ, we must continue to defeat our old sinful nature. It will keep rearing its ugly head, and with the power of Jesus, we must keep overcoming it.

So we need to resist blaming temptation on God. Instead, we need to call on him to help us resist temptation and avoid sin. We can pray and walk away from whatever is tempting us. ✤

PRAYER

Dear God, thank you for not tempting us to sin. When we are tempted, please help us to turn away from temptation and toward you. Amen.

day224

A WAY OUT

- Share a time when God provided you with a way to escape temptation.
- Name some things that are common to people.

No temptation has overtaken you except what is common to mankind. And God is faithful; he will not let you be tempted beyond what you can bear. But when you are tempted, he will also provide a way out so that you can endure it.   1 CORINTHIANS 10:13

This verse from 1 Corinthians may be one of the most encouraging verses from all of Scripture.

It tells you that even when you feel like you are facing the biggest temptation ever, someone who has gone before you has already faced it. And quite likely, someone else is facing it at the very same time you are.

Even when you feel like you can't stand the temptation anymore, this verse says you can because God will not allow you to be tempted beyond your strength.

And even when you feel like there is no way out, God has provided you with a way out. God will provide you with a way to tolerate, and not give in to, the temptation.

God is faithful. He will never let you down. When you feel like you are alone, you are not. Call on God. Ask him to give you strength, to send you help and to show you the way out. ✤

> **PRAYER**

Dear God, thank you for never allowing us to be tempted beyond our ability to withstand temptation. When we are tempted, please send us your strength and show us the way out. Amen.

THE APPLE OF YOUR EYE

- How would life be different if you did not have the Bible?
- How do you avoid temptation?

My son, keep my words and store up my commands within you. Keep my commands and you will live; guard my teachings as the apple of your eye. Bind them on your fingers; write them on the tablet of your heart.   PROVERBS 7:1–3

In these verses from Proverbs, King Solomon was teaching young men how to avoid temptation. And his words still apply to us today. We are to store up his commands within us. God's wisdom will keep us alive and well.

Today, "the apple of my eye" is a common phrase used to describe something precious. But it used to refer literally to the pupil of the eye. Because eyesight is so important, people began to also use the phrase to describe something that was incredibly important to them. This is how important God's commands should be to us. They are precious. They are important. Without them, we are blind.

We are also to bind the commands on our fingers. Imagine wearing Solomon's God-given wisdom engraved on rings. Not only would you be adorning yourself with God's commandments but you would also be able to read them at any time.

We are to write God's commands on the tablets of our hearts. When the Bible talks about our "heart," it's talking about our very being, the deepest part of us. This, ultimately, is the place we need to keep God's wisdom. ✤

PRAYER

Dear God, thank you for the wisdom you have provided us through your Word. Please help us to write this wisdom in our hearts and to live by it every day. Amen.

RUN AWAY! RUN AWAY!

- Try to remember who you were a year ago. How have you matured in your faith?
- How does God want you to deal with temptation?

Flee the evil desires of youth and pursue righteousness, faith, love and peace, along with those who call on the Lord out of a pure heart.   2 TIMOTHY 2:22

God doesn't tell us to casually avoid temptation, as if it were slightly dangerous. The most dangerous thing that we can do is to take temptation lightly. We are not to play around with it. God tells us to *run away* from temptation, to "flee the evil desires of youth."

This does not mean that the things we desire when we are young are evil things. However, young adults do often go through selfish and argumentative phases. These can be a normal part of growing up. Paul is telling us here that we must move past these phases. We must choose to seek God instead of ourselves and to pursue righteousness. We must work to mature in our faith.

And the best way to do this is alongside other believers. There is strength in fellowship. There is strength in numbers. Being in the company of other strong Christians can help us to flee from temptation. ✤

PRAYER

Dear God, thank you that we are maturing in our faith. Please help us to flee from temptation, and please send us other strong Christians to help us. Amen.

THE SERPENT

- Why did Eve eat the forbidden fruit?
- What is an example of one of Satan's lies?

Now the serpent was more crafty than any of the wild animals the LORD God had made. He said to the woman, "Did God really say, 'You must not eat from any tree in the garden'?" . . . "You will not certainly die," the serpent said to the woman. "For God knows that when you eat from it your eyes will be opened, and you will be like God, knowing good and evil."   GENESIS 3:1,4–5

Satan appears in the Garden of Eden to tempt Eve to sin. He does this by introducing doubt. He causes Eve to doubt God and her understanding of God's Word. He also accuses God of lying, and he promises Eve a reward for her sin.

Satan works in much the same way today. He does various things to cause us to doubt ourselves, to doubt the reality of God and to doubt our understanding of the Bible. He spread lies—lies that contradict God's Word. He also promises rewards for our sins. Satan promises that sin will make us happy, that sin will allow us to have fun, that sin will make us rich, that sin will make us popular.

Sometimes, there are rewards for sin, but they are short-lived and never worth the cost of the sin. Eve's eyes were opened, and she did receive the knowledge of good and evil. But at what cost? All creation fell into sin because of her and Adam's sin.

Satan will continue to tempt us throughout our lives, but we never have to give in to him. We have God on our side, and God is far more powerful than Satan. ✤

PRAYER

Dear God, thank you for protecting us from Satan and his lies. Please help us to stay strong in our faith. Please protect us from Satan's temptations. Amen.

day228

SUBJECT TO JUDGMENT

- What does God think about name-calling?
- Which is worse, daydreaming about hurting someone or actually hurting them? Why?

"You have heard that it was said to the people long ago, 'You shall not murder, and anyone who murders will be subject to judgment.' But I tell you that anyone who is angry with a brother or sister will be subject to judgment. Again, anyone who says to a brother or sister, 'Raca,' is answerable to the court. And anyone who says, 'You fool!' will be in danger of the fire of hell." MATTHEW 5:21–22

We know that it is wrong to commit murder. But sometimes we forget that it is just as wrong to think murderous thoughts and feel murderous feelings.

Now, you're probably not going to murder your brother or sister today, but you might think hateful thoughts toward someone or spout a few cruel words, and that is what Jesus is talking about in these verses from Matthew.

Sin can begin in the mind, before we actually do anything. Sometimes sin begins and ends in the mind, and we never take action at all. But these thoughts are still sin. Just because it happens in our heads doesn't mean that we're not accountable. Nothing is hidden from God.

We are accountable for the words we say, the insults we hurl and the thoughts we think. So, before we allow anger to lead us to sin, we need to take a moment to pray for grace instead. ♣

PRAYER

Dear God, please help us to avoid temptation. Please help us to keep our thoughts on you and to avoid sinning in our minds and hearts. Amen.

day**229**

THORNS AND THISTLES

- Why does God give us commandments?
- What are some of the consequences of sin?

To Adam he said, "Because you listened to your wife and ate fruit from the tree about which I commanded you, 'You must not eat from it,' Cursed is the ground because of you; through painful toil you will eat food from it all the days of your life. It will produce thorns and thistles for you, and you will eat the plants of the field. By the sweat of your brow you will eat your food until you return to the ground, since from it you were taken; for dust you are and to dust you will return." GENESIS 3:17−19

God does not give us commandments because he wants to hide something from us. He does not give us rules to punish us or to keep us from having fun. God's commandments are given to protect us. Not only does sin lead to eternal separation from God, but sin always has consequences in our life on earth.

You may think it's no big deal to cheat on that homework assignment. But then you don't learn the material, which you might need to know later in life. And you could lose the trust of your teacher, and later you might find it difficult to have someone write you a letter of recommendation for college.

You may think it's no big deal to drink a few beers. Everyone is doing it, and nothing bad ever happens, right? But then you do something really embarrassing at a friend's house, or you get into a vehicle with a drunk driver who gets into an accident on the way home.

We never really get away with anything. Even when sin has no obvious consequence, it takes its toll on our hearts. There's no such thing as sin without consequence. ✣

> **PRAYER**

Dear God, thank you for giving us your Word to protect us. Please help us to be obedient to your commandments. Amen.

BAD COMPANY

- Describe a time when you experienced peer pressure.
- Do choices regarding our friendships matter to God? Why or why not?

My son, if sinful men entice you, do not give in to them . . . These men lie in wait for their own blood; they ambush only themselves! Such are the paths of all who go after ill-gotten gain; it takes away the life of those who get it.　　　Proverbs 1:10,18–19

There's a reason people often talk about peer pressure. It's an incredibly powerful thing. We are created with a desire to belong. We want to fit in. Ultimately, we will belong to and fit in with the body of Christ.

Peer pressure takes advantage of this need for fellowship, but that doesn't mean that believers are powerless to resist it. We can resist it. We must resist it. As this chapter from Proverbs tells us, if people try to get us to sin, we must not give in to them.

First Corinthians 15:33 tells us that "'Bad company corrupts good character.'" The best way to avoid the temptations that come from peer pressure is to be careful about the kind of friends we hang out with. Some people seem like fun, but when we spend time with them, we always seem to get into trouble. Or they do things that make us uncomfortable.

We are called to love others, but we need to keep a healthy distance from people who will try to lead us to sin. ❖

PRAYER

Dear God, please help us to make good decisions. Please help us to keep a healthy distance from people who will try to lead us into sin. Amen.

day231

THE GOOD THEY OUGHT TO DO

- Share a time when you helped someone out.
- How do you know what "good works" God wants you to do?

If anyone, then, knows the good they ought to do and doesn't do it, it is sin for them.

JAMES 4:17

You're riding your bike down the street. You see an older woman, someone you know from church. She is carrying a large grocery bag and is just about to cross the street. As you ride by, the bottom of her bag tears and her groceries fall onto the ground, with some of them rolling into the street.

You know that you should stop and help her, but you've got somewhere to go and don't want to stop, so you ride on by. Since she didn't see you, can't you get away without helping?

As Christians, we know what is right, and because of this knowledge, we will be held to a higher standard. Sometimes, we don't sin by *doing* but by *not doing*.

We should always be on the lookout for the work that God wants us to do. We need to be open to, and obedient to, the voice of the Holy Spirit as he leads us. ❖

PRAYER

Dear God, please help us to be obedient in action as well as knowledge. Please help us to know what we should do, and help us to do it. Amen.

UNFAILING LOVE, GREAT COMPASSION

- What do you need to do in order for God to forgive you for sin?
- How does God show compassion?

Have mercy on me, O God, according to your unfailing love; according to your great compassion blot out my transgressions. Wash away all my iniquity and cleanse me from my sin ... Create in me a pure heart, O God, and renew a steadfast spirit within me.

PSALM 51:1–2,10

King David had sinned with Bathsheba. He then sent her husband, Uriah, to the front of the battlefield and ordered the other soldiers to move away from him so that he would be killed.

This story is one of the most scandalous stories in the Bible. It would be difficult to bounce back after a sequence of such sins, but as we see in Psalm 51, David did. David fell to his knees and prayed to God. David begged God for mercy, believing in God's unfailing love and great compassion.

If David could confess his awful sins and be forgiven, then so can we. God promises that he will forgive our sins. All we have to do is ask. No matter what you've done, you too can count on God's unfailing love and great compassion. No matter what offense you've committed, you can be forgiven. All you have to do is confess your sins to God and ask for his forgiveness. ✤

PRAYER

Dear God, thank you for your unfailing love and great compassion. Please forgive us of our sins and renew a steadfast spirit within us. Amen.

day233

A FRIEND LIKE YOU

- When you hear the words "good friend," what names or descriptions pop into your head?
- What's the worst thing a friend can do? Explain.

Many claim to have unfailing love, but a faithful person who can find? PROVERBS 20:6

Having a BFF sounds great, but it's not always possible to be best friends forever. Unfortunately, friendships don't run smoothly all the time. There are bound to be bumps in the road, conflicts, arguments and misunderstandings that can disrupt the bond of friendship between two people.

The secret to a faithful, lasting friendship is to make sure that conflicts and misunderstandings don't have a chance to take root. In Ephesians 4:26, the apostle Paul instructs us not to let the sun go down on our anger. That's good advice. When we have a conflict with a friend, we need to talk it through as soon as possible. We cannot give grudges time to build.

As Christians, we have a chance to honor God with the way we treat our friends. Proverbs 20:6 says faithful friends are hard to find. If we can be the kind of friends who are trustworthy, encouraging and honest, we will stand out from others.

The more people see what good friends we are, the more they'll be drawn to us. If they look closely enough, they'll see our friendships are rooted in something deeper than popularity. ✤

PRAYER

Dear God, thank you for the faithful friends you've given us. Bless our efforts to be faithful friends to others. We will give you all the glory. Amen.

GOAL!

- What was the last goal you set for yourself? Did you reach it? If so, how? If not, why not?
- What did you learn from that experience that you can use the next time you try to achieve a goal?

In all your ways submit to him, and he will make your paths straight.   PROVERBS 3:6

Ready or not, for most of us the new school year is starting up. And with it comes a whole new set of opportunities. If we take advantage of them, we could have the best year yet. The secret is setting the right goals. Here are some things to consider in planning goals for the year.

First, remember your priorities. God comes first. That's important because Proverbs 3:6 says if you put him first, he will help you with everything that comes after. If you're setting goals, it's good to have the all-knowing Creator of the universe helping you.

Second, be realistic. Consider your schedule. If your goals require a lot of time, figure out where it will come from. What might you need to sacrifice in order to work toward your goals?

Third, stretch yourself. Step outside your comfort zone. Test yourself for skills you may not be aware of. Try out for a play. Join a club. Run for student council.

Fourth, do not let failure have the last word. If you set ambitious goals, you may not accomplish them on your first try—or your second or third. That doesn't make you a failure. Learn from your mistakes, adjust your strategies and try again. ❖

PRAYER

Dear God, thank you for the new school year and the fresh start it gives. Give us the wisdom to choose goals that honor you, as well as the strength and endurance to reach them. Amen.

day**235**

SALT AND LIGHT

- Why is salt a good illustration of what Christians can do in this world?
- Why is light a good illustration of what Christians can do in this world?

"You are the salt of the earth. But if the salt loses its saltiness, how can it be made salty again? It is no longer good for anything, except to be thrown out and trampled underfoot. You are the light of the world. A town built on a hill cannot be hidden. Neither do people light a lamp and put it under a bowl. Instead they put it on its stand, and it gives light to everyone in the house." MATTHEW 5:13–15

Is it a compliment to be called "salt"? How about "light"? It must be, since that's what Jesus wants his followers to be.

Salt doesn't make itself known in a bold way, but it changes whatever it comes into contact with. It brings out goodness. That's the kind of influence God wants us to have—at school, in the office, around the neighborhood. He wants us to influence those around us, not in a showy, look-at-me way, but in subtle ways. What we say, what we do, the way we treat other students, the way we treat teachers, the way we go about our work—all of it matters.

If we live in a way that's pleasing to God, people will notice. Even better, some of them may get the courage to follow our example. In that way, we bring out goodness in others.

As light, we reflect God's goodness on others. We treat them as he instructs in his Word. We let them know through our actions and words that we care about them and that God cares about them.

If we commit ourselves to the principles of Matthew 5, we'll discover what God can do with a little salt and light. ✤

PRAYER

Dear God, thank you for giving us such key roles in your work here on earth. Give us the wisdom, courage and creativity to help people in need—at work and at school. Amen.

day236

HONORABLE WORK

- What's the hardest test or assignment you've ever had? What made it so difficult?
- Why is it tempting to give half-hearted efforts on some assignments?

All hard work brings a profit, but mere talk leads only to poverty.   Proverbs 14:23

In the story of creation in Genesis 2, one important verse often gets overlooked: "The Lord God took the man and put him in the Garden of Eden to work it and take care of it" (v. 15). Even from the beginning, humans had a job to do. We were designed to work. That's why we feel a sense of satisfaction for a job well done. We feel fulfilled because we're doing what we were made to do.

The urge to get out of work, to take a shortcut or to do less than our best is unnatural. It's part of the sinful nature that came after Adam and Eve's disobedience.

When we work hard—whether it's at a job, at home, in school or on the sports field—we honor God. Impressive results are nice. Who wouldn't like straight A's? But results are not as important as effort. If you give our best effort at something, God is pleased.

A strong work ethic can also be a silent witness. Co-workers notice. Teachers notice. Other kids notice. They may not say anything, but they make a mental note. We earn respect for ourselves and the Lord we serve. ✤

PRAYER

Dear God, thank you for giving us the ability to think, reason and accomplish complicated tasks. We commit ourselves to honoring you with our work. Amen.

A HELPING HAND

- If you've ever been a new kid at school, who reached out to you? What did that mean to you?
- What might keep some kids from reaching out to others?

Carry each other's burdens, and in this way you will fulfill the law of Christ.

GALATIANS 6:2

There's one thing everyone takes to school that can't be carried in backpacks. Galatians 6:2 calls them "burdens." We call them problems, issues, weaknesses or fears. Some people carry more than others, but we all have them. And they can make school a miserable place to be.

That's why God calls those of us who follow him to help lighten other people's loads. If we want to honor him, we can reach out to people who are struggling. We can do something about the needs we see.

New kids need someone to show them the ropes. Bullied kids need someone to stand up for them. Shy kids need someone to bring them out of their shells. Ignored kids need someone to notice them. Lonely kids need someone to include them. Hurting kids need someone to listen to them. Younger kids need someone to ease their fears. Older kids need someone to encourage them. You can't be all things to all people, but you can help more kids than you might imagine.

An amazing thing happens when you start to carry other people's burdens: God puts people in your life to help carry yours. ✤

PRAYER

Dear God, make us instruments of your goodness. Bless our efforts to carry the burdens of others and make life easier for them. We will give you all the praise and glory for it. Amen.

day238

OUR RESPONSIBILITY TO AUTHORITY

- Who was your favorite teacher? Why?
- What is the difference between a good teacher and a bad teacher?

The authorities that exist have been established by God. Consequently, whoever rebels against the authority is rebelling against what God has instituted, and those who do so will bring judgment on themselves.   ROMANS 13:1–2

Most people have a "horrible teacher" story—the tale of a time when they were falsely accused, unfairly punished, grossly mistreated or just plain misunderstood by an authority at school. Some of the stories may be true. Some may be exaggerated. Some may be completely made up. Whatever the case, many kids enjoy getting whatever revenge they can on teachers they don't like.

This is an area in which Christians can really stand out. The fact is, it doesn't matter whether we like certain teachers or not. God has put them in positions of authority in our lives for a reason. The way we treat them reflects our attitude toward him. If we obey them, we obey God. If we honor them, we honor God.

The best way to show honor and respect in the classroom is to listen. Give your teachers your full attention. Listen to what they say. Respond when it's appropriate. Ask relevant questions. Be respectful when you speak. Obey the class rules. But don't be fake or insincere. Teachers can smell a phony "teacher's pet" a mile away.

Remind yourself who *really* gets honored when you honor your teachers. Think of it as a way of worshiping God. ✤

> **PRAYER**

Dear God, thank you for the authority you have put in our lives. Though we may not always like it, we know that obeying authority honors you. Help us show the authority figures in our lives the respect they deserve. Amen.

BUILDING BETTER RELATIONSHIPS

- How many friends do you have? How many really *good* friends do you have?
- What's the difference between a friend and a really good friend?

A friend loves at all times, and a brother is born for a time of adversity. PROVERBS 17:17

Do you know the difference between a friend and an acquaintance? A friend is someone you respect, someone you enjoy being around, someone you share a bond with, someone whose happiness means a lot to you, someone who fills an important role in your life. An acquaintance might be someone you hang out with occasionally, someone who makes you laugh or someone you see around school a lot.

Sometimes it's easy to get the two confused. We assume that if we hang out with someone a couple of times, we become friends. But friendship is much more involved than that. To be friends with someone means to make that person a priority in your life. It means to be there when that person needs you. It means to notice when something is wrong and work to help make it right. It means to bring out the best in that person.

If you have a good friend, you should be thankful. They are more valuable than money. If you can *be* a good friend, that's even better. If you're not sure how to do that, check your Bible. God has filled his Word with instructions on how to love others. ♣

PRAYER

Dear God, thank you for the wisdom and examples of genuine friendship you've given us in your Word. Help us keep those things in mind as we try to build friendships that honor you. Amen.

THE (BIG) FAMILY OF GOD

- How do you think God wants us to treat the older people in our church family?
- Name an older person whose company you enjoy.

Do not rebuke an older man harshly, but exhort him as if he were your father. Treat younger men as brothers, older women as mothers, and younger women as sisters, with absolute purity. 1 TIMOTHY 5:1-2

God wants believers to act like one big family, to love and care for one another. We know that God wants us to honor our mother and father, but these verses take this commandment one big step further. God wants us to treat every older woman like she is our mother and every older man like he is our father. God wants us to honor and care about all the members of this big believer family, especially the older members.

This caring includes being respectful. God wants us to listen to these older voices. Sometimes, caring just means spending time with someone. It also means lending a helping hand. Older people often struggle to do tasks that we find simple, like mowing the lawn or shoveling snow.

God tells us to care for these people because it's good for them. But it's also good for us. When we care for older people, we learn so much about love, life and God. When we obey God by caring for older people, everyone benefits. ✤

PRAYER

Dear God, please show us a way to help an older person today. Please help us to be patient, respectful and caring to everyone, especially to our elders. Amen.

THE HARDEST COMMANDMENT OF ALL

- Which of God's commandments do you find the hardest to obey?
- How does God want us to treat people we don't get along with?

"But to you who are listening I say: Love your enemies, do good to those who hate you."

LUKE 6:27

We all know that people can be cruel sometimes. No matter how hard we try, or how nice we are to others, at some point someone will be mean to us. Sometimes people are unkind to us *because* we are kind to others and because we love Jesus.

But God wants us to love everyone. Even our enemies. *Especially* our enemies.

It's easy to love the people who love us back. But to love our enemies, we really need to draw on God's power. The truth is that we can't love our enemies on our own. We need to ask God for help. We need to let God's own love for these enemies move through us.

And when it's really hard, we need to remember that the love we're giving to the person who is mean to us might be the only love that person gets. Our enemy might meet God through us. ✣

PRAYER

Dear God, please help us to forgive people who are unkind to us. Please help us to love our enemies, to care about them and to show them kindness. Please let your love shine through us. Amen.

day242

RELIGION IN ACTION

- What do you think of when you hear the word *needy*?
- Who is someone you know who needs help?

Religion that God our Father accepts as pure and faultless is this: to look after orphans and widows in their distress and to keep oneself from being polluted by the world.

JAMES 1:27

Love is a great feeling. But love is an even greater action. Jesus gave away a lot of love when he walked on this earth, but there was a lot more to his love than words and feelings. He helped people who needed his help.

In this Bible verse, James is asking us to do the same. James mentions orphans (children without parents) and widows (women whose husbands have passed away) because at the time that he wrote this verse, those were the people who needed the most help.

Orphans and widows still do need help, and so do lots of other people. Can you think of a person at school who you could help? Can you think of an older person who might enjoy spending some time with you?

If we ask Jesus to show us someone in need, someone who needs our help, he will. This might mean sharing a favorite toy, sharing our food or spending time with someone who is lonely. ✤

PRAYER

Dear God, thank you for making sure we have everything we need. Please show us someone we can help today. Please help us understand how we can help and have the courage to do what you want us to do. Amen.

SEEK JUSTICE

- Describe a time when you saw someone being treated unfairly. How did this make you feel?
- What do you think of when you hear the word *justice*?

"Learn to do right; seek justice. Defend the oppressed. Take up the cause of the fatherless; plead the case of the widow." ISAIAH 1:17

God tells us in this verse to seek justice. Justice means fairness. We seek justice when we both *believe* in what is right and *work* to make sure people are treated fairly. God wants us all to shine and to glorify him as his creations. But when people are oppressed, or held back, by unfair treatment, they are unable to shine the way they are designed to.

Think of Martin Luther King Jr., who devoted his life to the Civil Rights Movement. He dedicated his hard work to make sure that people of all races were treated fairly. Now, you might not give a speech in front of thousands of people or lead a march tomorrow, but you can work to treat people fairly and to be kind and helpful to people who have been treated unfairly.

In this verse, God mentions children without fathers and women without husbands because those were examples of people who were treated unfairly in Isaiah's time. There are people in our time too who are treated unfairly, and God wants us to care about them. ❖

PRAYER

Dear God, show us how to help people who are being treated unfairly. Help us to help others shine the way you designed them to. Give us the courage to seek justice. Amen.

day244

september 1

THE FIRST COMMANDMENT WITH A PROMISE

- How do you "honor" someone?
- Who do you honor in your life?

"Honor your father and mother"—which is the first commandment with a promise.

EPHESIANS 6:2

In this verse, the apostle Paul reminds his young readers that God wants them to honor their parents. This commandment is first given in the Old Testament, and it is the first commandment given with a promise—"that you may live long and that it may go well with you in the land the LORD your God is giving you" (Deuteronomy 5:16). The mentioned "land" is the promised land, Canaan, which God promised to Abraham's descendants.

This promise also applies to children today. Your parents were not given to you by accident. God has a plan for your family, and God chose your parents especially for you. He gave them the difficult task of teaching and training you to be a man or woman of God.

Your God-given job is to honor the parents you have. You do this by trusting that God will help your parents do their job, that your parents have your best interests at heart and that your parents know what is best for you.

But what if your parents have made some mistakes? No parent is perfect, but no matter what your parent has done, you still need to pray for them, love them as best you can and honor them by wanting what is best for them. ♣

PRAYER

Dear God, thank you for parents. Please forgive us when we don't honor and obey them. Please help us to love and honor you by loving and honoring them. Amen.

day245

THE ULTIMATE AUTHORITY

- Have you ever been put in charge of a group of people? Describe that experience.
- How does it feel when an authority figure is unkind?

Masters, provide your slaves with what is right and fair, because you know that you also have a Master in heaven.   COLOSSIANS 4:1

Slavery was a normal part of life when Paul wrote the book of Colossians. Slavery is no longer a normal or acceptable part of life for most of us, but we can draw a parallel between the situation described in this verse and situations we find today.

The key here is that one person has authority over other people. This is a common occurrence for almost everyone. Most people have a boss at work. Some of us are the bosses at work, but we still have to obey the laws of our state or country. Kids are subject to teachers or others in authority, but they can also be leaders in school and in church. Whatever the specific situation, God wants us to treat people fairly, because in God's eyes, we are all equal. God is the one who places people in different positions of authority over others. But God is the ultimate authority over all of us, and we all answer to God.

Let's say you earn the position of stage manager for a play. God does not want you to bark orders at people, be cruel or use your power to hurt people and make them feel bad. Quite the opposite. God wants you to use whatever position you are in to show his love to others.

God calls us to care for our co-workers, our peers and everyone else we come in contact with. ✣

PRAYER

Dear God, please help us remember that you are our ultimate authority. Please help us care for and be kind to others, especially those you have put us in charge of. Amen.

day246

O GRACIOUS AND MERCIFUL ONE

- Think of a time when you deserved to be punished for something but weren't. How did you feel?
- Share something that you know about the Israelites from the Old Testament.

"But in your great mercy you did not put an end to them or abandon them, for you are a gracious and merciful God." NEHEMIAH 9:31

This verse from Nehemiah comes from the longest prayer recorded in the entire Bible. In this prayer, the Israelites confess that they have been sinful, rebellious and evil, and they praise God for never abandoning them.

If anyone was familiar with God's grace and mercy, it was the Israelites. Over and over again, throughout the Bible, God would rescue his people and set them straight, and they would turn against him. He would rescue them again and set them straight, and they would turn against him.

Sound familiar? We do the same thing. God has saved us. He has forgiven us. He has given us his Word. And yet, time and time again, we turn away. But he is always there for us when we need more rescuing.

God has shown incredible mercy to us by sending his Son to die in our place and forgiving us of our sins. God doesn't treat us the way we deserve to be treated. Instead, he treats us with mercy, showering us with constant grace. ✤

PRAYER

Dear God, thank you for your grace and mercy. Thank you for not treating us the way we deserve to be treated. Amen.

HE WHO IS HOLY

- Name something that disgusts you, something you can't stand to be around. Why do you react so strongly to it?
- How does that compare to the way God feels about sin?

In the year that King Uzziah died, I saw the Lord, high and exalted, seated on a throne; and the train of his robe filled the temple. Above him were seraphim, each with six wings: With two wings they covered their faces, with two they covered their feet, and with two they were flying. And they were calling to one another: "Holy, holy, holy is the LORD Almighty; the whole earth is full of his glory." ISAIAH 6:1–3

If you ask ten different people at church what the word *holy* means, you'll probably get ten different answers. It's important to understand the definition, though, because that word is going to be a big part of our future. Revelation 4:8 tells us that four creatures will stand in front of God's throne in heaven and say, "'Holy, holy, holy is the Lord God Almighty,' who was, and is, and is to come"—*for all eternity.*

We cannot understand God without understanding his holiness. To be holy is to be completely separate from sin. It's more than just taking a strong stand against sin. It's more than just judging people who do evil. The fact that God is holy means sin cannot exist where he is—just as darkness cannot exist where the sun is.

God's holiness is what makes salvation necessary. Anyone who is guilty of sin cannot be in God's presence. And since we're all guilty of sin, we need Jesus' perfect sacrifice to make us pure and reconnect us with God.

Praising God for his holiness should be a big part of our worship. Thanking him for his gift of salvation should be a big part of our praise. ✤

PRAYER

Dear God, we praise you for your holiness. You make us aware of our sin and stand willing to forgive us and make us pure. Thank you for loving us in your holiness. Amen.

day248

THE ONE WHO IS KNOWABLE

- How would your friends describe you? Would you describe yourself the same way?
- What's the best way to get to know someone?

I keep asking that the God of our Lord Jesus Christ, the glorious Father, may give you the Spirit of wisdom and revelation, so that you may know him better.   EPHESIANS 1:17

God is infinite; humans are extremely limited. God exists outside of time; humans live only in the present. God is beyond imagination; humans know only what our brains tell us. God is a spirit; humans can see only physical things. How can we possibly know anything about God?

First, we can know God because he has made the effort to reveal himself to us. He gave us his Word, which tells us what he's done and what he will do. He communicates to us through our limited senses, the only way we can understand him.

Second, we can know God because we are created in his image. The fact that we can think and love and make our own choices reflects our likeness to God. When we see those aspects of ourselves, we understand a little more about him.

Third, we can know God because he doesn't change. The information we have on him will always apply. He is now as he always has been and as he always will be.

The opportunity to get to know God and form a personal relationship with him is the greatest invitation we'll ever receive. If you've already accepted it yourself, you probably know others who haven't. How can you help them get to know God? ✤

PRAYER

Dear God, we praise you for your unchanging nature. Thank you for not making us guess at how you feel or what you're like. Thank you for allowing us to know you. Amen.

day249

THE SOURCE OF LOVE

- Do you think you are ever hard to love?
- Think of someone who is hard to love. What would it take for you to be able to show that person love?

Dear friends, let us love one another, for love comes from God. Everyone who loves has been born of God and knows God. Whoever does not love does not know God, because God is love. 1 JOHN 4:7–8

What if someone told you they loved you, but then spread a terrible rumor about you behind your back? Would you believe that person? Maybe if it happened once, you could forgive and move on. But if it happened over and over again, you'd have a good reason to doubt that person's love.

As believers, we are supposed to love others as we love ourselves. Yet often we are guilty of treating people in unloving ways. We all do it, and that's a shame, because it doesn't have to be that way. In fact, there's no reason for it to be that way.

We can use the excuse that we're only human, but it's not human love that we rely on. According to 1 John 4:8, the God we serve *is* love. Everything that is loving or shows love comes from him. He is the source of all love.

As his children, we have constant access to his love. When we have a hard time feeling love for other people, we only need to ask God for his love. That's what he wants us to do. If we're not showing God's love to others, we give people a reason to doubt whether God's love is really in us or if God's love is even real. And once doubt creeps in, trust is hard to regain. ❖

PRAYER

Dear God, thank you for loving us. Thank you for making your love available to us. Give us your love for others when we can't do it ourselves. Amen.

day250

THE ONE WHO IS ALWAYS NEAR

- Have you ever felt abandoned by God? Explain.
- Some people say, "If you feel far away from God, guess who moved?" What does that saying mean to you?

We praise you, God, we praise you, for your Name is near; people tell of your wonderful deeds.　　　　　　　　　　　　　　　　　　　　　　　　PSALM 75:1

It's interesting that this verse about God's nearness comes from the book of Psalms. Elsewhere in the book, we find several examples of psalmists feeling abandoned by God, or at least feeling distant from him. Psalm 13:1 and Psalm 22:1 are just two examples.

Yet Psalm 75:1, not to mention many, *many* other passages, shows us that those feelings of abandonment are just our human emotions playing tricks on us. Some people think that if hard times come, it's because God has left. But God never promised us that life would be easy. In fact, he makes it clear that hard times are unavoidable.

That doesn't change the fact that God will not abandon his people. We never have to ask, "God, where were you while I was going through that difficult time?" He never left. He was there every step of the way.

If you ever doubt God's closeness, pray. Tell God how you feel. Ask him to make himself known to you. He will answer your prayer, although it may not be immediately. Sometimes faith is a matter of believing in God's faithfulness and closeness even when there is no sense of his presence. In those cases, we need to remember, like the psalmist, what God has done in the past and affirm his faithfulness today. ✤

PRAYER

Dear God, if we whispered this prayer, you would still be close enough to hear every word. Thank you for never leaving our side. Amen.

day251

OUR HEAVENLY FATHER

- What does a good father do?
- How would you explain that God is your heavenly Father to someone who never had a good experience with his or her earthly father?

"This, then, is how you should pray: 'Our Father in heaven, hallowed be your name.'"

MATTHEW 6:9

The ideal father is one who provides for his family and protects them. He is brave, strong and compassionate. He knows how to do just about everything. He is a role model to his sons, showing them how to be a man. To his daughters, he provides an example of how men should treat women and shows them what to look for in a husband. He instills a godly set of values and a solid work ethic in his children.

Unfortunately, we don't live in an ideal world. Even the best earthly fathers have flaws. And the worst can do unspeakable harm to their children. Many kids have fathers who deserted them, abused them or abused others in front of them. As a result, their image of a father—earthly or heavenly—isn't a very good one. They can't imagine any father who will truly love and protect them.

God understands that, but he won't be deterred by it. He wants to protect us and give us good things. He invites us to call him not just "Father" but "Daddy," which is much more intimate. Our heavenly Father is compassionate and full of mercy. He wants to heal us, comfort us and encourage us. He wants to be our loving Daddy. ✤

PRAYER

Dear Father, thank you for the privilege of calling you "Father." Thank you for adopting us and treating us as your beloved children. Guide us as we try to bring glory to our family name. Amen.

day252

OUR ROCK AND FORTRESS

- Have you ever built your own fort? If so, how did you design it?
- How did you feel when you were inside it? Were you trying to keep anyone out?

Truly he is my rock and my salvation; he is my fortress, I will not be shaken. PSALM 62:6

In Old Testament times, having a refuge was important to survival. Depending on the circumstances, people could go to different places for refuge. For example, many small, unprotected villages were built around large stronghold cities. When an enemy attacked, the people of the villages would flee to the stronghold city. The city's high towers and fortified walls gave them protection from enemies who were many times their size. As long as the people stayed inside the stronghold city, they were safe.

King David's fortress, on the other hand, was probably a mountainous area with caves and steep heights—a hiding place from his enemies.

The fact that God is our rock and fortress means we can run to him whenever our enemies threaten to overwhelm us. Sometimes those enemies will be real flesh-and-blood people who want to harm us. Other times, though, they may be difficult circumstances or health issues or painful emotions.

If we had to fight those enemies on our own, we would be in trouble. We would have no protection on any side. We would be vulnerable. When we run to God, though, he acts as our stronghold. He gives us comfort and security in the midst of our daily battles. ❖

PRAYER

Dear God, thank you for being our fortress. Thank you for giving us a place to run to when we feel threatened. Remind us to turn to you whenever attacks come. Amen.

WRONG FOR WRONG IS WRONG

- Share a time when you wanted to get some payback.
- How are believers supposed to treat one another?

Make sure that nobody pays back wrong for wrong, but always strive to do what is good for each other and for everyone else.   1 THESSALONIANS 5:15

In this section of his letter to the Thessalonians, Paul is explaining to new believers how they are supposed to treat one another. Believers are not supposed to seek revenge when wronged. Instead, we are to always strive to do what is good for one another, and for everybody else too.

A desire for revenge is incompatible with the Christian life for several reasons:

Wanting and getting revenge wastes time and energy. We could be spending our time and energy helping others and serving God.

If someone wrongs us and we wrong them back, we have sinned. We have allowed someone else to lead us into sin, sin which we will be accountable for.

When we seek revenge, we do damage to the entire church. We hurt more people than just the person we are trying to hurt.

Even though at times it can be difficult, God asks us to love and forgive one another. We need to work together as the body of Christ, so that we can best serve God. ✤

PRAYER

Dear God, please help us to forgive people who have wronged us. Please help us to always strive to do what is good for one another. Amen.

day254

DO NOT SEEK REVENGE

- How do you feel when you are holding a grudge against someone?
- How is it possible to hold a grudge against someone and love him or her at the same time?

"Do not seek revenge or bear a grudge against anyone among your people, but love your neighbor as yourself. I am the LORD.'"   LEVITICUS 19:18

This verse from Leviticus shows us that from the very beginning, God did not want his people seeking revenge or holding grudges. Even way back then, God was instructing his followers to love their neighbors as themselves.

And still today, God's people should not seek revenge. God's people should be motivated by love and should strive to glorify God with every thought they think and every action they take. The idea of revenge cannot mesh with love or with glorifying God.

Revenge is a sin, and just like any other sin, Christians must work to avoid it. We need to avoid the temptation of revenge. We need to pray for strength to avoid this sin. And if we do make a mistake and think vengeful thoughts or actually take revenge on someone, we need to ask for forgiveness and turn away from this sinful behavior. A vengeful attitude will only separate us from God. ✤

PRAYER

Dear God, please help us to not seek revenge or hold grudges against people. Please help us to forgive others as we have been forgiven and to love our neighbors as ourselves. Amen.

day255

NO PAYBACK!

- Share a time when someone said something about you that wasn't true.
- How does God want us to react when people tell lies about us?

Do not say, "I'll do to them as they have done to me; I'll pay them back for what they did."
PROVERBS 24:29

Imagine that your friend is jealous because you aced your Spanish test. So she tells everyone that you used your phone to look up the answers during the test. Of course, this isn't true, and it was wrong of her to say this about you. And you could retaliate by spreading an equally damaging lie about her. But then you will have sinned too.

This verse from Proverbs tells us not to say, "I'll do to her what she did to me!" As believers, we're not supposed to be seeking payback. We're not supposed to be retaliating at all when we are wronged. We are supposed to forgive and walk in love.

In extreme cases, the authorities will work out an offender's consequences. In all cases, God will work out an offender's consequences. In no case are we to do it. Believers are never supposed to pay back evil for evil. ✤

PRAYER

Dear God, please help us to not seek payback when we are wronged. Please help us to give our hurt and anger to you instead of acting on it. Amen.

THE PERFECT EXAMPLE

- In what ways did Jesus set an example for us during his time on earth?
- Why didn't Jesus take revenge on the people who persecuted him?

To this you were called, because Christ suffered for you, leaving you an example, that you should follow in his steps. "He committed no sin, and no deceit was found in his mouth." When they hurled their insults at him, he did not retaliate; when he suffered, he made no threats. Instead, he entrusted himself to him who judges justly. 1 PETER 2:21–23

As followers of Jesus, we may be wronged even though we don't deserve it. We may be persecuted. We may be made fun of. But we are not to seek revenge. Jesus himself gave us the best possible example of this.

The people and soldiers made fun of Jesus. They pounded a crown of thorns onto his head, mocking his kinghood. They spat on him. They stole and destroyed his clothes. And he never retaliated.

Jesus has the power of God. He could have called down an army of angels and completely destroyed his persecutors. But he didn't. Instead, he calmly relied on God. And even as he hung on the cross dying, he used his precious breath to pray for the people who were crucifying him.

If we ever need an example of turning the other cheek, this is it. Jesus gives us a perfect example of relying on the Father to set things right. Because we love Jesus and are grateful for what he did for us on that day, we need to make every effort to follow this example. ✤

PRAYER

Dear God, thank you for the cross. Thank you for Jesus' example. Please help us to avoid vengeful attitudes. Please help us to forgive and love those who wrong us. Amen.

ROOM FOR GOD'S WRATH

- What does it mean to be *just*?
- Give some examples of evidence of God's power.

Do not take revenge, my dear friends, but leave room for God's wrath, for it is written: "It is mine to avenge; I will repay," says the Lord.   ROMANS 12:19

One of the best parts of choosing to live for God is that it sets us free from vengefulness. Feeling vengeful takes up a lot of energy. It hurts us. Anger and scheming wear a person out and are ultimately unsatisfying.

But because we follow God, we never need to seek revenge. God promises us that he will be the Judge. He will avenge. He will repay. Obviously, he will do a far better job of it than we ever could, and we get to leave it in his capable hands. Why would we want to worry about our measly revenge plots when the Lord of all creation is going to take care of all that for us?

When we find it hard to forgive someone, we can remember that God will take care of it. God has set us free from the pain and anger that comes with a grudge. We serve a just God. We can trust that he will take care of it. ❖

PRAYER

Dear God, thank you for being a just God. Thank you for setting us free from vengefulness. Please help us to put our pain and anger in your hands and leave it there. Amen.

day258

NO LAUGHING MATTER

- When you hear something shocking about someone, do you believe it? Why or why not?
- Has anyone ever spread a false rumor about you? How did it (or would it) make you feel?

"Do not go about spreading slander among your people. Do not do anything that endangers your neighbor's life. I am the LORD.'"　　　　　　　　LEVITICUS 19:16

When you slander someone, you say something about them that isn't true, something that damages their reputation. Slander is a form of lying, and it is a sin. Slander hurts people. For this reason, slander is illegal in many countries and states. It is certainly against God's law. It is truly no laughing matter.

Slander can be a tricky monster. We may participate in slandering someone without even realizing we are doing it. What we think may be news about someone could be packed full of dangerous lies.

When you hear something about someone that may be shocking or strange, realize that there's a very good chance that it isn't true. Do not reward a gossiper by reacting to their gossip. You don't even have to participate in the conversation. Walking away is always an option. And whatever you do, don't repeat what you've heard. This never helps anyone, and it certainly doesn't glorify God. ✤

PRAYER

Dear God, please help us to think before we speak. Please help us to not gossip, to not tell lies and to never slander anyone. Amen.

FALSE REPORTS

- Why do you think it is so hard to stop gossip from spreading after it has started?
- How can you avoid gossiping?

"Do not spread false reports. Do not help a guilty person by being a malicious witness."

EXODUS 23:1

To gossip means to share someone else's personal details with others, often without knowing if the details are true. People who gossip want attention, so they often exaggerate, sensationalize or simply create the gossip from scratch in order to get more attention.

Gossip hurts people. God doesn't want us to hurt people. He wants us to control our tongues and to think before we speak. Just imagine how you would feel if you learned that people were discussing the personal details of your life—and not even getting them right!

There are several ways to avoid gossiping. The best way is to simply physically walk away. You can make quite a statement without saying a word. If this is not possible, put a hand up and say, "Please stop." You don't have to say anything else. If the gossiper is a Christian, you could say something like, "It sounds like this person needs some prayer support. We should pray for them right now." You can stop a gossiper in their tracks. ❖

PRAYER

Dear God, please forgive us for the gossiping we've done in the past, and help us to not gossip in the future. Amen.

CHOICE MORSELS

- What is the tastiest thing you can think of eating right now?
- How do you feel when you are about to hear a secret about someone else?

The words of a gossip are like choice morsels; they go down to the inmost parts.

PROVERBS 26:22

Sin is usually very attractive. The serpent in the Garden of Eden didn't say, "This fruit is only average. It won't do much for you." On the contrary, he made the fruit incredibly attractive to Eve by telling her it would make her like God.

The enemy is no dummy—he knows what it takes to get us to misbehave. He knows that the more attractive sin is, the more likely we are to choose sin over obeying God. And gossip is no different than other sins. It can be very attractive. It can seem almost irresistible.

This verse from Proverbs compares gossip to a choice morsel, something we would really love to eat, like a warm, gooey, chocolate chip cookie, or a dish of cold, creamy ice cream.

But just because something tastes good doesn't mean we should eat it. Gossip, like all sin, is poisonous. We need to recognize that the attractiveness of gossip is a lie. ♣

PRAYER

Dear God, please protect us from the attractiveness of sin. Please help us to see sin for what it really is. Please help us to not gossip. Amen.

day261

STOP THROWING WOOD ON THE FIRE

- Why do people gossip?
- What happens when you refuse to participate in gossip?

Without wood a fire goes out; without a gossip a quarrel dies down. PROVERBS 26:20

If you have ever sat around a campfire on a cool autumn night, you know how important it is to keep adding wood to the fire. Once you stop adding wood, the fire dies.

This verse from Proverbs teaches us that gossip and arguments have the same relationship as wood and fire. Gossip will feed an argument and keep it burning hot. But if we remove gossip, if we stop gossiping, the argument will die.

When people are caught up in an argument, they will often use whatever weapons they can to defeat their opponent. This includes gossip. People will gossip in an attempt to sway people toward their side of the argument. Some people will gossip in an attempt to keep the argument going because they like the drama. None of this is okay.

The Bible tells us that instead of getting caught up in quarrels, we should look for ways to make peace. When gossip stops, peace follows, because there is nothing left to fuel the fire. As you spend time with your friends and family today, look for ways to make peace by refusing to be a gossip. ✤

PRAYER

Dear God, thank you for your proverbs that give us wisdom and guidance in our lives. Please help us to remember this proverb and to avoid feeding a fire with gossip. Amen.

GOSSIP-PROOF YOUR FRIENDSHIPS

- Who are your closest friends?
- What does gossip do to friendship?

A perverse person stirs up conflict, and a gossip separates close friends. PROVERBS 16:28

There are few things more valuable than a close friend. And there are few things that can destroy a friendship as quickly and efficiently as gossip can. Friendships are built on trust, and gossip shatters trust instantly. Think about it: If you found out your good friend was telling other people personal things about you, how could you ever trust that friend again?

We all know people who like to stir up trouble. These people know that one of the easiest ways to do this is to spread gossip. They enjoy creating drama and turning friends against friends. God calls these individuals "perverse"—probably not a word you want to use to describe yourself!

If someone is gossiping about a friend, don't listen; walk away. If you do hear gossip, don't believe it. Certainly don't repeat it. No one can make you participate in gossip. And if you are one of the few people who refuses to do so, your friends will take notice. ✤

PRAYER

Dear God, thank you for the close friends that you have given us. Please protect these friendships and help us to avoid gossip. Amen.

day263

GOOD FRIEND HOW-TO

- Which of your friends do you trust the most?
- What does it mean to be trustworthy?

A gossip betrays a confidence, but a trustworthy person keeps a secret.   PROVERBS 11:13

What does it mean to be a good friend? Part of being a good friend is honoring your friend's trust. If someone confides in you, be grateful for that person's trust, and honor it by keeping secrets secret. Never betray your friends' trust by gossiping about them or sharing their secrets.

However, if a friend ever tells you that they are in danger or that someone is hurting them, you need to tell a trustworthy adult, such as a parent or teacher, immediately. Friends protect each other, and if you know that a friend is being abused, bullied or threatened, you need to tell someone who can help. Similarly, if a friend is hurting themselves or doing something dangerous, then you need to tell someone who can help. This is not gossiping or tattling. This is being a good friend.

Being a good friend means looking out for your friends. ❖

PRAYER

Dear God, thank you for our friends. Please help us to be good friends. Help us to honor our friends' trust. Amen.

day264

A CLEAR CONSCIENCE

- What's the first thing you remember feeling guilty about?
- How easy is it to ignore your conscience?

But in your hearts revere Christ as Lord . . . keeping a clear conscience, so that those who speak maliciously against your good behavior in Christ may be ashamed of their slander.
1 PETER 3:15–16

If you follow Jesus, there's a good chance you're going to rub people the wrong way occasionally. Some may accuse you of being narrow-minded. Others may accuse you of being judgmental. Still others may call you uncaring or gullible.

If you hear those kinds of accusations long enough—or if you hear them from people you like and respect—you may be tempted to start believing them. That's where a clear conscience comes in handy.

If you live your life the way Jesus wants you to live it—loving God with all your heart and loving others as yourself—people will have no reason to question you. If you build a reputation as someone who can be trusted, someone who goes out of their way to help others, someone who's always willing to listen and someone who genuinely cares, people will have no reason to question you. More importantly, you'll have no reason to question yourself.

With a clear conscience, you can make a real difference in the lives of the people around you. ✤

PRAYER

Dear God, thank you for forgiving our sins and giving us a chance to have clear consciences. Help us become the people you want us to be. Amen.

HIDDEN NO MORE

- When was the last time you felt like hiding?
- If we know God sees everything, why do we try to hide our sin from him?

Whoever conceals their sins does not prosper, but the one who confesses and renounces them finds mercy.   PROVERBS 28:13

Have you ever seen a little kid try to hide just by closing her eyes? She thinks if she can't see anyone, no one can see her. That kind of thinking is cute when it's a little kid doing it. When it's someone who should know better, it's a different story.

Why do we try to hide sin from God by closing our eyes to it and pretending it doesn't exist? Why do we hide it from other people and assume God can't see it either? God sees everything. He knows the sin is there, and he knows it's keeping us away from him.

At every moment of every day, God stands ready to forgive us—no matter what we've done. All we have to do is ask him. Trying to hide our sin is a sure way to make a bad situation worse. Confessing our sin and receiving God's mercy is a sure way to feel a giant sense of relief. ✤

PRAYER

Dear God, thank you for the way you treat us when we bring our sins to you. Please help us remember that no matter what we've done, we can always receive forgiveness from you. Amen.

day266

A BROKEN CONSCIENCE

- How can you tell when a little kid has done something wrong?
- How can you tell when someone very close to you has done something wrong?

Such teachings come through hypocritical liars, whose consciences have been seared as with a hot iron. 1 TIMOTHY 4:2

You've heard of a broken leg and a broken nose, but a broken conscience? It can happen. The conscience is that little voice in your head that tells you when you've done something wrong and encourages you to make it right. Even though it's not a part of the *physical* human body, it's as vulnerable as any limb or organ. If you're not careful, your conscience can be weakened to the point that it's no longer useful. And that's a serious problem.

Think of your conscience as a carbon monoxide detector. It senses poisonous influences in your life, influences you may not even be aware of, and warns you about them before it's too late. Without it, you're in trouble.

When you've hurt someone, your conscience bugs you to make it right. When you pick up a damaging personal habit, your conscience prevents you from feeling good about it and encourages you to stop. Without a conscience, your social and personal life suffers.

The best way to keep your conscience healthy is to listen to it. Don't ignore it. Don't roll your eyes at it. Don't silently accuse it of ruining your fun. Listen to it. ✤

PRAYER

Dear God, thank you for creating us with a conscience. Open our ears to what it tells us, and what you tell us through it. Amen.

CALLING THE PLAYS

- Who is the best coach you ever had?
- Why is it sometimes tempting to ignore a coach's advice?

I speak the truth in Christ—I am not lying, my conscience confirms it through the Holy Spirit. ROMANS 9:1

In softball or baseball, coaches give signals to batters and base runners from their positions next to first base and third base. In football, offensive coordinators use a sound system in the players' helmets to give instructions from a booth high above the field. In basketball, coaches call out plays from the sidelines.

The coaches are experts. They have experience, and they can see the big picture. They know what a player has to do to help the team win. The players who follow their coaches' instructions are the ones who succeed. The ones who ignore their coaches usually don't last long.

As Christians, we too have a Coach—a Coach who has a perfect view of our lives, a Coach who knows exactly what we should and shouldn't do, a Coach who offers instructions constantly. The Holy Spirit is our Coach, and the way he communicates is through our conscience.

He nudges us when it's time to take a stand. He triggers guilt feelings when it's time to repent. He gives us a sense of peace inside when things get intense outside. And if we follow his lead, we will have success in pleasing God. ✤

PRAYER

Dear God, thank you for being our Coach and for showing us how to succeed. Please help us remember your instructions. Amen.

CREATURES OF HABIT

- In what ways are you a creature of habit?
- What might someone do to hide a bad habit?

"So do not fear, for I am with you; do not be dismayed, for I am your God. I will strengthen you and help you; I will uphold you with my righteous right hand."   ISAIAH 41:10

A creature of habit is someone who does the same thing over and over again because it's comfortable. For example, some people eat the exact same thing for breakfast every morning. Others drive the same route to school or work every day, even if it's faster to go another way. Creatures of habit don't like it when they have to change their routine. They prefer to stay in their comfort zones.

Though it may seem odd to some people, there's nothing wrong with eating the same cereal or driving the same road every day. But when the habit is something bad, something sinful, it can cause big problems in our relationship with God.

Quitting a habit like that can be tough. We need something to shake us up and make us recognize the negative effects of our habit. That's where our conscience comes in.

The conscience says, "Hey, you don't have to do this anymore. Your habit is hurting you. It's time to step out of your comfort zone and put an end to this. Yes, it will be hard. But if you do it, God will make it worth your while." ♣

PRAYER

Dear God, thank you for loving us enough to confront us when we're hurting ourselves. Please open our eyes to the things we do that displease you. Amen.

GOOD FOR THE SOUL

- What would happen if every criminal in the world suddenly confessed their crimes?
- What keeps people from confessing things they've done?

Then I acknowledged my sin to you and did not cover up my iniquity. I said, "I will confess my transgressions to the LORD." And you forgave the guilt of my sin. PSALM 32:5

It's nice to be thought of as a good person, someone people can trust, depend on and count on to make wise decisions. It's good for our self-image when others compliment our generosity or our helpfulness or some other part of our character.

When the compliments start to flow, though, it's easy to lose sight of some not-so-honorable parts of our character. It's easy to start thinking of ourselves more highly than we should. It's easy to overlook—or start trying to hide—things that might ruin our good reputation.

So we ignore God's command to confess our sins. Admitting that we're not as good as people think we are—or as *we* think we are—is a tough thing to do. It seems like the surest way to blow our cover and ruin our reputation.

Confession, though, actually makes us better people. It's real; there's nothing pretend about it. Admitting our sins to God and asking for his forgiveness changes us from the inside. And that's the kind of change people really notice. ✤

PRAYER

Dear God, thank you for forgiving us and changing us from the inside when we confess our sins. Help us remember that your opinion of us is the only one that really matters. Amen.

UNWASTED OPPORTUNITIES

- Have you ever chosen not to do something and regretted it later? Explain.
- Why do you sometimes choose not to take advantage of what God offers you in his Word?

"If my people, who are called by my name, will humble themselves and pray and seek my face and turn from their wicked ways, then I will hear from heaven, and I will forgive their sin and will heal their land."   2 CHRONICLES 7:14

God is speaking to the Israelites, his chosen people, in this passage. Notice he didn't say, "Start acting right or I'm going to do bad things to you." What he said was, "Follow these instructions because I have some amazing things I want to do for you." He knew all the good things that would happen if the Israelites followed his instructions, and he really wanted them to experience those things.

The same goes for us today. God knows the blessings that are in store for people who turn away from sin to follow him. And he wants us to take advantage of that opportunity. If we don't, we have no one to blame but ourselves. We can't say we didn't know. God gave us his Word so we could see for ourselves what he has to offer.

The Bible is full of stories of people whose lives were changed in incredible ways after they chose to follow God. If we want to enjoy the same kind of changes in our lives, all we have to do is confess our sins and follow after God. ❖

PRAYER

Dear God, thank you for always keeping your promises. Never let us forget the incredible things you offer to people who turn to you. Amen.

WHO'S SORRY NOW?

- How often do you say "I'm sorry"? How often do you mean it?
- How would you react if someone who'd hurt you asked for your forgiveness but didn't seem sorry about hurting you?

While Ezra was praying and confessing, weeping and throwing himself down before the house of God, a large crowd of Israelites — men, women and children — gathered around him. They too wept bitterly.   EZRA 10:1

How many times a day do you hear someone say "Sorry" or "Oops"? Whether it's a forgotten line in the school play, an accidental elbow to the ribs in the hallway or an attempt at humor that went bad, life is full of apology-inspiring situations.

How often are those apologies genuine? That's hard to say. Sometimes the word *sorry* is nothing more than a reflex, a way of moving past a situation as quickly as possible. If someone says, "You hurt my feelings," we say, "Oh, sorry," and expect the matter to be dropped — without a second thought.

That's not the attitude God wants from his people when we confess our sins. He wants us to see the damage we've done and feel the pain we've caused. He wants sin to bother us as much as it does him. More than anything else, though, he wants to relieve our pain and guilt by forgiving us. ✤

PRAYER

Dear God, create in us a proper attitude toward our sin. When we disobey you, help us feel the kind of remorse Ezra and the Israelites felt. Amen.

day272

A CHANGE WILL DO YOU GOOD

- What has been the biggest change in your life in the past year?
- Why does God expect you to change when he forgives you for doing something wrong?

Nevertheless, God's solid foundation stands firm, sealed with this inscription: "The Lord knows those who are his," and, "Everyone who confesses the name of the Lord must turn away from wickedness."　　　　　　　　　　　　　　　　　　2 Timothy 2:19

Some things are pretty easy to change. If you don't like the color of your room, you can repaint it. If you don't like your first name, you can ask people to call you by your middle name or a nickname.

Other changes are more difficult. The apostle Paul tells us that in order to receive God's forgiveness after we sin, we have to repent. That means we have to change the thoughts and actions that caused us to sin in the first place. It's not enough just to say "I'm sorry, God" and move on. We have to show him we feel bad about our sin and want to change.

That's not always an easy thing to do. Some sinful habits are hard to break. The key is to replace bad choices with good ones and old ways of thinking with new ones. Staying away from people or places that have gotten us in trouble in the past is a great strategy. So is saying a quick prayer when we feel our self-control start to slip. Remember, any change is possible with God in our corner. ♣

PRAYER

Dear God, thank you for forgiving us and giving us second chances when we repent of our sin. Show us how to make the changes you want to see in our lives. Amen.

day273

KEEP IT SIMPLE

- Have you ever made a pinky swear? Or heard someone swear on something, like the Bible, in order to be more convincing? What did they swear on?
- Why do you think people expect Jesus' followers to be honest?

"All you need to say is simply 'Yes' or 'No'; anything beyond this comes from the evil one."
MATTHEW 5:37

Isn't it great when God gives us simple instructions? When Jesus spoke these words from Matthew, he was teaching a large crowd. It was common for the people in this crowd to convince others of something by swearing by something else. And it's still common today. You've probably heard someone say, "I swear on my grandmother's grave!" or "I swear to God!"

Jesus was telling these people, and is telling us now, that as his followers we do not need to swear by anything to make our words believable. This type of "swearing" is commonly used to deceive people, and Christians should have no reason to deceive other people, ever. We are to be known for and recognized by our honesty.

Our sincerity should be a sign to others, believers and nonbelievers alike, that we are followers of Jesus. Our yes should mean yes. Our no should mean no. It should be that simple. We shouldn't need to beg people to believe us. If we are living the way God wants us to live, then people will already know us for our honesty and will trust us. ❖

PRAYER

Dear God, please help us to mean what we say and to always be honest, in order to glorify you. Amen.

day**274**

PUT OFF ALL DISHONESTY

- Share a time when you were dishonest with someone.
- How do you feel when someone is dishonest with you?

Therefore each of you must put off falsehood and speak truthfully to your neighbor, for we are all members of one body.   EPHESIANS 4:25

In this verse from Ephesians, the apostle Paul is teaching us that we, as Christians, are to put off all dishonesty. This means all *forms* of dishonesty. We know better than to tell outright lies, but sometimes we allow ourselves to be dishonest in small ways. We manipulate others to get our own way. We tell "little white lies." We exaggerate to make a story better. We cheat on our homework. Paul is telling us to cut it out! Put it off!

Paul also reminds us here that we are all members of one body—the body of Christ. What we say and do affects not only Christ himself but other members of the body of Christ. When we are dishonest, we do damage to the testimony of the church. When we are dishonest with others, we separate them from God's truth.

God wants us to speak truthfully to our neighbors, our friends, our teachers, our bosses, and our brothers and sisters. We need to work together if we are going to accomplish God's work here on earth. ✤

PRAYER

Dear God, thank you for your truth. Please help us to put off all forms of dishonesty so that others may learn about you through us. Amen.

day275

WHAT GOD HATES THE MOST

- What does it mean to hate something?
- What does God hate?

There are six things the LORD hates, seven that are detestable to him: haughty eyes, a lying tongue, hands that shed innocent blood, a heart that devises wicked schemes, feet that are quick to rush into evil, a false witness who pours out lies and a person who stirs up conflict in the community.　　　　　PROVERBS 6:16–17,19

Hate is a strong word. And we know that God is a God of love, grace and mercy. So if the Bible tells us that God hates something, we should probably pay attention.

In fact, King Solomon wrote these verses in a form designed to get our attention. He wrote "There are six things" and then wrote "seven." This used to be a common way for writers to build suspense and to make sure they had their audience's attention. The knowledge shared in these verses is incredibly important. If we know what God hates, then we can make sure we avoid these things.

Solomon names seven things that God hates. And out of these seven, he mentions lying twice. He writes that God hates a lying tongue and that God hates a false witness who pours out lies. He hates it so much that Solomon said it twice.

It is important that we work to avoid lying of all kinds. Our lies do nothing for us; they only hurt us. And more importantly, they hurt God. ❖

PRAYER

Dear God, please keep our tongues from lying and let us tell the truth. Please give us the courage and confidence to always be honest. Amen.

day276

GOD IS TRUTH

- What does God want from you?
- What do people mean when they say that "God is truth"?

Yet you desired faithfulness even in the womb; you taught me wisdom in that secret place.

PSALM 51:6

God created the universe, right? He created everything. So, he knows everything too. God, by definition of being the Creator, knows all the truth there is to know. He *is* the truth.

And he created us in his image. Yes, we are born into a broken and fallen, sin-filled world. But we are each designed to want God's truth. We are designed to want, need and be faithful to God. We were designed to be an example of his truth.

God wants us to believe in the truth, to seek it, to be faithful to it, and to be faithful to him by always telling the truth. He desires us to honor him by always striving to live the truth. Yes, this will be hard. But we were built for this. ♣

PRAYER

Dear God, thank you for designing us as unique creations. Please help us to be faithful to you. Let us honor your truth by living truthfully. Amen.

THE NINTH COMMANDMENT

- What are the Ten Commandments? Try to list them.
- Why do you think there are ten?

"You shall not give false testimony against your neighbor."   EXODUS 20:16

Some of the Ten Commandments are harder to keep than others. We probably haven't thought about killing anyone lately. But what about that ninth commandment? The one that tells us not to lie? That one can be pretty tough.

In fact, the Bible tells us that no one can tame the tongue. This means that it is very difficult to control the words we say. It is too easy to speak without thinking, and it is easy to base our words on our emotions.

However, we are *commanded* to tell the truth. Even when it is hard. *Especially* when it is hard. When we are faced with a difficult situation, and we find it hard to tell the truth, we know that God will help us. He wants us to tell the truth, and he will give us the strength to do so.

We also need to remember that the little lies, those "white lies" that we think are no big deal, are a big deal to God. God doesn't tell us to be truthful only when it matters. He commands us to tell the truth. ✤

PRAYER

Dear God, please help us to keep all your commandments. Please help us to control our tongues and not to lie. Give us the courage to tell the truth. Amen.

STARSTRUCK

- Who is the biggest celebrity you've ever met?
- Why don't more people recognize what an awesome opportunity prayer is?

Let us then approach God's throne of grace with confidence, so that we may receive mercy and find grace to help us in our time of need.   HEBREWS 4:16

Imagine that you have five minutes to say anything you want to your favorite sports star, singer or celebrity. It's just the two of you. No one else is around. You have the person's undivided attention. What would you say? How starstruck would you be? What if you had five minutes to say anything you want to the president of the United States? Would you be able to go through with it?

Most of us would likely get at least a little tongue-tied in the presence of a world leader or big celebrity. That's just the way we're wired. So why don't we get nervous when we pray? You'd think that talking to the all-powerful, all-knowing Creator of the universe would be much more nerve-wracking than chatting with a celebrity.

And it would be—if we didn't have his encouragement. God invites us to talk to him. He gives us permission to approach him any time we need him—not with fear and trembling, but with confidence and purpose. ❧

PRAYER

Dear God, it is amazing that you allow us to talk to you anytime we want. Let us never forget what a privilege it is. Amen.

ON GUARD

- What's your biggest fear or phobia?
- When was the last time you did something you were nervous about?

Be on your guard; stand firm in the faith; be courageous; be strong.

1 CORINTHIANS 16:13

When the apostle Paul wrote this letter back in the first century AD, Christians *had* to be courageous. The threat of persecution hung over their heads constantly. They were in danger of being thrown into prison, beaten and even killed for following Jesus. Courage went hand in hand with their faith.

We may not face the same type of persecution today, but we still need courage to live the way God wants us to. It takes courage to obey his laws when other people treat them as jokes. It takes courage to stand up for people who can't stand up for themselves. It takes courage to store treasures in heaven and not chase after money and possessions. It takes courage to identify ourselves as Christians when we know it will make us targets.

Here's the good news: Courage is available. All we have to do is ask God for it. He won't prevent us from facing tough situations, but he will give us what we need to get through them. ✤

PRAYER

Dear God, thank you for being available every moment of every day to hear our prayers and give us what we need. Let us never forget that our courage comes from you. Amen.

COVER ME

- Which of your friends is most likely to have your back when you really need it?
- If you know the Holy Spirit is protecting you, how might that change the way you live?

After they prayed, the place where they were meeting was shaken. And they were all filled with the Holy Spirit and spoke the word of God boldly.　　　ACTS 4:31

If you're watching a police drama, war movie or western, there's a good chance there will be a scene where the good guys get pinned down by gunfire. They'll be trapped behind a car or in a building with bullets flying all around them.

One person—usually the star—will volunteer to run out into the gunfire to get help or to get a better position on the bad guys. And that's when they'll turn to the others and say, "Cover me." In other words, "Give me the protection I need in order to do something brave."

That's what the Holy Spirit does for us. It's risky to be a Christian. People may not fire actual bullets at us, but they will oppose us, challenge us and mock us. And when we're under attack, it's tempting to just lay low and protect ourselves.

With the Holy Spirit behind us, though, we can take risks. We can be bold in representing Christ because we know he's covering us. He has our back. ✤

PRAYER

Dear God, thank you for giving us your Holy Spirit. Encourage us to act boldly in our faith, knowing the Holy Spirit is protecting us. Amen.

VICTORY IS OURS

- What is your biggest win ever?
- Why do Christians sometimes lack confidence about living their faith?

Their hearts are secure, they will have no fear; in the end they will look in triumph on their foes.   PSALM 112:8

Back in 1969, New York Jets quarterback Joe Namath predicted that his team would beat the Baltimore Colts in Super Bowl III. This prediction was a bold one because the Colts were considered to be a much better team than the Jets. To make Namath's prediction come true, the Jets would have to pull off one of the biggest upsets in sports history. And that's exactly what they did.

The psalmist's prediction in Psalm 112:8 is even bolder. The psalmist doesn't even name the foes because it doesn't matter who they are. God's people will triumph over all.

Of course, the important words to remember in this verse are "in the end." God doesn't promise that we will win every battle. Sometimes we'll be embarrassed and be made to look foolish. Other times we'll lose our cool and make people question what we're really like. Other times we'll give in to temptation and question ourselves.

What God does promise is that if we keep plugging away, if we stay faithful to him, eventually we will overcome our opponents. Victory will be ours. ✤

PRAYER

Dear God, thank you for giving us the confidence to face every day, knowing that eventually we will prevail. Let us never lose sight of our ultimate victory. Amen.

day**282**

COURAGE UNDER FIRE

- Who is the bravest person you know?
- What is the most recent courageous thing you've done?

Pray also for me, that whenever I speak, words may be given me so that I will fearlessly make known the mystery of the gospel, for which I am an ambassador in chains. Pray that I may declare it fearlessly, as I should. EPHESIANS 6:19–20

When you think of courage, what kind of situations do you think of? Do you picture firefighters rushing into a burning building? Do you picture police officers chasing dangerous criminals? Do you picture soldiers fighting in enemy territories? Courage certainly plays a role in each of those situations. But courage isn't just physical action.

For Christians, courage plays a role in almost every decision we make. If we follow Christ, we're going to make choices that are unpopular. We're going to go against the crowd. We're going to stand up for people who are being bullied or made fun of or ignored. We're going to speak up when we see things that are wrong.

That takes guts—more than most people have. So where does that courage come from? God himself. No matter what situation we're facing, we can get the personal strength we need directly from him. ✤

PRAYER

Dear God, thank you for sending your Son to give us the greatest example of courage in history. Give us the courage we need to carry out your will. Amen.

day283

GOD CARES ABOUT YOUR RELATIONSHIPS

- How do you know that God cares about you?
- Why do you think God created people to live in families?

The LORD God said, "It is not good for the man to be alone. I will make a helper suitable for him." GENESIS 2:18

In this verse from early Genesis, God is just about to create Eve. God didn't want Adam to be alone. See, even way back then, God was concerned about our loneliness. And he still is today. God doesn't want us to be lonely—that's why he gives us families and friends.

It's healthy to spend some time alone. It's healthy to spend some time alone with God. But we are not designed to spend all our time alone. God wants us working together, sharing one another's tough times and triumphs.

There is tremendous power in fellowship. We are supposed to lift one another up, support one another and keep one another company. Relationships like this honor God.

If you are feeling lonely, talk to God about it. He does care. Ask him to send you friends to help you in life; ask him to help you strengthen your bonds within your family. He will. ♣

PRAYER

Dear God, thank you for caring about us. Thank you for giving us friends and family to help us, support us and love us. Amen.

day284

WHAT FRIENDS ARE FOR

- Think of a friend whom you really appreciate. What do you appreciate about them?
- Who do you talk with when you are facing a tough time?

If either of them falls down, one can help the other up. But pity anyone who falls and has no one to help them up. Also, if two lie down together, they will keep warm. But how can one keep warm alone?　　　　　　　　　　　　ECCLESIASTES 4:10–11

God created people with a gift for and a need for companionship. Friendship is one of the most beautiful experiences life has to offer, especially when we are going through tough times or struggles.

Friends make work easier and more fun. Friends make it easier to get back up when we get knocked down. Friends listen to us and teach us about life. And friends provide us with company and companionship.

God designed us to support, encourage and lift up one another. When we are feeling troubled or alone, God wants us to reach out to our friends for companionship. And when we know of someone who is going through a difficult time, God wants us to reach out to that person and offer our friendship. We can show our love for God by loving one another. ✤

PRAYER

Dear God, thank you for the gift of friendship. Please help us to be good friends to the people you have placed in our lives. And please remind us to be available to our friends when they need us. Amen.

day285

A BRUISED REED HE WILL NOT BREAK

- When do you feel lonely?
- When you feel lonely, what do you do?

"A bruised reed he will not break, and a smoldering wick he will not snuff out. In faithfulness he will bring forth justice."   ISAIAH 42:3

In this verse from Isaiah, God is talking about Jesus. He is saying that Jesus will not break a bruised reed, meaning that Jesus does not kick us when we are down. Jesus will not snuff out a smoldering wick, meaning that Jesus does not discourage those who are barely hanging on.

God cares about people who are hurting, people who are lonely—he does not crush them. He is a gentle and merciful God who wants to help us in our sorrows.

When we are feeling small, weak and all alone, it is then that we need to go to God, and he will comfort us, lift us up and make us strong. During those lonely times God is close to us, just waiting for us to reach out to him. ✤

PRAYER

Dear God, thank you for caring for the lonely. When we feel alone, please remind us to reach out to you. And when we can help someone else who is lonely, please show us how to do so. Amen.

day286

A REALLY BAD DAY

- Share a "bad day" that you've had.
- Who in your life helps you serve God?

The LORD said to him, "Go back the way you came, and go to the Desert of Damascus. When you get there, anoint Hazael king over Aram . . . Yet I reserve seven thousand in Israel—all whose knees have not bowed down to Baal and whose mouths have not kissed him."   1 KINGS 19:15,18

Elijah was having a bad day. He had been working hard to convince people to worship the real God instead of the false god Baal. Elijah had just miraculously defeated 450 prophets of Baal. And because of this, the evil Queen Jezebel threatened to kill Elijah. Elijah ran for his life and ended up hiding in a cave.

But God did not leave Elijah alone to suffer. God sent angels to visit and feed him, and then God himself visited Elijah and named specific people who would help him destroy Baal worship in Israel.

Can you imagine being completely discouraged, at the end of your rope, and having God himself say to you, "Here are some people to help you. There are seven thousand people who do not worship Baal. You have seven thousand people on your side!"

When we are on God's side, we are never truly alone. Even when we feel alone, God has a plan. When we are feeling lonely, scared or discouraged, we can ask God for encouragement. Who knows, he may have seven thousand people lined up to help. ✤

PRAYER

Dear God, thank you for encouraging us when we are lonely. Thank you that we are never really alone. Amen.

day287

STAYING POWER

- Describe a time when you have felt God's presence in your life.
- How do you know that God will never leave you?

"And surely I am with you always, to the very end of the age."   MATTHEW 28:20B

Matthew chose these words to conclude his Gospel account. He chose to end the story of Jesus on earth with the reminder that Jesus will always be with us.

Jesus spoke these words after his resurrection. He spoke them to his disciples before he ascended into heaven. They would soon not be able to see Jesus the way they were used to seeing him, as a man walking on earth. So he wanted to assure them, and us, that even though we can't see him, he hasn't left us.

God will never leave us. He does not abandon his children. He promises this over and over in his Word, and he has shown this over and over in the lives of believers. Romans 8:39 tells us that nothing can separate us from the love of God that is in Jesus.

We can try to run away from God. We can commit sins that come between us and God. We can try to ignore God. But he will not leave us. He stays with us through thick and thin, through this life on earth and through eternity in heaven. ✤

PRAYER

Dear God, thank you for not giving up on us. Thank you for remaining with us no matter what. Please help us to feel you working in our lives and give us opportunities to share your love with others. Amen.

STIRRERS OF CONFLICT

- What's the difference between wanting a good life for your family and being greedy?
- Why is greed especially bad in a Christian?

The greedy stir up conflict, but those who trust in the LORD will prosper.

PROVERBS 28:25

There's an old Christian song called "They'll Know We Are Christians by Our Love." Love isn't the only thing that might mark someone as a Christian, though. God's people are called to be generous, selfless and self-controlled. We are also instructed to be unified. Ephesians 4:1 – 13 says we are one body, working together in unison.

One of the biggest obstacles to Christian unity is greed. Greed destroys unity because it looks out for self first. Greed creates disagreement. People who are pursuing earthly riches have little in common with people who are pursuing heavenly riches.

Greedy people who call themselves Christians wreck their own lives by chasing after wealth and possessions. And they wreck Christian unity in the process, giving outsiders a reason to doubt what Christians say. Of course, God will judge them severely on both counts.

And who does this proverb say will ultimately prosper? Not greedy people, who get tripped up by their own sinful attitude. Their greed keeps them from ever feeling content with what they have. The ones who ultimately will prosper are the ones who commit themselves to Christian unity and trust in the Lord. ❖

PRAYER

Dear God, forgive us for the times when we've let our greed get the better of us. Help us to understand that trusting in you is the only way to really prosper. Amen.

day289

GIMME, GIMME, GIMME

- Why do some people believe greed is good?
- How do you battle temptations to give in to greed?

For of this you can be sure: No immoral, impure or greedy person—such a person is an idolater—has any inheritance in the kingdom of Christ and of God.   EPHESIANS 5:5

Everyone knows the old saying, "You can't take it with you." But many people, including some who call themselves Christians, give it their best shot. They spend their lives chasing after money and expensive possessions. For them, having more than other people is a reason to be happy and proud.

Unfortunately, greedy people who don't repent of their sins will find out too late that their time on earth was completely wasted. God makes it clear that there are two choices in this world: We can pursue treasures on earth or we can pursue treasures in heaven. We can serve God or we can serve money (see Matthew 6:19–24).

Though the right choice seems obvious, it's not always an easy decision to make. Greed has a strong pull, and it seems harmless at first. After all, what's wrong with wanting something nice?

But it's a slippery slope. If we give in to greed once, it makes it easier to give in to it again. Before we know it, we're pursuing earthly treasures full-time and becoming a slave to money. God leaves the choice to us. But we must choose wisely, because our decision will have a big impact on our lives—in this world and the next. ❖

PRAYER

Dear God, thank you for providing us with everything we need. Help us see things from an eternal perspective so that we may be content and not give in to greed. Amen.

THOSE GREEDY PHARISEES!

- How do you recognize greed in someone?
- Besides money, what are people greedy for?

"Woe to you, teachers of the law and Pharisees, you hypocrites! You clean the outside of the cup and dish, but inside they are full of greed and self-indulgence."   MATTHEW 23:25

In the New Testament, the Pharisees are often the bad guys. You can almost hear the villain's music whenever they arrive on the scene. They're the ones who are always trying to trick Jesus into saying something that goes against Scripture or accusing him of doing something wrong. One of their favorite schemes was to claim he was an agent of Satan.

Even though their reputation as enemies of Jesus is well earned, the Pharisees weren't completely evil. They weren't necessarily born with arrogant spirits and hard hearts. They were teachers of God's law. They knew his Word better than almost anyone else. They went to great lengths to obey every word in Scripture. And the Jewish people respected them for it. In fact, they put the Pharisees on a pedestal.

That's where the trouble started. Once leaders get a taste of the perks that go with leadership, there's a great temptation to want more—whether it's power, fame or money. That's where greed is born.

That same temptation exists for Christian leaders today. That's why we need to pray regularly for our pastors and teachers. We need to ask God to protect them from greed and keep their hearts pure. ✤

PRAYER

Dear God, make yourself known today in the hearts of the pastors and teachers in our church. Give them the strength to resist temptation and keep their hearts pure. Amen.

PRETTY SIMPLE

- If you could change one family rule, what would you choose?
- What do you think the purpose behind this rule is?

Children, obey your parents in the Lord, for this is right.　　　　Ephesians 6:1

Sometimes the Bible makes things simple. "Children, obey your parents." Pretty simple, right?

This verse doesn't say to obey your parents when you feel like it, or when you think they're right about something, or when you think it will work for you. It just says to obey.

Even if you don't want to.

While you may sometimes think that your parents are from outer space, the truth is that God assigned them to you. God has a plan, remember? And your parents are part of that plan. And their job is to love you, raise you, protect you, train you and teach you. When they tell you to do something, realize that they are just doing the job that God gave them.

The job God gave *you* is much simpler: Obey your parents.

When this is difficult, remember that when you are obeying your parents, you are really obeying God. ✤

PRAYER

Dear God, thank you for parents. Please help us to obey them, even when we don't want to. Amen.

ESTABLISHED BY GOD

- How does God feel about governmental laws?
- When is it okay to break the law?

Let everyone be subject to the governing authorities, for there is no authority except that which God has established. The authorities that exist have been established by God. Consequently, whoever rebels against the authority is rebelling against what God has instituted, and those who do so will bring judgment on themselves. For rulers hold no terror for those who do right, but for those who do wrong. Do you want to be free from fear of the one in authority? Then do what is right and you will be commended.

ROMANS 13:1–3

Second Corinthians 6 tells us that, as followers of Jesus, Christians must be careful not to do anything to discredit Jesus' name. We need to be aware that the world is watching us and learning about God through us. It is important that we act like model citizens, obeying the laws of the government and submitting to the government's authority.

God is the ultimate authority, and he is well aware of everything that is going on. We need to trust that he is control. When we rebel against the government, we rebel against God.

The only exception to this rule would be if the government asked us to sin. In this case, we would follow God's law instead of the government's law. But in every other case, we are to obey the government's laws. We are submit in order to bring honor to God's name. ✣

PRAYER

Dear God, please help us to obey the law—both governmental laws and your laws. Please help us to bring nothing but honor and glory to your name. Amen.

NO QUESTIONS ASKED

- Give an example of a sin and its consequence.
- Why does God give us commandments?

Your kingdom will not endure; the LORD has sought out a man after his own heart and appointed him ruler of his people, because you have not kept the LORD's command.

1 SAMUEL 13:14

Saul's had an obedience problem. He knew God's laws, and he was given a big responsibility: to be the king of Israel. As king, people looked to him to be a leader and to provide an example of the right way to do things. But Saul thought he could do things his own way.

When Saul was faced with an enemy army, he could have turned to God for help and guidance. He could have also turned to God's messenger, Samuel. Instead, Saul took matters into his own hands and offered a sacrifice to God on his own.

It was a good thing to want to offer a sacrifice, but only the priests were allowed to do that. Saul had good intentions, but he disobeyed a rule that God had put in place.

God doesn't want us to follow him and make up our own rules. God tells us to obey his commands. Period. Yes, God will forgive us, but once we disobey, the damage has been done. Disobedience always has consequences.

In Saul's case, God removed his blessing from his life and told him that there would soon be a new king. Saul didn't know this would happen, but he didn't have to know. He should have just obeyed God. Even when we don't understand why God commands what he does, we need to recognize that God knows what he's doing. We need to trust in God's commandments and obey them—no questions asked. ✤

PRAYER

Dear God, thank you for your commandments. Please help us to trust you and to be obedient to your Word. Amen.

BLESSED ARE THOSE

- Share a time when you have been rewarded for doing the right thing.
- What does it mean to be blessed?

He replied, "Blessed rather are those who hear the word of God and obey it." LUKE 11:28

Jeremy was walking home from school when he found a wallet half-buried in the snow. Back in the warmth and privacy of his bedroom, he opened the wallet to find five twenty-dollar bills folded neatly inside, along with several credit cards and a driver's license.

Jeremy was tempted to take the money. He knew how much stuff $100 could buy. But he also knew that God commands us not to steal. So Jeremy gave the wallet to his mother.

Later that evening, the owner of the wallet came to Jeremy's house. The man looked inside his wallet and then looked at Jeremy. He said, "I can't believe that everything is still here. I didn't think there were any honest people left in this world, and for this honesty to come from such a young man, well—you must be a very special boy." And then he handed Jeremy one of the neatly folded twenty-dollar bills and said, "Here you go, son, buy yourself something fun."

In this case, the owner of the wallet was kind enough to reward Jeremy on the spot, and while that doesn't happen, doing the right thing is always its own reward. Obedience brings blessings—sometimes physical, sometimes spiritual, sometimes both. When we obey God's Word, we open up our lives to God's blessings. ✤

PRAYER

Dear God, thank you for your commandments. Please help us to be obedient to your Word. Amen.

day**295**

CHILLING WORDS

- Give an example of someone famous who has a "bad reputation."
- How long does a bad reputation last?

If you take your neighbor to court, do not betray another's confidence, or the one who hears it may shame you and the charge against you will stand. PROVERBS 25:9–10

"The charge against you will stand." These are chilling words. These verses from Proverbs deal with how we are to settle conflicts. If we have a conflict with someone, we are not supposed to blab about it all over town. When we speak poorly of someone, we damage their reputation and our own. And we expose ourselves to shame—a shame that doesn't just fade away.

Our reputation follows us. It takes a lot of time and effort to build a good reputation and one thoughtless comment can damage it. We need to think before we speak.

We are not supposed to worry about what other people think about us, but we're also supposed to behave in such a way that gives people no cause to speak ill of us. What people say about us does matter because those outside the church may judge all Christians by the words and actions of one. Words have power. Our reputation has power. We need to guard it wisely. ✤

PRAYER

Dear God, please help us to think before we speak and to build reputations that honor and glorify you. Amen.

day296 october 23

A WISE AND UNDERSTANDING PEOPLE

- What do you think people say about you when you are not around?
- Why is a good reputation important?

Observe them carefully, for this will show your wisdom and understanding to the nations, who will hear about all these decrees and say, "Surely this great nation is a wise and understanding people." DEUTERONOMY 4:6

In this verse from Deuteronomy, Moses is telling the Israelites to observe God's commandments carefully, so that other people and other nations would see that God's followers have wisdom and understanding. Moses wanted his people to understand that obedience to God's Word would earn them a good reputation, and that other people would learn about the one true God through Israel's testimony.

The same principle applies today. When we obey God's Word, we earn good reputations and we become living testimonies for God. Obedient Christians are trustworthy, reliable and admirable people. Obedient Christians work hard at their jobs and love their families. Obedient Christians stay out of trouble and are content with their lives. People who do not yet know God notice these things.

Your reputation is a significant part of your testimony. And being obedient to God's Word is the best possible way to build a good reputation. ✤

PRAYER

Dear God, thank you for giving us your Word to teach us, guide us and protect us. Please help us to be obedient and to earn good reputations that will lead others to you. Amen.

day297

THE OUTSIDERS

- How does God want you to act when you are around people who do not know him?
- Share a time when you were tempted to "join the crowd" in sin.

Be wise in the way you act toward outsiders; make the most of every opportunity.

COLOSSIANS 4:5

When Paul refers to "outsiders" here, he is referring to unbelievers. We need to be careful about how we act when we are around people who do not know God. It can be tempting when around unbelievers to act the way they do. Sometimes we feel like "no one's watching" if the people we are with do not know how God wants people to behave. But this is precisely when others are watching—the unbelievers are watching. Whether they consciously think about it or not, they are observing our behavior.

And if our behavior is godly, it will often lead to opportunities for us to share our faith with others. Someone is bound to ask us why we won't let them cheat from our homework or why we won't steal that lipstick. Someone will ask us why we don't swear or drink or sneak out at night.

Our time on earth is limited. We need to make the most of it by honoring God with our actions, especially toward "outsiders." ❖

PRAYER

Dear God, please give us wisdom to act the way you want us to act when we are around people who do not know you. Please give us opportunities to share your truth with others and the courage to do so. Amen.

day298

WALK THE TALK, AND PEOPLE TALK

- What does it mean to have integrity?
- What does it mean to "walk the talk"?

At this, she bowed down with her face to the ground. She asked him, "Why have I found such favor in your eyes that you notice me — a foreigner?" Boaz replied, "I've been told all about what you have done for your mother-in-law since the death of your husband — how you left your father and mother and your homeland and came to live with a people you did not know before. May the LORD repay you for what you have done. May you be richly rewarded by the LORD, the God of Israel, under whose wings you have come to take refuge."

RUTH 2:10–12

Boaz did not yet know Ruth, but he had heard all about her. He had heard how she stood by her mother-in-law, Naomi, and he was impressed. Not only did he give Ruth food to feed Naomi and herself, but he also blessed her by wishing that God would reward her for her integrity.

To have integrity means to have a solid foundation of values and the courage to stand by your beliefs. It takes strength to have integrity, and Ruth's integrity had earned her a good reputation.

Integrity will earn you a good reputation too. Through God's Word, you are learning the difference between right and wrong. You are learning what pleases God and what doesn't. It takes a lot of strength to stand up for what you believe in. It's also well worth the effort — living with integrity builds a good reputation, which pleases the Lord. ✤

PRAYER

Dear God, thank you for giving us a solid set of values to live by. Please help us to live with integrity and to earn reputations that honor and please you. Amen.

ABOVE SUSPICION

- Share a time when you got into trouble for being in the wrong place at the wrong time.
- Do Christians need to be concerned about what others think of them? Why or why not?

And we are sending along with him the brother who is praised by all the churches for his service to the gospel . . . We want to avoid any criticism of the way we administer this liberal gift. For we are taking pains to do what is right, not only in the eyes of the Lord but also in the eyes of man.   2 CORINTHIANS 8:18,20–21

In these verses from 2 Corinthians, Paul and Titus are collecting a large offering. So that no one could ever accuse them of stealing the money or using it sinfully, Paul sent an unbiased person to help carry the offering.

Paul knew that he was being watched. He knew how important his reputation was among the different churches. He knew that people judged the gospel by his own behavior, so he took great pains to make sure that nothing dishonest could happen or even be said to happen.

Paul did not put himself in compromising situations. And neither should we. We can choose to go to a party where we know there will be drinking. We can try to justify it by not drinking anything, but we will be judged based on our proximity to sin.

While it might not seem fair, as Christians we must take pains to avoid situations that may lead others to question the reality of the gospel. We need to work to keep ourselves above suspicion. ✤

PRAYER

Dear God, please help us guard our reputations and stay above suspicion. Please help us to make wise decisions. Amen.

day300

ALL OVER THE WORLD

- What would you like to be famous for?
- What do you think life was like for the early Christians?

Everyone has heard about your obedience, so I rejoice because of you; but I want you to be wise about what is good, and innocent about what is evil. ROMANS 16:19

Laura was a quiet woman who lived in a small town. She was very busy at home, taking care of her children and animals and tending her garden, so she didn't even go out much. Yet everyone knew that Laura was a Christian. Even though most people in the town didn't know her personally, everyone knew that she lived for the Lord. And when there was a crisis, when someone was sick and dying, or abused and scared, or grieving and confused, they came to Laura's door.

Paul opens his letter to the Romans by telling them, "Your faith is being reported all over the world" (Romans 1:8). Sixteen chapters later, he uses the verse above to help close his letter. Obviously, the believers in Rome had a widespread reputation for faith and obedience.

Word travels. Obedient believers attract attention. As followers of Jesus, we are not supposed to blend in with the world around us. ❖

PRAYER

Dear God, thank you for the Bible. Please help us to be obedient to your Word. Amen.

day301

IMAGE IS EVERYTHING

- If you could be anyone in the world, who would you be?
- Would you ever insult or make fun of God? Why or why not?

Then God said, "Let us make mankind in our image, in our likeness, so that they may rule over the fish in the sea and the birds in the sky, over the livestock and all the wild animals, and over all the creatures that move along the ground." So God created mankind in his own image, in the image of God he created them; male and female he created them.

GENESIS 1:26–27

God created human beings in his own image, in the likeness of the Trinity—God, Jesus Christ and the Holy Spirit. God did not create human beings as powerless and miserable creatures. He created Adam and Eve—and he created *you*—in his own image.

So when a voice, either from another person or from inside of you, tells you that you are not worthwhile, remember that this just isn't true. These are lies from the enemy, who doesn't want you to remember who you are—God's beloved child.

When you feel bad about who you are, when you cut yourself down or say negative things about yourself, you are insulting God's image. You are not seeing yourself as a child of God.

We need to open our hearts to God's love, open our minds to God's Word and let his power into our lives, so that we will know who we are. When we do this, we will understand who we belong to: our awe-inspiringly magnificent God. And we will know that we are awe-inspiringly magnificent too. ✤

PRAYER

Dear God, thank you for creating us in your image. Please help us to remember this when we are feeling down on ourselves, and let us glorify you. Amen.

# day302

A LITTLE LOWER THAN THE ANGELS

- What is something that you know about angels?
- What do you think is God's most impressive, most beautiful creation in the whole universe?

When I consider your heavens, the work of your fingers, the moon and the stars, which you have set in place, what is mankind that you are mindful of them, human beings that you care for them? You have made them a little lower than the angels and crowned them with glory and honor. PSALM 8:3–5

If you ever want to experience a tiny glimpse of God's immense creative power, look at pictures taken by telescopes in outer space. Look at the "close-up" photographs of Saturn's moons or an icy comet. The God that we serve each day created these extraordinary features of our universe. How powerful is he, really?

When we look at these awesome creations, we quickly realize how small we are. But we are not insignificant; God is mindful of us. God cares for us. God created us and put us in charge of this earth. He placed us just beneath the angels, and because he loves us, he crowned us with glory and honor.

How often do we think of ourselves as just below the angels? How differently would we act if we kept this in mind? We are truly holy beings, created by and belonging to our perfect Creator. ✤

PRAYER

Dear God, thank you for creating us and for placing us a little lower than the angels. Thank you for crowning us with glory and honor. Please help us to remember this when we forget how much you love us. Amen.

MANY SPARROWS

- How many hairs are on your head?
- Describe a sparrow. What does it look like? What does it act like?

"Are not five sparrows sold for two pennies? Yet not one of them is forgotten by God. Indeed, the very hairs of your head are all numbered. Don't be afraid; you are worth more than many sparrows."   LUKE 12:6−7

Have you ever really looked at a sparrow? They are small, insignificant birds. They don't have flashy colors. They don't sing loudly. They eat seeds and small insects. Sparrows are seemingly unimportant creatures, and yet not one of them is forgotten by God. In Matthew 10, Jesus tells us that not one sparrow will fall to the ground outside of our Father's care (see vv. 29−30).

If God cares for the *sparrows* this much, how much more does he care for us? He made human beings last, in his own image, and put us in charge of the earth. We are of tremendous value to God. God knows our every thought, our every feeling. He is with us every second of every day. He knows exactly how many hairs are on our heads.

We are never insignificant to God. He takes care of the small, unimportant sparrow. How much more will he take care of us? God loves us. He will take care of us completely. For eternity. ✤

PRAYER

Dear God, thank you for caring about us. Thank you for valuing us. Please help us to remember how much you love us. Amen.

THE ULTIMATE POTTER

- What words would you use to describe modeling clay?
- Why do you think artists sign their work?

Yet you, LORD, are our Father. We are the clay, you are the potter; we are all the work of your hand.   ISAIAH 64:8

Young children often love clay because it does whatever you want it to. It is easy to bend, fold and squish. And if you make a mistake, you can fix it instantly by pushing the clay back into place.

Some of these children go on to become potters. They form intricate sculptures that sell in art galleries for thousands of dollars. They create gorgeous clay pots, mugs and bowls. These potters are artists. They put their heart and soul into their work. They are diligent, making sure that every aspect of their creation is just the way they want it. They know it has to be perfect because it will be a reflection of who they are as artists. In the hands of these talented artists, the clay becomes a masterpiece, bearing their signature.

We are God's artwork. He forms us like clay, modeling us with his own hands. We bear his signature. He does not make mistakes. He is God—the ultimate potter. And we are God's masterpieces. ✤

PRAYER

Dear God, thank you for creating us. Thank you for intentionally making each of us unique. Thank you for loving us. Amen.

GOD DOESN'T GRADE ON THE CURVE

- How do you feel when you are around someone who is arrogant?
- How do you know if you are doing a good job of living for God?

If anyone thinks they are something when they are not, they deceive themselves. Each one should test their own actions. Then they can take pride in themselves alone, without comparing themselves to someone else, for each one should carry their own load.

GALATIANS 6:3–5

Most teachers award grades based solely on the work students do. If a student does all of their work correctly, they get a good grade.

Some teachers grade "on the curve." The teacher considers all the work that all the students do and then awards the student with the best work the best grade and the other students get averaged in after that.

God never grades on the curve, so Christians do not need to compare the work they do for God against the work of other Christians. We certainly shouldn't be arrogant about what we are doing. We must not overestimate ourselves.

So how do we rate ourselves? We need to test our actions against God's Word. We are responsible for how we live for God. Therefore, we are responsible for evaluating how we are doing. We need to examine ourselves through prayer, reading the Bible and taking the time to honestly reflect on our lives.

If we find that our relationship with God is strong, we can rejoice. But we should never rejoice because we are "doing a better job" than other Christians. ✤

PRAYER

Dear God, please keep us from comparing our works to other Christians. Please help us to test our own actions and carry our own load. Amen.

day306

THE FIRST STEP

- Why is it important to have a healthy self-esteem?
- How do you know that God loves you?

The commandments, "You shall not commit adultery," "You shall not murder," "You shall not steal," "You shall not covet," and whatever other command there may be, are summed up in this one command: "Love your neighbor as yourself." Love does no harm to a neighbor. Therefore love is the fulfillment of the law. ROMANS 13:9–10

God commands us to love our neighbors. In fact, we obey *all* of God's commandments when we love others. And in order to love others, we need to accept that God loves us, and we need to love God.

When we let God's love into our lives—into our hearts—it overflows, and we have plenty to give to others. If we don't open our hearts to God's love, we won't be able to love others.

If you have given your life to God, you should have a healthy self-esteem and a knowledge of God's love. If you are struggling in these areas, it is important to determine why and work on healing. Ask for help if you need it. Find a Christian whom you trust and talk to that person. Also, spend some time reading God's Word and talking to him in prayer. You will not be able to grow in God or serve him until you accept his love for you, allow it to heal your wounds and learn to see yourself as he sees you. ✤

PRAYER

Dear God, thank you for loving us. Please help us to accept this love, loving who we are in you. Please allow our hearts to overflow with love for others. Amen.

day307

FOREVER AND EVER

- Name something you wish would never end.
- How do you picture heaven?

Brothers and sisters, we do not want you to be uninformed about those who sleep in death, so that you do not grieve like the rest of mankind, who have no hope. For we believe that Jesus died and rose again, and so we believe that God will bring with Jesus those who have fallen asleep in him. 1 THESSALONIANS 4:13–14

Have you ever been sad to get to the end of a movie or book? Did you wish that the story could just go on forever and ever? Most people feel that way about life. Of course, not every day is great. There are ups and downs, good times and bad. But few people are eager to get to the end; most people would like it to last forever.

And it does. For believers, life on earth is like being on the first page of a trillion-page book. The apostle Paul's words to the believers in Thessalonica are meant to give us comfort. Christian loved ones who have passed away aren't gone from our lives forever—just for one page. One day we'll be reunited with them, and we'll spend eternity—trillions of pages—together.

Death is not the end for a person who follows Christ. Reminding ourselves of that can help us keep the right perspective on this life. No matter what happens, good or bad, it's temporary. What matters is what lasts: our relationship with the Lord. ✤

PRAYER

Dear God, thank you for allowing us to have an eternal relationship with you. Help us keep our eyes on eternity even when things in this world try to interfere. Amen.

day308

THE FINITE AND THE INFINITE

- If you had more time in the day, how would you spend it?
- Name something that lasts a long time.

For the wages of sin is death, but the gift of God is eternal life in Christ Jesus our Lord.
ROMANS 6:23

If a pickup truck runs for 10 years, we call it long lasting. But we say the same thing about a stick of deodorant that keeps a person dry for 12 hours. If a couple stays together for 50 years, we call it a long marriage. If someone celebrates their 100th birthday, we say they've had a long life.

We look at the world around us in a finite way. Things have a beginning and an end. We use time to measure the space between the two. Time is what we understand because it hangs over everything we do in this world. We only have a certain amount of time given to us, a specific number of days, hours and minutes to live our earthly lives. Our daily decisions are driven by the question of whether we have enough time.

Thinking outside of time can be difficult. Yet outside of time is exactly where we'll be if we receive God's gift of eternal life. Time itself will end, but we will go on and on. We will exist *forever* with God—perfectly happy, perfectly healthy and perfectly content. ✤

PRAYER

Dear God, we praise you for being eternal, and we thank you for giving us the same opportunity. Help us understand and appreciate, even in some tiny way, what it means to live with you forever. Amen.

NO TEARS IN HEAVEN

- Describe what you want your funeral to be like.
- What's the worst thing about funerals?

"'He will wipe every tear from their eyes. There will be no more death' or mourning or crying or pain, for the old order of things has passed away."   REVELATION 21:4

Did you know the average cost of a funeral in the Unites States is about $7,000? If there's any comfort to be found in the business of death, it's this: Funerals only occur in this world. There is no death or mourning in heaven.

Death wasn't part of God's original plan. His original plan was for his human creation to live endlessly and sinlessly with him. Death didn't come into the picture until after Adam and Eve disobeyed him. Death was part of the consequences of their sin. In heaven, things will return to their original design. Once again, life will have no end. Death will not exist.

What does that mean for us? It means we will never have to worry about losing a loved one again. We will never have to wonder how we can live another day with the hole in our hearts that death causes. We will never have to watch a family member slowly die from an incurable disease. We will never have someone tell us that a good friend was killed in an accident. When God wipes the tears from our eyes in eternity, we will never be sad again. ✤

PRAYER

Dear God, in this world of death and loss, thank you for giving us something to look forward to. Watch over the people who are grieving right now. Give them a sense of peace and hope. Amen.

day310

CONQUEROR OF DEATH

- What scares you most about death?
- How do you think most people would react if you told them about Jesus' death and resurrection?

But Christ has indeed been raised from the dead, the firstfruits of those who have fallen asleep. For since death came through a man, the resurrection of the dead comes also through a man. For as in Adam all die, so in Christ all will be made alive. But each in turn: Christ, the firstfruits; then, when he comes, those who belong to him.

1 CORINTHIANS 15:20–23

Mark 5:21–43 tells the story of a man named Jairus whose daughter had died. He asked Jesus for help. Jesus told the mourners who had gathered that the girl wasn't dead but was merely sleeping. The mourners laughed at him. Jesus took the girl by the hand and told her to get up. She got up. The mourners stopped laughing.

Jesus showed his ultimate power over death three days after his crucifixion. His heart, which had stopped beating, started again. His lungs, which had stopped breathing, filled with air. His eyes, which had been closed, opened. His muscles, which had stopped working, regained their power. His enemies, who thought they'd gotten rid of him for good, and his followers, who thought they'd lost him forever, were all in for the surprise of their lives.

Jesus conquered death once and for all through his resurrection. But that's not all he did. He also blazed a trail for everyone who follows him. The apostle Paul tells us that Jesus will raise everyone who has died. If we believe in him, death ultimately can have no power over us. ✤

PRAYER

Dear God, thank you for sending your Son to defeat death once and for all. Help us remember that death can have no power over us. Amen.

NO GUARANTEE OF TOMORROW

- What would you like to be doing 20 years from now?
- How often do you tell your family and closest friends how you feel about them?

Now listen, you who say, "Today or tomorrow we will go to this or that city, spend a year there, carry on business and make money." Why, you do not even know what will happen tomorrow. What is your life? You are a mist that appears for a little while and then vanishes. JAMES 4:13–14

Few people say, "I'll see you tomorrow . . . unless I die before then" or "If I'm still alive this weekend, we should go see a movie." We all make plans, whether it's a summer vacation, a college choice or a career. We naturally assume that we will live long enough for those plans to come to fruition.

There's nothing wrong with that approach. Those verses in James aren't telling us that God gets mad when we make plans for the future. They are pointing out that our plans are always secondary to God's plans for us. We can assume we'll get old before we die, but that doesn't mean it will happen. None of us knows for sure how long we'll live.

We can either be depressed by that thought or we can use it as an inspiration to make every moment count. If there's no guarantee of tomorrow, let's make sure we spend today wisely. Feel like telling a loved one how much you appreciate them? Do it today. Feel like apologizing to someone you've hurt? Do it today. There's no guarantee you'll have a chance to do it tomorrow. ♣

PRAYER

Dear God, we praise you for the fact that you hold today and tomorrow in your hands. Give us the wisdom to know how to spend our time in the best way possible. Amen.

day312

HAPPILY EVER AFTER

- Will you read a book or watch a movie if you know it has an unhappy ending? Explain.
- What are you looking forward to most in heaven? Why?

And I heard a loud voice from the throne saying, "Look! God's dwelling place is now among the people, and he will dwell with them. They will be his people, and God himself will be with them and be their God."　　　　　　REVELATION 21:3

When you're grieving, the hurt and sorrow can seem endless. Wave after wave of pain crashes down on you. You can feel your strength draining away. In times like these, it's natural to ask, "Will it ever end?" The good news? The answer is yes. Revelation 21 gives us a glimpse of eternity in heaven—and grief, pain and suffering are nowhere in sight.

The reason is simple. In heaven there will be no more death. Unlike earth, where best friends, beloved grandparents, friendly neighbors, young kids and countless really, really good people die every day, heaven is all living, all the time.

That may not seem like much of a consolation to someone who's suffered a devastating loss here on earth. But if we hold on to that truth—if we trust that God always keeps his promises—we will find comfort. ♣

PRAYER

Dear God, thank you for giving us eternity with you to look forward to. When we are hurting, remind us that our pain is temporary. Amen.

WITH FRIENDS LIKE THESE

- Think of the last time you tried to comfort someone who was hurting. What did you do right? What did you do wrong?
- What will you do differently next time?

When they saw him from a distance, they could hardly recognize him; they began to weep aloud, and they tore their robes and sprinkled dust on their heads. Then they sat on the ground with him for seven days and seven nights. No one said a word to him, because they saw how great his suffering was.   JOB 2:12–13

One way God comforts hurting people is to put caring friends in their lives. And if we're following God, one day we'll be one of those caring friends. The apostle Paul says, "Praise be to . . . the God of all comfort, who comforts us in all our troubles, so that we can comfort those in any trouble with the comfort we ourselves receive from God" (2 Corinthians 1:3–4). God uses our experiences to reach out to others with compassion and comfort. Here are some tips to keep in mind when talking with someone who is hurting:

Ask God to guide you before you speak. He will give you the right words to say.

Give your hurting friend a chance to share their feelings. Listen closely and ask questions. Don't try to correct anything the person says.

Don't use clichés or try to give simple answers. Instead, talk about how much you care about your friend.

Pray with your friend.

Ask if you can do simple things, like chores or errands, to make your friend's life a little easier. ❖

PRAYER

Dear God, thank you for putting loved ones in our lives who care about us and comfort us. Teach us to be people who can offer care and comfort to other hurting people. Amen.

EVEN IN THE DARKEST TIMES

- When was the darkest time of your life?
- Who or what helped you get through it?

But no one says, "Where is God my Maker, who gives songs in the night?"   JOB 35:10

The quote from Job 35:10 comes from Elihu, a friend who tried to comfort Job after tragedy struck. Job was devastated because he didn't know why such suffering had been heaped on him. He prayed to God about it but only seemed to get silence in return. Elihu emphasized that God does hear our cries, even when it seems he doesn't.

If we're struggling with grief, we need to do three things. First, we need to let the grief run its natural course. A devastating loss isn't something we recover from in a day or a week or even a month. God will not make all pain go away in an instant, because that's not how grief works. In order to make a healthy recovery, we need to experience the pain.

The second thing we need to do is believe in God's love and concern. We need to put our faith in his promises and trust that the help and comfort he offers is exactly what we need when we need it.

The third thing we need to do is to accept the comfort that God offers. Through praying and studying his Word, we can feel safe and consoled. ✤

PRAYER

Dear God, thank you for always being there for us, no matter what we face. Thank you for never failing us. Remind us to look to you when we are in pain. Amen.

COMFORT ABILITY

- What kind of comfort do you want when you're hurting?
- What kind of comfort do you *not* want? Why?

Comfort, comfort my people, says your God.　　　　　　　　ISAIAH 40:1

The Lord isn't a stranger to grief. He understands it because he experienced it. The apostle John tells the story of Jesus' encounter with his friends Mary, Martha and Lazarus. The three of them were siblings. One day Mary and Martha sent word to Jesus that Lazarus was very ill. By the time Jesus reached them, Lazarus was dead.

Jesus knew he was going to raise Lazarus from the dead. He knew that in a matter of minutes Mary and Martha and all their friends and family would be rejoicing. But in that moment, he looked around and saw people he loved weeping and mourning. And do you know what Jesus did? He wept. He allowed himself to feel—and show—deep, deep sorrow. Other people's sadness touched his heart, and he shed tears. (For the complete story, see John 11:1–45).

The Lord knows the kind of comfort we need when we're grieving. He knows even better than we do. All we have to do is call on him. We don't need to give him instructions. We don't even have to tell him what's wrong. All we have to do is say, "Lord, I need you," and he will be right by our side. ❖

PRAYER

Dear God, thank you for sending your Son, who experienced pain and suffering and knows how to comfort us when we are hurting. Let us always remember to turn to you in times of grief. Amen.

day316

A COMFORTER FOR ALL SEASONS

- What do you know about the Trinity? What's the difference between God the Father, Jesus and the Holy Spirit?
- What does the Holy Spirit do?

"And I will ask the Father, and he will give you another advocate to help you and be with you forever."   JOHN 14:16

As Jesus was preparing for the end of his life, his disciples were understandably upset. With Jesus gone, who would guide them, teach them and make them feel better in times of trouble? The Lord eased his disciples' fears by promising them the Holy Spirit—also called the Comforter—who would do for them in spirit what Jesus did for them in the flesh.

That same Holy Spirit accompanies believers today. The fact that we cannot see him does not make him any less real. His work is vital to us. If we don't recognize his presence in our lives, we may fool ourselves into thinking that we're alone when tough times come. And that would be a terrible mistake.

The apostle Paul gave this encouragement: "Do not be anxious about anything, but in every situation, by prayer and petition, with thanksgiving, present your requests to God. And the peace of God, which transcends all understanding, will guard your hearts and your minds in Christ Jesus" (Philippians 4:6–7). If we turn to God for help, the Holy Spirit will give us peace, even in the midst of suffering. That's his promise to us. ✣

PRAYER

Dear God, thank you for giving us your Holy Spirit. Remind us always that he offers constant comfort and healing when we need it most. Amen.

day317

A DECISION TO MAKE

- What is a verdict?
- Why do you think the Bible refers to Jesus as "light"?

Whoever believes in him is not condemned, but whoever does not believe stands condemned already because they have not believed in the name of God's one and only Son. This is the verdict: Light has come into the world, but people loved darkness instead of light because their deeds were evil. JOHN 3:18–19

In this verse from John, the phrase "believes in him" means more than just saying "Jesus is real." This kind of belief includes committing your life to Christ and putting your trust in his salvation.

Each and every person in this world must make such a decision. Each and every person in this world must choose between light and darkness, between serving God and serving self. Sadly, some people do choose darkness. Some people do choose themselves over their Creator.

And that's *their* choice. No one can make this decision for someone else. Parents cannot make their kids choose Jesus. Church leaders cannot get church members to heaven. And you will not be able to make this decision for your friends or loved ones. You are called to share the gospel with people, to present it in a way that makes the truth clear through both actions and language. The rest is between each individual and God. ❖

PRAYER

Dear God, thank you for Jesus. Thank you for our faith in him. We pray for those individuals who still need to make the right decision. Please help them to do so. Amen.

day**318**

THE SLIPPERY SLOPE

- Describe a time when you were tempted to sin.
- What is an example of one sin leading to another?

When tempted, no one should say, "God is tempting me." For God cannot be tempted by evil, nor does he tempt anyone; but each person is tempted when they are dragged away by their own evil desire and enticed. Then, after desire has conceived, it gives birth to sin; and sin, when it is full-grown, gives birth to death. JAMES 1:13–15

God is 100 percent good. He cannot sin, and he cannot be tempted. Neither will he tempt anyone. When we are tempted to sin, it's not God who is tempting us. He may allow the temptation to happen, but he doesn't whisper "go ahead and do it" into our ears.

We are tempted by our own sinful natures. We tempt ourselves, and therefore, we are responsible for each of our decisions. We are responsible for our actions. It doesn't do any good to try to blame other people, or God, for our sin. God knows the truth, and ultimately, so do we. If we don't accept responsibility for our sins, then we cannot repent—and cannot be forgiven.

Sin is a slippery slope. If we don't deal with it, it leads to death. Of course, not every sin will result in devastating consequences, but all sin is unhealthy and breaks down relationships (with us and God). Seemingly "small" sins lead to bigger, more dangerous sins. It is up to us to avoid this slippery slope. We need to deal with our sin, turn away from it and turn toward God. ♣

PRAYER

Dear God, thank you for forgiving us for our sins. Thank you for setting us free from our sins. Please protect us from temptation, help us to make good decisions and help us to take responsibility when we do slip up. Amen.

THE CENSUS SIN

- What does it mean to "accept responsibility"?
- How do you feel after you sincerely apologize for something?

Then David said to God, "I have sinned greatly by doing this. Now, I beg you, take away the guilt of your servant. I have done a very foolish thing." 1 CHRONICLES 21:8

David had become a powerful king, and at one point he told his general to go count all the men in Israel. Taking a census is not necessarily a sin, but David's motivation was sinful. The Bible doesn't explain his motivation, but there was no godly reason to take this census. Maybe David had become anxious. Maybe he had begun to rely more on his army and less on God, so he wanted the count to assure himself of his security. Or maybe he had become arrogant, and he wanted to know how great his kingdom was so that he could brag about it. We don't know his motivation, but we know from the Bible that David was guilty.

And it didn't take him long to realize it. When he did, he repented. David was no stranger to sin, but David always admitted when he was wrong. He always asked God for forgiveness.

So it should be with us. The Bible says that we will sin. We will give in to temptation, and we will make mistakes. But we need to admit when we are wrong. We must repent and ask God for forgiveness. We cannot be set free from our guilt until we admit we are guilty. ✤

PRAYER

Dear God, please give us the humility and courage to admit when we are wrong. Please help us to accept responsibility for our actions. Amen.

FAITHFUL WITH A FEW THINGS

- Name some things that God has given to you that you can use for him.
- What does it mean to be faithful with your money?

"To one he gave five bags of gold, to another two bags, and to another one bag, each according to his ability. Then he went on his journey . . .

The man who had received five bags of gold brought the other five. 'Master,' he said, 'you entrusted me with five bags of gold. See, I have gained five more.'

His master replied, 'Well done, good and faithful servant! You have been faithful with a few things; I will put you in charge of many things. Come and share your master's happiness!'" MATTHEW 25:15,20–21

In this parable from Matthew, a man leaving on a journey left his money behind with three servants.

Two of his servants went to work with their master's money. They invested it and got a return for their efforts, which they gratefully gave to their master when he returned. The third servant, however, was "wicked" and "lazy" and did nothing with the money that his master had given him. He had nothing to show for it and offered up excuses for his lack of responsibility.

In the same way, God gives each of us a certain amount of "wealth," which we are to use in his service. This wealth could be actual money. It could be time. It could be a skill. What he gives us and the amount it is not the point. The point is what we do with it. Do we use it wisely? Or do we behave wickedly and lazily and do nothing with it?

God has entrusted us with a portion of his wealth so that we can use it for his glory. We need to be faithful with what we have been given. We need to put it to work. ✤

PRAYER

Dear God, thank you for entrusting us with a portion of your wealth. Please help us to use it wisely, so that we will increase it and be able to give back to you. Amen.

ABILITIES AND LIMITATIONS

- What would happen if you tried to work every hour of every day?
- Share a time when you worked with a group of people who cooperated well together.

So the Twelve gathered all the disciples together and said, "It would not be right for us to neglect the ministry of the word of God in order to wait on tables. Brothers and sisters, choose seven men from among you who are known to be full of the Spirit and wisdom. We will turn this responsibility over to them" . . . So the word of God spread. The number of disciples in Jerusalem increased rapidly, and a large number of priests became obedient to the faith. ACTS 6:2–3,7

These verses explain one of the ways that the believers in Acts organized their efforts. They worked together to form a system. It wasn't chaotic. They didn't waste energy, time or resources. They wanted to work efficiently for God.

They recognized their own abilities and their own limitations. They didn't run around trying to do everything at once. They didn't try to do more than they could do, and they worked hard at what they could do. As a result, the church grew, and more and more people came to know Jesus.

Believers today also need to share responsibilities. No one can do it all. And everyone should be doing something. We need to prayerfully consider where our abilities best fit into God's work. We need to ask God to assign us to tasks that will allow us to best serve him. And as a result, the Word of God will spread. ♣

PRAYER

Dear God, please help us to know and use the abilities you have given us. Please also help us to know our own limitations. Amen.

day322

WHO NEEDS THE DOCTOR?

- Why do we go to the doctor?
- What does it mean to be brokenhearted?

The LORD is close to the brokenhearted and saves those who are crushed in spirit.

PSALM 34:18

This verse from the book of Psalms is one of many Bible verses that teach that God cares about our emotions. He cares when we are hurting. God heals broken hearts.

It can be tempting to think that our problems are too small for God, or that God is too busy for our pain, but this is just not true. God wants us to cast all our cares on him.

Jesus said, "It is not the healthy who need a doctor, but the sick" (Matthew 9:12). Jesus came to this earth to help, heal and save those who needed him. When we are brokenhearted, we need Jesus, and it is through this broken heart that we can grow closer to him.

When someone shares a testimony, listen closely. Nearly all believers have, at one point or another, experienced God's healing power. He truly does save those who are crushed in spirit. ✤

PRAYER

Dear God, thank you for caring about our emotions. Thank you, Jesus, for coming to earth to heal the sick. Help us to bring our emotional pain to you. Amen.

GUARD YOUR HEARTS!

- What does it mean to guard something?
- How do you behave when you're upset?

Above all else, guard your heart, for everything you do flows from it.   Proverbs 4:23

When this verse talks about the "heart," it is referring to our thoughts, emotions and will. Basically, our "heart" is who we are on the inside.

God wants us to keep his truth in our hearts. The state of our hearts affects how we behave, the decisions we make and the words we say. It is so important that we "guard our hearts," watching over and guarding them from dangers.

God cares about our hearts, about our feelings. He doesn't promise that our feelings will never be hurt, but he does tell us to guard our own hearts. When we guard our hearts, we can protect ourselves from many situations that will bring us pain. We also prevent ourselves from making bad decisions based on our emotions, decisions that will often bring us even more pain.

We guard our hearts, in part, by spending time with God. Filling our hearts with God's truth is one of the best ways to guard and protect our hearts. Another way to guard our hearts is to keep bad things out. If we know something isn't good for us, we should stay away from it. ✤

PRAYER

Dear God, please help us to guard our hearts, to carefully guard our emotions. Help everything that flows from our hearts to be honoring to you. Amen.

day324

THE EMOTION SNOWBALL

- How do you act when you are angry?
- Share a time when you got angry with a sibling or a friend.

In the course of time Cain brought some of the fruits of the soil as an offering to the LORD. And Abel also brought an offering—fat portions from some of the firstborn of his flock. The LORD looked with favor on Abel and his offering, but on Cain and his offering he did not look with favor. So Cain was very angry, and his face was downcast.

GENESIS 4:3–5

You may know the story of the brothers, Cain and Abel. Shortly after this Genesis scene, Cain says to his brother, "Let's go out to the field." When they get there, Cain attacks and kills Abel. When God asks Cain where Abel is, Abel lies and says he does not know (see Genesis 4:8–9).

Sin can have a snowball effect if we let it. And Cain's devastating snowball began with emotions—anger and jealousy. On their own, anger and jealousy are only emotions, but emotions can lead us to sinful actions if we let them. And then sin can lead to more sin, which leads to more anger and hurt.

We need to recognize emotions for what they are: emotions, and only emotions. We do not have to act on them. If our emotions make us want to sin, we need to resist this temptation and bring our emotions to God. We need to pray about whatever we are feeling. ✤

PRAYER

Dear God, please help us to recognize and respect our emotions. Help us to learn to deal with the emotions that we experience by praying about them, talking about them and expressing them in appropriate ways. Amen.

day325

NEVER FOLLOW A GUIDE WHO DOES NOT KNOW THE WAY

- Describe a time when you were tempted to sin.
- Describe the process you go through when you need to make a decision.

So I say, walk by the Spirit, and you will not gratify the desires of the flesh. For the flesh desires what is contrary to the Spirit, and the Spirit what is contrary to the flesh. They are in conflict with each other, so that you are not to do whatever you want.

GALATIANS 5:16–17

The flesh desires what is contrary to the Spirit. In the Bible, "the flesh" does not just refer to our physical bodies but also to our minds and emotions. Basically, "the flesh" refers to all the parts of us that are susceptible to sin.

God has given believers the Holy Spirit to show us a better way. The Holy Spirit lives inside each and every believer to help us make good decisions. When we listen to the Holy Spirit, we make good and safe decisions that honor and please God. When we listen only to our emotions, we can make poor decisions that land us in trouble.

We all have feelings, and we need to be aware of and able to name our emotions. We were not designed to be robots. But we shouldn't depend on our emotions to guide us. Our emotions are not always reliable—only the Holy Spirit is a reliable guide. ✤

PRAYER

Dear God, thank you for giving us the Holy Spirit to guide us. Please help us listen to and obey the Holy Spirit. Amen.

FOR ANSWERED PRAYERS

- What's the last prayer you remember the Lord answering?
- Why is it important to remember God's answers to your prayers?

I will praise you, LORD, with all my heart; before the "gods" I will sing your praise. I will bow down toward your holy temple and will praise your name for your unfailing love and your faithfulness, for you have so exalted your solemn decree that it surpasses your fame. When I called, you answered me; you greatly emboldened me.　　　PSALM 138:1–3

David understood that he wasn't throwing prayers into a void. He knew God was listening to every word. He knew because God answered his prayers—just as he answers ours.

Do you remember the Lord's answers to a prayer? Do you have a record of your prayers and their answers? Sometimes it's easy to forget about yesterday when today's needs become pressing. As a result, we can forget God's amazing work in our lives.

That's why a prayer journal is a great idea. A prayer journal is a place to write down our requests and how God answered them. With a journal, we can look back on past answers and thank God for his continuing goodness in our lives.

We can also use our journal as a confidence builder when we feel anxious about a current need. We can remind ourselves that God took care of us in the past and will take care of us in the future.

Let us be thankful that God hears our prayers and answers them. Let's thank him for the times he gives us exactly what we ask for, exactly when we need it. But let's also thank him for the times he *doesn't* give us what we ask for because he has something better in mind. ✤

PRAYER

Dear God, thank you for listening when we talk to you. Thank you for answering our prayers as you see fit because your way is perfect. Help us keep your answered prayers fresh in our minds. Amen.

A THANKFUL LIFE

- How many blessings do you think God sends your way every day? No need to be precise; you can just round to the nearest million.
- What keeps you from saying "thank you" to God as much as you should?

And whatever you do, whether in word or deed, do it all in the name of the Lord Jesus, giving thanks to God the Father through him.   COLOSSIANS 3:17

Every day is Thanksgiving for a Christian—at least, it should be. We certainly have more than enough to be thankful for. We don't need to look far for God's blessings in our lives. They're all around us: a place to live, a loving family or someone to care for us, supportive friends, food to eat, clothes to wear, assorted talents and abilities, the security of knowing we'll go to heaven when we die—just to name a few.

We have the material for a 365-day Thanksgiving celebration, but do we have the desire? After all, life gets busy. More important things come up. Right?

Actually, they don't. If we're serious about our relationship God, nothing is more important. We just need to rethink our schedules. How can we carve a little time out of every day to think about what God has done for us and tell him how much we appreciate it? One idea is to keep a running conversation. As good things come up, we can thank God for them. When we solve a problem or do well on a test, we can thank him for our reasoning skills. When we go to church, we can thank him for living in a place where we are free to worship him.

We can learn to appreciate every moment—and share our appreciation with the One who made it possible. ❖

PRAYER

Dear God, we praise you for the blessings you pour into our lives every day. If we were to list them, there would not be enough time in the day to get them all named. Thank you for taking care of us. Let us never lose sight of what you've done. Amen.

day328

THANK YOU, LORD

- When you pray, how much of your prayer is spent praising and thanking God, and how much is spent making requests?
- What's wrong with having too little gratitude in your prayers?

Do not be anxious about anything, but in every situation, by prayer and petition, with thanksgiving, present your requests to God. PHILIPPIANS 4:6

We should take advantage of every opportunity we get to say "thank you" to God in prayer. That's good advice whether we're feeling incredibly happy or incredibly down. If we're happy, our joy will be multiplied by sharing our gratitude with the One who made it possible. If we're down, we'll feel better when we focus on the good things God is doing in our life.

Too often our prayers, even during our family devotions, sound like a fast-food order: "I'd like good grades for my math test, a successful surgery for my grandmother and a way to make $250 before spring break. Amen." The problem with that approach is that it's one-sided. Prayer should be a conversation, a way of exercising and celebrating our relationship with God. Constant asking does not make for a good relationship.

If we're serious about having a relationship with God, a good rule of thumb is to begin our prayers with praise and thanksgiving. That way, if we run out of time, we will have gotten to the important, relationship-building part.

God will take care of our needs and honor our requests. He proves that every day. So, will we honor him with our thanks? ✤

PRAYER

Dear God, thank you for our family and for this time to come together in devotion. Forgive us for the times we forget to tell you how much we appreciate what you've done. Please help us remember your work in our lives. Amen.

IN ALL CIRCUMSTANCES

- How do you know God is always with you?
- Why is God's work hard to recognize when things get bad?

Rejoice always, pray continually, give thanks in all circumstances; for this is God's will for you in Christ Jesus.   1 THESSALONIANS 5:16–18

"Give thanks in all circumstances"? Is that even possible, or was the apostle Paul trying to make some ironic point to the Thessalonians? People can't really give thanks when they've just lost their jobs, can they? Or when they've just been told they have cancer? Or when they are being bullied at school? There is nothing to be thankful for in any of those circumstances, is there?

It turns out the apostle Paul wasn't joking. There are thing to be thankful for in *all* circumstances. We just need to know where to look. If we have trouble seeing beyond the bad in our lives, we can ask God to open our eyes to the things he's doing that we can't see. He'll help us see concerned friends, committed doctors, caring teachers and other resources we may not have noticed.

Even if we can't see what God is doing in our lives now, we can thank him for the things he's done in the past. There's no expiration date on God's blessings. We can still mention them in prayer, no matter how long ago we received them.

If we as a family learn to praise God in all circumstances, we will grow closer to him. ❖

PRAYER

Dear God, train our eyes to see your work in our lives. Keep our eyes open to the amazing things you do — even in the worst of times. We praise you for your wondrous love. Amen.

day330

FOR HIS GOODNESS

- When you think of someone who is "good," who comes to mind? Why?
- How is God's goodness different from human goodness?

Give thanks to the LORD, for he is good; his love endures forever.   PSALM 107:1

True goodness is a hard thing for humans to understand because we don't see very much of it. Sure, there are good people in the world. But a lot of actions we call "good" often have motivations that aren't. Some people may act nice and friendly but only because they expect something in return. If they don't get it, they withdraw their goodness. Other people are inconsistent. They do something good one day, then turn around and do something terribly destructive the next.

We're all guilty of it. Think of times in our family when someone was extra helpful and obedient because they wanted to go to a sleepover or a party. Human goodness is temporary.

The goodness that the psalmist talks about in Psalm 107:1 is different, though. God's goodness, like his love, endures forever. It's not motivated by selfish desire. He doesn't demand anything in return.

It's never inconsistent either. He knows exactly what we need, and he gives it exactly when we need it. He gives out of the pure goodness of his heart. He loves us and wants us to be fulfilled in him. That deserves our thanks. ✤

PRAYER

Dear God, in our broken world, your goodness shines. We celebrate that goodness today. Give us the words and the opportunity to tell others about it. Amen.

FOR OUR SALVATION

- How do you explain to your friends what it means to be saved?
- Why does God want you to know that you had nothing to do with your salvation?

For it is by grace you have been saved, through faith—and this is not from yourselves, it is the gift of God—not by works, so that no one can boast. EPHESIANS 2:8-9

We take certain things for granted every day. We never question whether we'll have oxygen to breathe or water to drink or gravity to keep us from floating off into space. We don't give those things a second thought; they are a given.

Some sure things, though, deserve more than a second thought. Our salvation, for one. If we've repented and put our trust in Christ, our salvation is more assured than oxygen, water and gravity.

Yet we can never take it for granted because it came at such a steep price. We are saved only because Jesus took the punishment for our sin. He died on the cross in our place. His blood covers our impurity. That deserves more than a second thought, wouldn't you say? It's certainly something to be thankful for—again and again and again.

A worthwhile goal for our family would be to thank God for our salvation at least once a day. We can do it during a private morning prayer, our mealtime prayer at dinner, our bedtime prayer or anytime in between. The important thing is that we tell God regularly how grateful we are for his gift of salvation. ✤

PRAYER

Dear God, we humbly thank you for our salvation. We were helpless to save ourselves, so you sent Christ to save us. We can never repay the debt we owe you. We can only praise you forever. Amen.

FOR HIS PROTECTION

- What's the most dangerous situation you've ever faced?
- How did God help you through it?

My shield is God Most High, who saves the upright in heart. PSALM 7:10

David made a powerful enemy in King Saul, though he couldn't understand why. David had been nothing but loyal to the king. He killed the giant Goliath because none of the Israelite soldiers would do it. How could he have known that would make him more popular than Saul in the eyes of the Israelites?

David took a job playing harp in the palace to ease the king's nerves. How could he have known that Saul was getting more and more crazed in his resentment? Saul twice tried to kill David with a spear. When that didn't work, he sent a team of assassins to execute him. David escaped into the mountains, where he hid until King Saul's anger cooled. While he was in hiding, David poured out his emotions to God in psalms.

You'd expect to find fear in his words, and there is some. But there's also a lot of thankfulness, which you may not expect. As powerful as King Saul was, he was no match for David's "shield," God Most High. God would not allow Saul to harm David, and David was grateful for it.

God is our shield too. He protects us and gives us comfort in whatever we are facing. How will we show him our thankfulness? ✤

PRAYER

Dear God, you are our shield. You protect us from harm. Give us the wisdom to trust you when we are afraid. Amen.

day**333**

FOR HIS FAITHFULNESS

- Are you a faithful friend? Explain.
- Give an example of how God has been faithful to our family.

Give praise to the LORD, proclaim his name; make known among the nations what he has done. Sing to him, sing praise to him; tell of all his wonderful acts. Glory in his holy name; let the hearts of those who seek the LORD rejoice. 1 CHRONICLES 16:8–10

If you ever need a praise role model, look to David. He was a shepherd, a giant-killer, a warrior, a musician and the most beloved king in Israel's history. More important than all that, though, is the fact that David knew how to praise God.

In Scripture, David is described as a man after God's own heart. He didn't get that reputation by ignoring the Lord. David knew God better than most people because David spent more time talking to him than most people do. And what did David talk about? Sometimes he talked about his enemies. Sometimes he talked about his failures. But most of the time, he talked about how great and how faithful God is.

The setting of 1 Chronicles 16 is Jerusalem, where David had just returned the ark of the covenant, one of the holiest relics in Israel's history. David was so excited that he started praising God for his faithfulness to Israel throughout history. And David didn't stop for 29 verses.

Do you think we could fill 29 verses with thanks to God for his faithfulness to our family? We'll never know until we try. ✤

PRAYER

Dear God, you have been faithful to our family. You have shown us what true, long-lasting love looks like. Bless our efforts to stay faithful to you. Amen.

FOR HIS PROVISION

- If your house was on fire and you had one minute to grab as many possessions as you could, what would you get? Why?
- What does your list say about you?

May the peoples praise you, God; may all the peoples praise you. The land yields its harvest; God, our God, blesses us. May God bless us still, so that all the ends of the earth will fear him.   PSALM 67:5–7

In this devotion, we're going to answer three questions. Here's question number one: What do we *need* in this world? That's a little tricky, isn't it? If the question were, "What do you *want* in this world?" we could probably make a list ten pages long. Wants are easy to think of, but what about needs?

For starters, we need oxygen to breathe. We need water to drink. We need food to eat. We need some kind of shelter from the elements. We need love. We need forgiveness. We might add other, less primal needs such as a job to support the family or a way to get food and water.

Here's question number two: How many of our family's needs has God supplied? That's an easier answer: all of them. God takes care of our needs—and a great deal of our wants.

Here's question number three: How often do we thank God for providing the basics that we need to survive? In Psalm 67:5–6, David calls on the people of the earth to praise God for the harvest that the land was about to produce.

Let's answer his call as a family. Let's spend some time thanking God for the basics, the things we need every day. ❖

PRAYER

Dear God, thank you for the air we breathe, the water we drink, the food we eat and everything else you provide to keep us alive. Your creation is amazing, and it sustains us. Amen.

FOR HIS GRACE

- Why did the Israelites keep disobeying God after all the things he did for them?
- Why do you disobey God after all the things he's done for you?

In that day you will say: "I will praise you, LORD. Although you were angry with me, your anger has turned away and you have comforted me. Surely God is my salvation; I will trust and not be afraid. The LORD, the LORD himself, is my strength and my defense; he has become my salvation." ISAIAH 12:1−2

The prophet Isaiah wrote the song of praise in Isaiah 12 to show his thankfulness for the Lord's deliverance of Israel. From Egypt, through the Red Sea, against the attacks of the Philistines and others, God kept his protective hand over his people. He delivered them safely to the promised land. Isaiah wanted to make sure that the Israelites showed God proper thanks.

Let's thank God for *our* deliverance too. As sinful creatures, we faced a bleak future. We had no hope of ever restoring our broken relationship with God. Heaven was beyond our reach. Our sin destined us to be separated from God forever.

Yet he would not let that happen. He loves us too much to allow us to stay trapped in our sin, apart from him. Someone had to take the punishment for wrongdoing, so he sacrificed his Son. Causing unimaginable pain to himself in the process, God gave us the gift of salvation. Thanks to him, we can have eternal life through Jesus.

Let us show him our gratitude. Beyond that, let's help others discover his mercy and salvation. Let's give them something to really be thankful for! ✤

PRAYER

Dear God, we have read about your deliverance in the Bible, and we have experienced it ourselves. Thank you for your miraculous work in this world. We love you. Amen.

FOR HIS DEEDS

- What is the best present anyone could give you?
- Besides salvation, what is the greatest thing you've ever received from God?

We praise you, God, we praise you, for your Name is near; people tell of your wonderful deeds.   PSALM 75:1

Psalm 75:1 is a perfect verse of thanksgiving: "People tell of your wonderful deeds." By telling of God's wonderful deeds, we show our thanks and bring him glory. That's the way to show gratitude!

In Psalm 75, the psalmist celebrates God's perfect justice, the fact that good will be rewarded and evil will be punished. He celebrates God's power in holding the world together despite all the wickedness in it. He celebrates the fact that those who are arrogant and wicked will one day get what's coming to them. Those are the deeds the psalmist wanted people to know about. Because his words have survived to this day, we can celebrate with him.

If we were to make a list, it probably would look much different than the psalmist's. We might celebrate the good things that have happened at work and school. We might celebrate the way we've grown spiritually at church. We might celebrate our family bond. We might celebrate our friends. We might celebrate our ministry opportunities.

It doesn't really matter what we celebrate, only that we praise God and share with others the amazing things he has done in our lives. ❖

PRAYER

Dear God, we celebrate your goodness in our lives in so many areas. You give us everything we need and more. Amen.

EVERY KNEE SHOULD BOW

- How well do you respond to authority?
- What kind of authority do you respond best to?

Therefore God exalted him to the highest place and gave him the name that is above every name, that at the name of Jesus every knee should bow, in heaven and on earth and under the earth. PHILIPPIANS 2:9–10

Jesus came to earth as a humble servant. Jesus humbled himself by choice. He gave up his heavenly glory to squeeze himself into a simple human body. He started life as a baby. He lived among us, his own creation. He allowed himself to be mocked, beaten and killed. And he did it for us because there was no other way for us to be saved.

Because of his willingness to humble himself, God the Father gave Jesus the highest authority. No one is above him. No one else inspires worship like him. God leaves no room for doubt as to who deserves our eternal praise.

In our eagerness to understand Jesus' humanity, we sometimes lose sight of just how awe-inspiring he is. This week, let's take some time as a family to think about Jesus' authority and what our proper response to him should be. ✤

PRAYER

Dear Lord, we humbly come before you as your servants. Because of your grace, you allow us to have a personal relationship with you. However, we will never lose sight of your power and authority. Amen.

day338

THE KING OF THE NATIONS

- Why is it important to praise Jesus?
- What happens when you neglect to praise him?

"Great and marvelous are your deeds, Lord God Almighty. Just and true are your ways, King of the nations."
REVELATION 15:3B

In Revelation 15:3, the people in heaven are playing harps and singing praises to the King of the nations. The scene takes place during the final judgment of the earth, not long before the end of the world. Jesus is on the verge of establishing a new order, and his subjects are glorifying him in song.

Because we often focus on the 33 years Jesus spent dwelling among us on earth, we can lose sight of his eternal nature and his awesome power as the King. The prophet Jeremiah said this about him: "When he is angry, the earth trembles; the nations cannot endure his wrath" (Jeremiah 10:10).

And the one Jeremiah was talking about—the King who has performed great and marvelous deeds and whose anger causes the earth and all of its nations to tremble—is the one who humbly subjected himself to humiliation, torture and death on the cross to save us.

That is the King we follow. That is the Lord we worship. ❖

PRAYER

Dear Lord, you have reigned forever and you will reign forever. We are blessed to call you King and Savior. Thank you for leaving your throne to save us. Amen.

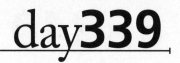

THE LAMB OF GOD

- How would you describe a lamb?
- Why is Jesus' sacrifice once and for all, instead of temporary, like the Old Testament sacrifices?

I did not see a temple in the city, because the Lord God Almighty and the Lamb are its temple. REVELATION 21:22

The idea of the Messiah being the Lamb of God goes way back to before Jesus was born. The Old Testament prophet Isaiah said, "He was oppressed and afflicted, yet he did not open his mouth; he was led like a lamb to the slaughter, and as a sheep before its shearers is silent, so he did not open his mouth" (Isaiah 53:7). Like a lamb, Jesus appears meek, humble and willing to submit to God's will. But in order to fully understand why Jesus is called a lamb, we need to look at the way things were in Old Testament times.

Before the Savior came, people had to atone for their sins by making sacrifices, usually using animals. Not just any animal would do for a sacrifice, though. It had to be a male without defect (see Leviticus 1:3), the firstborn of the flock or herd (see Numbers 18:15) and without any broken bones (see Exodus 12:46).

Jesus, the ultimate sacrifice, fits all those descriptions. He is male, without defect (or sin) and the firstborn of God. And even though he was crucified, none of his bones were broken (see John 19:36). He is the Lamb of God, and his sacrifice makes it possible for us to live forever. ✤

PRAYER

Dear Lord, thank you for humbling yourself to become the sacrificial Lamb for us. You are perfect. No other sacrifice can save us. We will praise you forever. Amen.

day340

ONE WAY

- What would you say if someone tried to convince you that Christianity isn't the only belief system that offers a path to God?
- How can you be respectful of someone's beliefs while pointing out areas in which you disagree?

Jesus answered, "I am the way and the truth and the life. No one comes to the Father except through me."   JOHN 14:6

Muslims believe that paradise can be earned through reciting a creed, praying five times a day, giving a certain percentage of money once a year, fasting during Ramadan and making a pilgrimage to Mecca. Hindus believe they can become one with God by living pure lives, free of earthly desires. Dozens of other religions teach dozens of other means of salvation.

Are any of them valid? Is there more than one way to be saved? As Christians, we must answer no—not because we're narrow-minded, but because if there's another path to salvation, it makes Jesus' sacrifice meaningless.

If there is another way to God—a back door to heaven—then Jesus didn't have to suffer on the cross. He didn't have to take the sins of the world on his shoulders. He didn't have to die in our place.

Jesus' sacrifice on the cross and his resurrection are the cornerstone of our faith. When we live in a way that points to Jesus, others will see that. We know Jesus is the only way; let's live in a way that shows that reality to others. ✤

PRAYER

Dear God, thank you for making salvation simple for us. Thank you for giving us one way to you. Bless our efforts to help other people understand that truth. Amen.

day**341**

THE FAITH LENS

- What do you think of when you hear the term *worldview*?
- What does it mean to be transformed?

Do not conform to the pattern of this world, but be transformed by the renewing of your mind. Then you will be able to test and approve what God's will is—his good, pleasing and perfect will.   Romans 12:2

Taylor was a star basketball player, but she was not a team player. She never passed the ball. She talked down to her teammates, constantly letting them know how lucky they were to have her. And if her coach created a play for someone else to shoot, Taylor refused to execute it.

When Taylor learned about Jesus, everything changed. She realized that life wasn't all about her. Her behavior changed, but more importantly, her thoughts changed. Even in the midst of competition, her thoughts were focused on glorifying God. She looked for, and found, evidence of God's image in her teammates.

When we become believers, we adopt a new worldview. Our old ideas get kicked out, and we begin to look at everything through the faith lens. We think about things differently. And if some old attitudes and thoughts do creep in, we need to get rid of them. It is our new worldview that will lead us to God's perfect will for our lives. ✤

PRAYER

Dear God, thank you for transforming us and renewing our minds. Please help us to always think like believers, as even our thoughts can glorify you. Amen.

day342 december 8

WHAT YOU THINK MATTERS

- Share a time when something you saw in a movie or television show bothered you.
- When you are in a good mood, what kinds of thoughts are you thinking?

Finally, brothers and sisters, whatever is true, whatever is noble, whatever is right, whatever is pure, whatever is lovely, whatever is admirable—if anything is excellent or praiseworthy—think about such things. PHILIPPIANS 4:8

You've probably noticed that thinking about certain things upsets you. While a violent or scary movie may not frighten you while you're watching it, it may well lead you to think disturbing thoughts after the movie is over. Or while you might find a certain friend fun, spending time with them might leave you feeling uncomfortable with what you've been talking about or doing.

God knows this and has given us instructions to help us protect ourselves. When we think thoughts that are pleasing to God, we are happier, healthier and better able to live for God and get his work done.

God tells us to think about what is true. Don't focus on the world's lies: that you're not beautiful enough, that money will make you happy, that you have to follow the crowd. Instead, focus your thoughts on what is noble, pure, lovely and admirable. Think about what is excellent and praiseworthy.

Your thoughts affect your life. God has given you the power to live a better life just by steering your thoughts toward him. ✤

PRAYER

Dear God, thank you for making our thoughts powerful. Please help us to obey this verse and to think on things that please you. Amen.

MENTAL SIN IS SIN

- Give an example of a mental sin.
- What are some ways that you can control your thoughts?

"You have heard that it was said, 'You shall not commit adultery.' But I tell you that anyone who looks at a woman lustfully has already committed adultery with her in his heart. If your right eye causes you to stumble, gouge it out and throw it away. It is better for you to lose one part of your body than for your whole body to be thrown into hell."

MATTHEW 5:27–29

The Old Testament teaches us about sin, but here in the Gospel of Matthew, Jesus takes it up a notch. We know from the Old Testament that murder is a sin, but Jesus tells us that just *thinking* about committing murder is sin. And this goes for all the other sins as well. It is a sin to think about cheating on a test. It is a sin to think hateful things about your brothers and sisters, even if you don't say them out loud. Mental sin is sin.

Jesus says to throw away our eye if it's causing us to sin. He doesn't want us to actually go gouge out our own eye, but he uses this language to convey the seriousness of mental sins. It would be better to lose an eye than to go to hell because our mental sins kept us away from God.

We can control our thoughts. God gives us the strength to do this. It is not easy, and it takes time and effort to learn to control our minds. But with God's help, we can keep our minds pure. ✤

PRAYER

Dear God, thank you for your Word. Please help us to keep away from mental sins. Please help us to keep our minds trained on you. Amen.

THINGS ABOVE

* Do you look forward to heaven? Explain.
* Give an example of how a person might set their mind on earthly things. Give an example of how a person might set their mind on heavenly things.

Since, then, you have been raised with Christ, set your hearts on things above, where Christ is, seated at the right hand of God. Set your minds on things above, not on earthly things.   COLOSSIANS 3:1–2

Before a person becomes a Christian, it's natural for them to have an earthly outlook. We can't really blame someone for pursuing wealth, fame, popularity, fun and everything else this world has to offer. After all, from their perspective, what else is there? Life is short, so grab everything you can while you can.

When a person makes a decision for Christ, though, the perspective changes. We shift our eyes away from this earth and toward heaven. We see things with an eternal view. We shift our priorities to reflect what's really important. We recognize the things of this world for what they can be: distractions, wastes of time, empty pleasures.

We turn our attention to heaven. We consider the possibilities. If heaven is where God is, and God is the source of all joy and happiness, what does that say about our eternal life there? What kind of place has Jesus prepared for us (see John 14:3)? What will it be like not to have to worry about pain, sickness, sorrow or death? We may not know a lot about heaven, but we know enough to get our curiosity going. ✤

PRAYER

Dear God, thank you for giving us an unimaginable future beyond this life. Help us keep our minds focused on heavenly things, not earthly things. Fill us with an excitement for heaven. Amen.

NO MOURNING, NO CRYING

- How would you like people to remember you when you're gone?
- How would your life be different today if death didn't exist? Think of the friends and loved ones you've lost.

He will swallow up death forever. The Sovereign LORD will wipe away the tears from all faces; he will remove his people's disgrace from all the earth. The LORD has spoken.

ISAIAH 25:8

Unless you're very imaginative, heaven is a hard place to picture. Most of what we know about it comes from John's descriptions in the book of Revelation. And few people would describe them as easy to understand. "A sea of glass glowing with fire" (Revelation 15:2)? "Four living creatures . . . covered with eyes" (Revelation 4:6)?

Countless Bible scholars have made educated guesses as to what heaven will be like. But no one has any real concrete idea because no one has ever come back from heaven to tell us.

One thing we know for sure is that there will be no death in heaven. When Jesus rose from the grave, he defeated death once and for all. Anyone who believes in him will have life forever in heaven, with no death to end the joy of being forever in God's presence.

The eternal perspective allows us to look at death—especially the deaths of believers—as a temporary pain. It's a pain that certainly hurts, but it hurts only for a while. When we get to heaven, we will be free of death forever. ✤

PRAYER

Dear God, thank you for assuring us that one day death will be no more. Give us the strength and comfort we need when we lose a friend or loved one. Make us instruments of strength and comfort when other people suffer loss. Amen.

day346

december 12

HEAVEN ON EARTH

- How do you picture heaven?
- How would your life be different if you lived each day with a greater awareness of heaven?

Meanwhile we groan, longing to be clothed instead with our heavenly dwelling.

2 CORINTHIANS 5:2

Have you ever heard something described as "heaven on earth"? Usually the phrase is used when someone's talking about an exotic vacation destination or a cozy hometown. Most people likely have some very specific ideas about what heaven on earth is for them.

In reality, though, heaven and earth are two very different places. Heaven is our homeland, the place of our citizenship. The other is earth. No, that's not a mistake. That's reality for Christians. The earth is *not* our home.

The apostle Peter describes us as "foreigners and exiles" in this world (1 Peter 2:11). The apostle Paul urges us to hang on to our outsider status and warns, "Do not conform to the pattern of this world" (Romans 12:2). In other words, we shouldn't make ourselves too comfortable here because we're only passing through. Our lives will not be complete until we enter heaven.

That perspective allows us to look at the bad things in this world from a temporary point of view. Pain is temporary. Suffering is temporary. That perspective may not make our misery go away, but it does help a little to know it won't last forever. ✤

PRAYER

Dear God, we thank you for the world we live in and the blessings you give us here. We thank you especially for the heavenly home you are preparing for us. Let us never lose sight of what's really important. Amen.

350

WHERE YOUR TREASURE IS

- List the presents you got for Christmas last year.
- What do you want for Christmas this year?

For where your treasure is, there your heart will be also.   MATTHEW 6:21

Christmas is coming. You know this. Are you already tired of Christmas music and decorations?

With all the hype, it can be very easy to get caught up in the materialism of the season. You are being absolutely pummeled by advertisements and other forms of media, all of them telling you which stuff you should want the most. Everything is bigger, shinier, faster and smarter than last year.

This materialistic philosophy tells us that life is about what we own. But we know life isn't about stuff. It really doesn't matter what presents we want or what presents we get. None of that stuff will satisfy. If we get caught up in that mentality, it is never enough, and we always end up wanting more than what we already have.

Where is your heart? Is it with God this Christmas? Where is your treasure? This Christmas, think about what you really want. Think about wanting something that will truly satisfy. ✤

PRAYER

Dear God, we are so grateful that we know the truth, that we know what really matters. Please help us to not get caught up in the mania of the season. Amen.

day348

MORE BLESSED TO GIVE

- Have you ever given a gift that brought someone joy? How did that make you feel?
- What is the best gift someone can give?

"In everything I did, I showed you that by this kind of hard work we must help the weak, remembering the words the Lord Jesus himself said: 'It is more blessed to give than to receive.'"   ACTS 20:35

In this verse from Acts, Paul tells us that Jesus once said, "It is more blessed to give than to receive." If you've ever given a gift to someone who really appreciated it, then you know what an absolute thrill you get when that person's face lights up with joy. It is way better than the thrill you get when you unwrap your own present.

The best way to celebrate Christmas is to focus on the giving part, not the getting part. If you take the time to figure out how to bless someone, you won't believe how awesome you'll feel. What could you give to your family members that would really be meaningful? What could you give to someone in need? You might not even have to buy anything. Maybe you could give your time or your skills. Maybe you could make a gift, or give away something that you already own.

Jesus provided us with the best possible example of giving. He spent his whole life giving, and he ended his life on earth by giving his life on the cross. When we give a gift at Christmastime, we are honoring the gift that he gave us. ✤

PRAYER

Dear God, thank you for the Christmas season. Thank you for Jesus' example. Thank you for blessing us with joy when we give. Please show us a way to give this Christmas that honors your Son. Amen.

NO DOUBT!

- How would your life change if you couldn't talk for nine months?
- Share a time when you doubted God.

Zechariah asked the angel, "How can I be sure of this? I am an old man and my wife is well along in years." The angel said to him, "I am Gabriel. I stand in the presence of God, and I have been sent to speak to you and to tell you this good news. And now you will be silent and not able to speak until the day this happens, because you did not believe my words, which will come true at their appointed time." LUKE 1:18–20

Shortly before Mary became pregnant with Jesus, the angel Gabriel appeared to a righteous man named Zechariah. The angel told Zechariah that he and his wife would soon have a son who would grow up to be John the Baptist. And Zechariah, even though he was a believer and loved God, responded with, "Are you sure? We're pretty old."

Many, if not most, people would have had some doubts too in that situation. But not all of us will be silenced for nine months for our doubts. But that is what God did to Zechariah. The angel Gabriel said to him, "You will not be able to speak until your son is born."

How would you have responded to the news of a miracle had you been in Zechariah's shoes? How do you respond today to the revelations that you hear in the Bible or in Biblical teachings? It is normal to doubt, but we need to bring those doubts to God. James writes in James 1:6 that "the one who doubts is like a wave of the sea, blown and tossed by the wind." We must work to have complete faith that God will do what he says he will do. ✤

PRAYER

Dear God, please forgive us when we doubt. Please make our faith stronger. Amen.

day350

THE FORERUNNERS

- What is a forerunner?
- Share something that you know about John the Baptist.

"For he will be great in the sight of the Lord. He is never to take wine or other fermented drink, and he will be filled with the Holy Spirit even before he is born. He will bring back many of the people of Israel to the Lord their God. And he will go on before the Lord, in the spirit and power of Elijah, to turn the hearts of the parents to their children and the disobedient to the wisdom of the righteous — to make ready a people prepared for the Lord."

LUKE 1:15–17

Of all the people discussed in the Bible, it's tough to find anyone more fascinating than John the Baptist. People of all ages are drawn to him — he's tough, well spoken, smart and committed. He's committed to his work. He wears camel fur and eats honey and locusts. He's the stuff of legends, and he was very much real.

John the Baptist served a very important purpose. He was Jesus' forerunner. A forerunner is someone who is sent in advance to announce the coming of someone or something. And Jesus' cousin John took his job very seriously. He preached to anyone who would listen, and people came from miles around to hear what he had to say. He told them that the Messiah was coming, that he would soon be in their midst. Because of John the Baptist's powerful words, many people repented and were baptized before Jesus even began his ministry.

We too are Christ's forerunners, though we may never have to eat locusts. Jesus is coming back to earth, and we are to prepare the way for him. We can learn a lot from John the Baptist's boldness and dedication. He was a great and humble man. ✤

PRAYER

Dear God, thank you for John the Baptist. Please show us how to be forerunners for Jesus. Please help us to prepare the way for him. Amen.

THE FIRST MENTION OF JESUS

- Where in the Bible is Jesus first mentioned?
- At what point in history did Jesus' sacrifice on the cross become necessary?

"And I will put enmity between you and the woman, and between your offspring and hers; he will crush your head, and you will strike his heel."　　　GENESIS 3:15

It's almost Christmas, but let's go way back to the beginning for a moment. People sometimes think that Jesus first appears on the scene when he is born in Bethlehem, but in Genesis 3:15, we learn that this assumption isn't even close.

In this verse, God is talking directly to Satan. God tells Satan that he will put hatred between Satan's offspring and Eve's offspring. No surprise there. But it's a little bit more surprising when God says "he will crush your head." Who is this "he"? Jesus!

Just verses before, we read that humankind had fallen into sin. And already, God is telling Satan that he has a plan. Jesus will crush Satan's head, while Satan will only be able to strike his heel. Satan did strike Jesus' heal. He did cause him pain. But that pain was only temporary. Our victory in Jesus is eternal. And it's been the plan all along. ✣

PRAYER

Dear God, thank you for sending Jesus to this earth. Thank you for making us victorious in you. Amen.

THE WORD MADE FLESH

* Name something in God's Word that you don't understand.
* What would make it easier for you to understand the Bible?

In the beginning was the Word, and the Word was with God, and the Word was God.

JOHN 1:1

God's written Word has been around since humans have been alive. When God spoke to his people, they wrote it down and passed it on to others. When God did something amazing, they wrote that down too. The written Word got bigger and bigger. People taught their children from its pages. They changed their lives based on what it said.

They debated over which parts were most significant and put them together to form Scripture, God's written Word. The Old Testament, God's Word, served as mankind's primary source for knowing God—until Jesus came and the Word became flesh. Jesus is the Word of God. Everything he said came from God. Every miracle he performed told us something more about God. God's Word came alive—literally. Jesus gave us new words and made us rethink old ones. The Word was fresh, exciting, unpredictable and life-changing. Jesus taught us to live according to the Word.

As we celebrate this Christmas season, let's remember that God's Word is still as fresh, exciting, unpredictable and life-changing as it was to the people who encountered Jesus over two thousand years ago.

Jesus lives in our hearts. His Holy Spirit speaks to us through our conscience. That's how we can live according to his Word today. ✤

PRAYER

Dear God, thank you for giving us your Word in the flesh. Thank you for the life Jesus led and the things he taught. Guide us as we attempt to follow his example. Amen.

MARY, DID YOU KNOW?

- Do you think it was hard or easy to be Jesus' mother? Explain.
- How do you think Joseph felt about God's plan for Mary?

But the angel said to her, "Do not be afraid, Mary; you have found favor with God. You will conceive and give birth to a son, and you are to call him Jesus."   LUKE 1:30–31

If God had asked the women of Israel who wanted to be the mother of the Messiah, every one of them would have raised her hand. If they had known what that privilege would actually involve—becoming pregnant before marriage, enduring terrible gossip, watching helplessly as their Son was mocked, ridiculed, tortured and crucified—those hands would have come down in a hurry.

Mary certainly didn't volunteer for the job. And she was stunned to discover she'd been selected for such an important role. She handled the extraordinary situation with grace and humility. She asked one question to help her understand God's plan, then agreed to it immediately.

God has a plan for each of us. Ours may not be as earth-shattering as Mary's. Ours may not be miraculous. Ours may not be announced by an angel. But God's plan for us is important, and someone somewhere may be counting on us to be faithful to it.

Mary didn't completely understand what God was going to accomplish through her. But she obeyed. She trusted God and gave him her life to do with as he pleased. What could God do with us if we gave him our lives? ❖

PRAYER

Dear God, thank you for using humble, unassuming people to carry out your work. Use us as you see fit to accomplish your will. Amen.

A FRIEND WHO UNDERSTANDS

* If God gave you an awesome assignment, who would be the first person you would tell? Why?
* What would you say to a friend who told you she was being led by God to do something extraordinary?

"Blessed is she who has believed that the Lord would fulfill his promises to her!"

LUKE 1:45

When the angel Gabriel appeared to Mary to tell her what God was going to do, he mentioned Elizabeth, Mary's much older cousin. Elizabeth was well past her childbearing years. Yet she was pregnant—miraculously, as Mary was.

Mary went straight to Elizabeth's house to share her extraordinary news. She didn't need to. As soon as she arrived, the baby inside Elizabeth, John the Baptist, leapt in her womb. In that instant, the Holy Spirit revealed everything to Elizabeth, and she celebrated joyfully with Mary. Mary stayed with Elizabeth for three months before returning home to prepare for the Savior's birth.

What an amazing gift God gave Mary—someone to empathize with her and share her struggles. Someone who knew a lot about what she was going through. Someone who would encourage her when she started to get anxious. Mary knew she had a big responsibility ahead of her. She needed support from a trusted friend. She got it from Elizabeth.

What friends has God has put in our lives? Where would we be without them? This Christmas season, let's thank God for his gift of friends. And let's thank our friends for their godly support. ✤

PRAYER

Dear God, thank you for bringing people into our lives who encourage us to grow in our spiritual life and be faithful to your plan. Give us the wisdom we need to do the same for our friends. Amen.

BC BECOMES AD

- What's the best way to keep your attention focused on Jesus during the Christmas season?
- What do you think was the biggest sacrifice Jesus made when he came to earth?

While they were there, the time came for the baby to be born, and she gave birth to her firstborn, a son. She wrapped him in cloths and placed him in a manger, because there was no guest room available for them.   LUKE 2:6–7

Christmas is a time for celebration. The weary world rejoices because a Savior is born. Heaven and nature sing because God's plan to save the human race has been put into motion.

Yet there's another side to the Advent season that we should not forget. You see, everything that brings us joy about this season cost Jesus dearly. By being born as one of us, Jesus made himself vulnerable to pain, rejection and loneliness. He put aside his heavenly glory to live a painful 33 years on earth.

He was mocked by people who should have been on their knees worshiping him. He was beaten by people who would have trembled in fear if they could have seen who he really is. He was crucified by people who would later trust in him to save them from eternal death. Everything that benefited us hurt Jesus. Yet still he came, because there was no other way.

This Christmas, as we celebrate Jesus' birth—God's gift to us—let's remember how much that gift cost. ❖

PRAYER

Dear Lord, we can't imagine what it was like for you to give up your glory to come to earth as one of us. Remind us always of the sacrifice that made this joyous season possible. Amen.

day356 december 22

THE FIRST WITNESSES

- What would you do if an angel suddenly appeared to you?
- Do you think the shepherds really understood what they were witnessing? Explain.

When they had seen him, they spread the word concerning what had been told them about this child, and all who heard it were amazed at what the shepherds said to them.

LUKE 2:17–18

As anyone who has ever been part of a living nativity can tell you, the shepherds played an important role in the Christmas story. Angels announced Jesus' birth to them. Since angels only do God's bidding, it's safe to say God wanted the shepherds involved.

Naturally the shepherds were overwhelmed and frightened at first. But the angels calmed their fears. They headed off to Bethlehem, as the angels directed, unsure of exactly why they had been summoned by God. They had no gifts to give the baby or the young couple. They really had nothing to offer at all. Yet they went to see all that the angels had told them about.

As a result, the shepherds were the only witnesses, besides Mary and Joseph, to Jesus' first hours on earth. After they had seen the baby, their purpose became clear: They had been chosen to spread the news about Jesus' arrival. The shepherds were the very first Christian witnesses.

Those of us who know who Jesus is and what his birth means to the world have been chosen by God to make the Good News known everywhere. This Christmas, let's follow the shepherds' example. ✤

PRAYER

Dear God, thank you for making us witnesses of your amazing work. Help us to follow the example of the shepherds and spread your Good News far and wide. Amen.

SIMEON

- How would it have felt to hold the baby Jesus?
- How can we make sure that we don't take Jesus' presence for granted?

Now there was a man in Jerusalem called Simeon, who was righteous and devout. He was waiting for the consolation of Israel, and the Holy Spirit was on him. It had been revealed to him by the Holy Spirit that he would not die before he had seen the Lord's Messiah.   LUKE 2:25 – 26

Simeon was an older man who loved God. Simeon believed the Scriptures and knew that the fate of the world rested in the coming Messiah. More than anything, he wanted to see the Messiah, and the Holy Spirit told him that he would — that he would not die until he had seen the Christ.

The Holy Spirit led Simeon to the temple, where he saw Mary and Joseph with Jesus. They let him hold the baby, and Simeon was filled with joy. He said, "Sovereign Lord, as you have promised, you may now dismiss your servant in peace. For my eyes have seen your salvation, which you have prepared in the sight of all nations: a light for revelation to the Gentiles, and the glory of your people Israel" (Luke 2:29 – 32).

Simeon was honored to be in the presence of Jesus. At that moment, he felt that his life had been fulfilled, and he was ready to leave this earth. It never occurred to Simeon to take the Messiah for granted. And it shouldn't occur to us either. We have constant access to the presence of Jesus. He is living within us. Let us treat Jesus with the same reverence, love and awe that Simeon did on that day long ago. ✤

PRAYER

Dear God, help us to treasure every second we spend in the presence of Jesus. Amen.

day358

A NEW HOPE

- Have you ever made a prediction that came true? Tell us about it.
- Why didn't more people recognize Jesus as the Messiah, especially since he fulfilled all the Old Testament prophecies?

For to us a child is born, to us a son is given, and the government will be on his shoulders. And he will be called Wonderful Counselor, Mighty God, Everlasting Father, Prince of Peace. Of the greatness of his government and peace there will be no end. He will reign on David's throne and over his kingdom, establishing and upholding it with justice and righteousness from that time on and forever. The zeal of the LORD Almighty will accomplish this. ISAIAH 9:6–7

Seven hundred years before the birth of Christ, the prophet Isaiah predicted the coming of one who would shake the earth to its very foundations. He would arrive as a child—a Son, but not just any Son. He would be the Son of David, a descendant of Israel's beloved king. He would be a Wonderful Counselor, a king capable of carrying out a royal plan that would change the world.

And then Isaiah dropped the bombshell: This child would be Mighty God himself, a warrior with unmatched power. He would be the Everlasting Father, whose kingdom would endure forever. He would be the Prince of Peace, the one who ends conflict and strife. The peace he offered would last forever.

And when that much-anticipated child arrived 700 years later, no one was there to greet him but his mother and stepfather, a few shepherds and some barn animals. When he talked about his kingdom, he was mocked. When he revealed his identity, he was killed. Yet he was everything Isaiah said he would be. And if we believe in him, we will enjoy his kingdom forever.

On this Christmas Eve, we celebrate the arrival of Isaiah's prophesied child, our Lord and Savior Jesus Christ. ♣

PRAYER

Dear God, as we prepare to celebrate the birth of your Son tomorrow, we thank you for your plan of salvation. Jesus came to save us from our sin. That's what we really celebrate this Christmas. Amen.

THE WISE MEN ARRIVE

- How do you suppose the myth that the wise men were at the manger got started?
- Why is it meaningful that they brought very expensive gifts to Jesus?

On coming to the house, they saw the child with his mother Mary, and they bowed down and worshiped him. Then they opened their treasures and presented him with gifts of gold, frankincense and myrrh. MATTHEW 2:11

If we were to ask people who aren't familiar with the Bible who came to visit Jesus on the night he was born, they would probably look at the closest nativity scene and name Mary and Joseph, the shepherds, the angel above the stable and the wise men. And we would have to tell them their answer is incorrect.

There were no wise men at the manger. They didn't show up until months later, when Jesus and his family were living in a house. And as long as we're talking about myths, we should point out that there weren't necessarily three wise men. The wise men, or Magi, brought three gifts to Jesus, but that doesn't mean there were three givers.

What we do know is that the Magi were kings from the East. They saw a star, realized it meant that the King of kings had been born, and followed it to Jesus' house. There they presented him with gold, incense and myrrh.

The fact that kings from a distant land knew who Jesus was and where he could be found shows us that God's hand was at work in every part of the Christmas story. For that, we can praise him. ✤

PRAYER

Dear God, on this Christmas Day, we thank you for the evidence in your Word that supports our faith. You are the truth, and we put our belief in you. Amen.

HIS FATHER'S HOUSE

- What do you think Jesus was like as a boy?
- Why do you suppose the Bible is almost completely silent about Jesus' childhood?

"Why were you searching for me?" he asked. "Didn't you know I had to be in my Father's house?" LUKE 2:49

The Festival of Passover is one of the most important dates on the Jewish calendar. In Jesus' day, the festival took place in Jerusalem, where thousands and thousands of Jewish people gathered to commemorate the holiday together.

When Jesus was 12 years old, his parents took him to Jerusalem for Passover. When his parents headed for home, they assumed Jesus was with someone else in their traveling party. He wasn't.

An entire day passed with no sign of Jesus. Joseph and Mary got worried and returned to Jerusalem. It took them three days, but they finally found Jesus sitting among the teachers in the temple, listening to them and asking questions. Even the most educated teachers were amazed at Jesus' knowledge and wisdom.

When Mary told Jesus that she and his stepfather had been searching for him, he asked, "Didn't you know I had to be in my Father's house?" He wasn't being rebellious or sarcastic. He was genuinely surprised. He clearly knew he had a special relationship with God; in fact, he may have known at this time who he was—God's Son—and what was expected of him. No matter what he knew when, he always followed God's perfect plan. And that's why we celebrate him at Christmas. ✤

PRAYER

Dear God, thank you for giving us Jesus' story in your Word. Thank you that we can keep learning new things about him today, over two thousand years since he left the earth. Amen.

FINDERS KEEPERS

- Do you think God would ever break a promise? Why or why not?
- Name some promises God has given us in the Bible.

"I will make an everlasting covenant with them: I will never stop doing good to them, and I will inspire them to fear me, so that they will never turn away from me."

JEREMIAH 32:40

We might imagine that God got pretty frustrated with the Israelites. Over the years, they repeatedly turned away from him. And yet, God never gave up on them. He never broke his promise to them. He told them that they were his people, and he remained true to his word. He told them that he would send them a Messiah to redeem them, and he did.

God doesn't break promises. He didn't break his promises to the Israelites, and he won't break the ones he's made to us either. And he's made many. He's promised to care for us. He's promised to exalt us. He's promised to love us. And he's promised us salvation through the blood of Jesus.

If you ever have any doubt about your salvation, talk to God about it. Take your doubt to the Word and ask the Holy Spirit to abolish it. Because once you belong to God, you belong to him for good. ✤

PRAYER

Dear God, thank you for your promises. Please help us to lean on them, believe in them and trust in them. We know that you don't break promises, Lord, and we thank you and praise you. Amen.

day**362**

NEITHER HEIGHT NOR DEPTH

- How do you know that your parents love you?
- What could you do to make God stop loving you?

For I am convinced that neither death nor life, neither angels nor demons, neither the present nor the future, nor any powers, neither height nor depth, nor anything else in all creation, will be able to separate us from the love of God that is in Christ Jesus our Lord.
ROMANS 8:38–39

Your parents love you. You may be able to do something that makes them angry, but you will never be able to do anything that makes them stop loving you. Try to imagine this kind of love and then multiply it by infinity. That's the love that Jesus has for you. That's the love that God has for you.

God *made* you. He loved you enough to create you. He loved you enough to give you free will. Then he loved you enough to give you his *Son*. He loved you enough to forgive you for turning away from him. This is an impossible love! This is a love that we may never understand. But we don't have to understand it. We just have to accept it. We just have to fall into the welcoming arms of our God, our heavenly Father.

Nothing on this earth — nothing spiritual, no power, no evil, no anger — can *ever* separate us from the love of God that is in Jesus. He's ours forever and ever. And we are his. ✤

> **PRAYER**

Dear God, we cannot possibly thank you enough for your love. Please help us to accept it, so that we don't have to live in fear. Wrap us in your loving arms. Amen.

WE ARE THE CHILDREN

- Why are you able to recognize the voices of your parents?
- How do you know that you are a child of God?

"My sheep listen to my voice; I know them, and they follow me."   JOHN 10:27

If you love and believe in Jesus, that is because he called to you. That is because God chose you. You are God's child. He picked you to be in his family. None of this is an accident. Your faith is not something that just happened. It was predestined. You were chosen before you were even conceived.

Your spot in God's family is secure. Jesus knows you. He knows everything there is to know about you. You may not necessarily hear him calling to you with your ears, but you can hear him calling to you in your heart. You can hear him in your soul. You know and recognize his voice. If you were not one of his "sheep," if you were not a child of God, you would not know his voice.

We spend a lot of time serving and working. We spend a lot of time learning about God and avoiding sin. We need to also spend some time just listening to Jesus' voice and remembering that we are children of God and that we always will be. ✤

PRAYER

Dear God, thank you for choosing us. Please help us to understand that you are our Father and that we are your children. Thank you for your love. Amen.

NEW YEAR'S RESOLUTIONS

- Share some of your New Year's resolutions.
- Have you discussed your resolutions with God? Why or why not?

My soul is consumed with longing for your laws at all times.   PSALM 119:20

If you choose to make some New Year's resolutions, you have countless options. You could resolve to study more. You could resolve to eat healthier or exercise more. You could decide to practice your musical instrument every day or shoot 100 free throws a day.

Or you could resolve to read your Bible every day. If you're going to make a New Year's resolution, why not make one that will change every aspect of your life? Why not make a resolution that will have eternal significance for you and for others?

Don't make this resolution just to make one. Make it prayerfully. Ask God what he thinks about the idea. But do consider it. If you are not already in the Word every day, you will not believe what it will do for you. If you are already in the Word every day, good for you. Resolve to step it up a notch. There are many programs out there designed to help you read the whole Bible in one year. This could be your year! ✜

PRAYER

Dear God, please guide us as we enter into this new year. And God, please give us a hunger for your Word. Let our souls long for it. Amen.

LAST DAY OF THE YEAR!

• What has been your favorite part of this year?
• What is something that you have learned this year?

I desire to do your will, my God; your law is within my heart.   PSALM 40:8

If you started this series of daily devotions at the beginning of the year, then you've finished. Congratulations! If you didn't start this series at the beginning of the year, then hopefully you'll keep right on going!

Devotions are a great way to study God's Word and get to know God's will. In Psalm 40, David wrote that he kept God's law within his heart. That's something we can do too, to keep God's truth in the innermost part of ourselves where no one can ever take it away.

An awesome way to keep God's Word close is through memorization. We may have been encouraged to memorize verses in Sunday school. Or we may have memorized poems in school. Memorizing God's Word shouldn't feel like an obligation. If we do it because we think we have to, then the Word will be stored in our minds but not our hearts. So let's think about giving it a try. If we do, we will etch God's truths right into the fabric of our being. ✤

PRAYER

Dear God, thank you for giving us so many ways to learn about you. We can never thank you enough for your Word. Please help us to learn it, understand it and keep it within our hearts. Amen.

SUBJECT INDEX

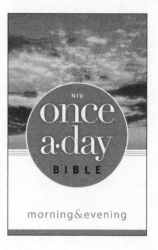

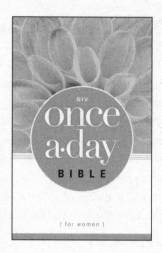

Go deeper with NIV Once-A-Day Bibles

NIV Once-A-Day Bible

The *NIV Once-A-Day Bible* organizes the New International Version—the world's most popular modern-English Bible—into 365 daily readings. This softcover edition includes a daily Scripture reading from both the Old and New Testaments, plus a psalm or a proverb, followed by a short devotional thought written by the staff at the trusted ministry Walk Thru the Bible.

Softcover: 978-0-310-95092-9

NIV Once-A-Day Bible: Chronological Edition

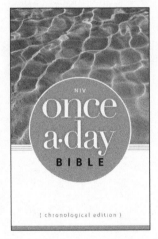

The *NIV Once-A-Day Bible: Chronological Edition* organizes the New International Version—the world's most popular modern-English Bible—into 365 daily readings placed in chronological order. This softcover edition includes a daily Scripture reading, followed by a short devotional thought written by the staff at the trusted ministry Walk Thru the Bible.

Softcover: 978-0-310-95095-0

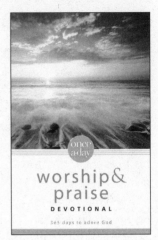

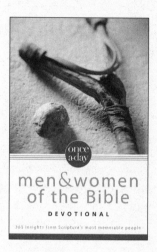

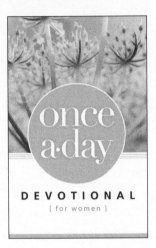
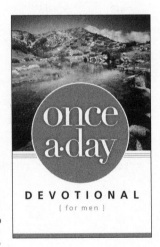